VISIONS of the MODERN CITY

VISIONS of the MODERN CITY

Essays in History, Art, and Literature

Edited by

William Sharpe and Leonard Wallock

1987
The Johns Hopkins
University Press

Baltimore / London

The original edition was sponsored and published by
the Heyman Center for the Humanities, Columbia University
in the City of New York, 1983.

The Johns Hopkins University Press
701 West 40th Street
Baltimore, Maryland 21211
The Johns Hopkins Press Ltd., London

Cover art is by Keith Haring, a New York City artist who is known for drawing with white chalk on the black paper covering unrenewed ads in the subway. Used with Mr. Haring's permission.

Library of Congress Cataloging-in-Publication Data

Visions of the modern city.

  Reprint. Originally published: New York: Columbia University, 1983. (Proceedings of the Heyman Center for the Humanities.)
  Includes bibliographies and index.
  1. Cities and towns in art.   2. Cities and towns—History.   3. Arts.   I. Sharpe, William.   II. Wallock, Leonard.
[NX650.C66V57   1987]   700   87-2764
ISBN 0-8018-3539-9
ISBN 0-8018-3540-2 (pbk.)

Contents

Editors' Note to the 1987 Edition

Since this book first appeared in 1983, changes have occurred in the city and in the ways it is described by writers and critics. We have tried to take these new developments into account by revising and expanding our introductory essay. While the ideas expressed in this essay are the result of a collaborative effort, the portions devoted to literature and the arts were written by William Sharpe and those concerning urban history and the social sciences were written by Leonard Wallock. Steven Marcus's essay has also been expanded; but the rest of the volume, which is devoted to urban history and culture, remains in its original form.

We are grateful to Thomas Bender, Robert Fishman, Michele Hannoosh, Heather Henderson, Gregory Jay, and Neil Smith for their criticism of the introduction. We also want to thank George Thompson and Anne Whitmore of the Johns Hopkins University Press for their critical insights and editorial expertise.

Acknowledgments

This volume is based on papers originally presented as part of the series of seminars on the modern city sponsored by the Society of Fellows in the Humanities and held at the Heyman Center for the Humanities, Columbia University, during February and March of 1983. Two other essays grew out of papers on the city delivered by Deborah Nord and Thomas Bender to the Society of Fellows at the Heyman Center during 1981 and 1982.

On behalf of the Society of Fellows in the Humanities, we wish to thank the Heyman Family for providing the funds for this first publication of the Proceedings of the Heyman Center.

In the course of arranging these seminars the editors received the gracious and indispensable assistance of Loretta Nassar, director of the Society of Fellows, and of staff members Sharon Kahn and Anthony Glover. We wish to thank our contributors for making the seminar series and this volume a success. We also want to acknowledge the help and guidance in planning this volume provided by the staff of the Columbia University Publications Office, particularly Janet Huet, Margaret Mulligan, Susanne Manheimer, and Sonia Murray.

Most of all we have to thank our colleagues in the Society of Fellows in the Humanities for creating an atmosphere in which this kind of multidisciplinary exchange could take place. First we should mention the generous assistance afforded us by the members of the Governing Board of the Society; and next the Fellows themselves, whose friendship and participation have made the Heyman Center a lively and rewarding place in which to learn.

Finally we owe a special debt of gratitude to Professor Wm. Theodore de Bary, whose encouragement and belief in the work of the Society has inspired us all. His own generous vision of the city, as a vital resource for artistic and intellectual creation, is mirrored in the essays which follow.

1983

VISIONS of the MODERN CITY

From "Great Town" to "Nonplace Urban Realm": Reading the Modern City

William Sharpe and Leonard Wallock

> . . . if the modern city has ceased to grow, the metropolitan region continues to expand. . . . We stand at the beginnings of a transformation as consequential as that which, two hundred years ago, brought the modern city into being.
>
> —Oscar Handlin[1]

When studying the modern city, we confront problems of language as well as of methodology, for language inevitably conditions our responses to the city. Our perceptions of the urban landscape are inseparable from the words we use to describe them and from the activities of reading, naming, and metaphorizing that make all our formulations possible. We are now at a point of transition to a new kind of city and are thus experiencing a crisis of terminology similar to that felt by observers of early industrial Manchester and later by the modernist investigators of Paris, London, and New York. In this third stage of the city's evolution, we find ourselves seeking to delineate a "decentered" city that does not conform to the definitions of the past.

This introductory essay relies on the work of artists and critics alike to analyze how, over the past two centuries, the conception of the city as a physical entity has gradually yielded to one based on intangible relationships. After surveying the treatment of the modern city in a variety of disciplines, we outline three phases in its evolution. We then explore some major characterizations or "readings" of the city since the nineteenth century and the metaphors they have employed. Such an analysis should help us in our struggle to define the decentered city of today. For if we are now confronted with a new type of city and new ways of describing it, then perhaps the foremost task we face is to keep our critical language honest through careful scrutiny. As Charles Olson admonishes in the *Maximus Poems*, his modern epic on the city of Gloucester,

> Let those who use words cheap . . .
> take themselves out of the way
> Let them not talk of what is good in the city.[2]

I. The City and the Disciplines

For the past two centuries we have been aware of unprecedented urbanization, but we are still uncertain about its precise outcome.[3] What is the modern city? How are we to define it? Many traditional disciplines have had to make room for the city as a subtopic of increasing importance—city literature and painting, urban psychology, sociology, and history. In the past few decades a new multidisciplinary field, urban studies, has attempted to integrate this knowledge. But in its complexity the city remains resistant to scholarly synthesis, and our working definitions of it continue to be determined by the individual disciplines involved. As the urban planner Melvin Webber recently pointed out, "There has been little basis for agreement or disagreement about the nature of the phenomenon under discussion . . . for each group of observers views the metropolitan communities through the colored glasses of its own discipline or profession, and each sees something different from what the others see."[4] The view of the city is often no less clouded within a single field of investigation. For example, the preface to an anthology of "New York Poets" includes the modest disclaimer, "This book . . . is not a collection of poems about New York, nor is it a collection of poets writing about New York—we don't think that any of them would agree as to what New York even is."[5]

A survey of the visions of the city offered by the major disciplines represented in this book—history, art, and literature—should help to clarify the current confusion in urban termi-

William Sharpe and Leonard Wallock

nology and conceptualization. Three traditions of analysis have shaped what historians define as the significance of the modern city. Not surprisingly, the earliest of these developed in nineteenth-century England, seat of the industrial revolution and home of the great metropolis, London. Struck by the rapid growth and widespread poverty of England's urban centers, several contemporaries conducted what became classic surveys of the modern city: Friedrich Engels, *The Condition of the Working Class in England;* Henry Mayhew, *London Labour and the London Poor;* and Charles Booth, *Life and Labour of the People in London.*[6] In carrying out their detailed investigations of the Victorian underworld (including Manchester's Old Town and "outcast London"), each pointed to what Booth called "the problem of poverty in the midst of wealth."[7] Their studies amounted to not only vivid exposés of current social conditions but also pioneering analyses of cities from a structural viewpoint. They demonstrated that the concentration of a heterogeneous population and the division of labor on an extended scale had given the city a new spatial order and a new social structure that were decidedly modern. In both its ecology and its class relations, this "classic" city was a product of the Age of Capital, whose internal dynamics could be specified.[8] Thus, far from being the chaotic, haphazard, and indecipherable environment perceived by many casual observers, the nineteenth-century city was an integrated, ordered, and knowable entity.

Members of the German School, even more than their English predecessors, were concerned with the social, cultural, and psychological consequences of life in the modern city. Writing at the turn of the century, Max Weber, Georg Simmel, and Oswald Spengler theorized about the impact of the urban environment upon patterns of human association and consciousness.[9] To them, an expanding market economy and an emerging large-scale bureaucracy were critical determinants of urban experience, for they bred among city dwellers a character that was rational, impersonal, alienated, unemotional, and autonomous. Yet, while the metropolis might lead to the corruption of "mental life," it might also serve as a site of human emancipation. "If one asks," wrote Simmel, "for the historical position of these two forms of individualism which are nourished by the . . . metropolis, namely, individual independence and the elaboration of individuality itself, then the metropolis assumes an entirely new rank in the history of the spirit."[10]

In the second and third decades of the twentieth century, the Chicago School expanded upon the earlier traditions of urban analysis by attempting to specify the relationship between the city's physical structure and its "moral order." Robert Park outlined the conceptual basis of this approach in his ground-breaking essay of 1916, "The City: Suggestions for the Study of Human Behavior in the Urban Environment." The ecological approach advocated by Park started from the assumption that "there are forces at work within the limits of the urban community . . . which tend to bring about an orderly and typical grouping of its population and institutions."[11] As Booth had already demonstrated in his study of London, the city could be defined as a spatial-distributive pattern with its own internal dynamics. Yet, following Simmel, Park felt that the city was "something more than . . . congeries of individual men and of social conveniences." Rather it was "a state of mind, a body of customs and traditions, and of the organized attitudes and sentiments that inhere in these customs and are transmitted with tradition." Thus, the city was not simply a physical artifact but possessed "a moral as well as physical organization, and these two mutually interact[ed] in characteristic ways to mold and modify one another."[12] Since Park believed that culture was constitutive of city life, he concluded that there were definite possibilities for human development in the urban environment. With the segmentation of social life and the breakdown of uniform standards of conduct, individuals would enjoy a greater freedom of behavior.[13]

In expanding his definition of the city to include the formidable presence of an urban state of mind, Park has much in common with the artists inspired by the atmosphere of the modern metropolis. Indeed, in painting and literature the idea of the modern city is often difficult to separate from the physical change, social turmoil, psychological trauma, and in-

William Sharpe and Leonard Wallock

tellectual ferment bound up with the idea of modernism in general. Malcolm Bradbury relates the concept of artistic modernism to the urban environment in which it took shape. The city not only molds artistic expression but almost parallels it: "the cultural chaos bred by the populous, ever-growing city, a contingent and polyglot tower of Babel, is enacted in similar chaos, contingency, and plurality in the texts of modern writing, the design and form of modernist painting."[14]

City and style, object and evocation quickly take on aspects of one another as the urban environment shapes an aesthetic perception, which in turn produces a new form and vision of the city. The city is the locus of modernism, and each aspect of city life seems to generate or demonstrate a characteristic of this artistic movement—multiplicity of meaning, loss of sequential or causal connection, breakdown of signification, and dissolution of community. For artists and writers the modern city has come to mean as much a style, a fractured syntax, a paratactic sign-system, as a physical construct with certain demonstrable boundaries.

For painters like Chagall, Stella, Marin, and Severini, in the early part of this century, being modern meant coming to terms artistically with the juxtaposition of urban sights and sounds, the compression of history and modern technology on a single street. Cubism, Futurism, abstract art of many kinds are all tied to an urban sensibility. While painting the city took the form of social criticism for artists like Shahn, Rivera, and Grosz, or meditative anatomies of melancholy in the work of Hopper, L. S. Lowry, Sickert, or de Chirico, for most modern painters the city meant excitement, liberation, energy. More preoccupied with aesthetic than social issues, the great modernists like Picasso, Léger, Kandinsky, and Boccioni, and the chief movements, from Futurism to Action Painting, celebrated the "universal dynamism" of modern urban life.

In determining the relation of earlier painting to the modern city, schools of thought are less important than a certain metropolitan sensibility which, although uncommon before 1880, is easily visible in some artists, such as Manet. For painters in Victorian England and America, the contemporary city was not a proper subject for art—it did not accord with the historical, mythological, or pastoral decorums of the time. But the Parisian artist displayed a clear concern for the representation of a highly articulated urban social world that revealed bourgeois values of dress, work, leisure, and social interchange. Moreover, he sensitively portrayed the plight of the urban poor, the tradesmen, and the street people left homeless by Haussman's "improvements." Finally, on a metaphoric level one can find in Manet and the painting of late nineteenth-century Paris—as Michele Hannoosh does in this volume—an expression of Baudelaire's "*vie moderne*," a modernist aesthetic founded on the celebration of the artificial, the transitory, the vibrantly colorful, the melancholy, all of which the city supplies in abundance. For much French painting of the Impressionist period, the city was defined by its capacity to express "the heroism of modern life"; it stood for the discovery of a lasting beauty in the new and ephemeral.

But painting also shared with literature certain traditional metaphoric associations concerning the city. The primary emphasis of a canvas or a novel might be its portrayal of social organization (as in Zola or Manet) or its rendering of specific areas of the city (as in T. S. Eliot or Charles Sheeler). In either case, the city as depicted often stood for the condition of the society as a whole. As such, this expression was most commonly tied to a number of ruling metaphors: as it symbolized human faith and aspirations, the contemporary metropolis took on aspects of the Heavenly City, the New Jerusalem; as it embodied the failure of these hopes, it partook of the depravity of Babylon or Sodom; its smoke, industry, and avarice suggested the Infernal City of Dante; and its confusion, noise, and lack of direction or community likened it to Babel, the original urban chaos.

Since the time of Dickens and Baudelaire, the city has been seen as social and psychological landscape, both producing and reflecting the modern consciousness. It is a setting that in the modernist period often takes center stage. In the Dublin of Joyce, the London of Eliot, and the New York of Dos Passos, the city becomes one of the most important characters of all, determining and imaging every human action. The same may

William Sharpe and Leonard Wallock

be said of the paintings of Stella and Boccioni, the films of Eisenstein and Lang. Yet at the height of its popularity as a special topic the city begins to lose whatever clear definition it might have had in earlier art and literature. The urban sensibility becomes increasingly a modern sensibility that we can as readily locate in Juan Gris's still-life collages or Monet's haystacks as in Pound's London "Vortex" or Janet Flanner's "Cubical City."

Speaking in the broadest cultural terms, the historian Carl Schorske has identified three major areas of urban self-perception since the eighteenth century: the Enlightenment city of Virtue, the Victorian city of Vice, and the modern city "beyond good and evil."[15] In essence, these stages correspond to the metaphors already outlined—a New Jerusalem indicating the perfectibility of man; a Babylon punishing him for his dedication to mammon; and a Babel, or decentered city, that seems to thrive on loss of connection and lack of reference to the values of the past, what Schorske calls a city of "permanent transience." Schorske's schema indicates something largely unprecedented in history: the gradual devaluation, over the past two centuries, of the city as a concept. Thus, American culture, which came to maturity during the latter two of Schorske's three stages, has never developed a positive image of the city. Leslie Fiedler and Leo Marx have made a strong case for antiurbanism as a preeminent motif in American literature; and other critics have noted that even where one would expect certain urban sympathies, in Hawthorne and James for instance, the American city is scorned, this time not for being too unnatural, but because it is not civilized enough, compared with its European counterparts.[16]

In some ways America presents a special case, but in many countries, after the industrial revolution the city acquired a negative image unequalled in the history of its representation from Augustan Rome to Georgian London. For all the artistic stimulation they provided, the cities of Wordsworth, Dickens, Baudelaire, Melville, Dostoevsky, Tennyson, Eliot, and Fitzgerald have predominantly negative connotations. This is possibly because, as Leo Marx argues in *The Machine in the Garden*, the nineteenth-century city's incursion into the countryside was for the first time in history an irreparable, *technological* one. Thoreau remarked the noise of the trains as they passed by Walden Pond every day.[17]

As the city and its technological extensions gradually become inescapable, it no longer seems possible for us to view them with detachment. If the failures of the city become a synonym for those of society, social criticism will inevitably take on an antiurban coloring. Ironically, it is city-dwelling writers, journalists, advertisers, artists, and so forth, who perpetuate this cultural devaluation of the city.

Nonetheless, recognizing the problems located in and exacerbated by the city has given birth to many of the most energetic reform movements, from the social protest and moralizing of Dickens and of Booth and the Salvation Army in London, and Henry Mayhew's less judgmental urban anthropology there, to Jane Addams' settlement houses and Jacob Riis's muckraking masterpieces in Chicago and New York. As the center of the modernist impulse, the city has also inspired movements dedicated to liberation in the arts and in culture generally: Cubism, Futurism, Vorticism, the International Style of architecture and, somewhat later on, the New York Schools of painting and poetry. Despite its failings, or perhaps because of them, the city has been a powerful source of both artistic stimulation and social reform. Some of the essays in this volume reflect an awareness of how the intensity of urban life encourages just such a sensitivity to urban problems and their artistic expression. For Manet and Mayhew, Baudelaire and Bellow, the city has afforded infinitely varied possibilities of *la vie élégante* and wretchedness, of sublime intensity and utter alienation. As the great urban artists show, from the city's immense disorder a new cultural and aesthetic order emerges.

As we look at images of the city in the social sciences and the arts over the past two centuries, we must recognize that our view is colored by certain preconceptions. It has been prepared for us by previous views of the urban field—artistic, social, and experiential. And the object scrutinized has itself been shaped by the actions and imaginations of earlier viewers, each having his own conception of the city. Whenever we

William Sharpe and Leonard Wallock

see the city, we regard it through a series of lenses, of which we are not always aware. The idea of the "naked city" is itself a fiction compounded of our desires for unmediated vision and a conflicting cultural predisposition that identifies the "naked" environment with violence, volatility, and a lack of order or control. The city that we seek conditions the city we will find.

There is, moreover, an important temporal dimension to the problem of seeing the city clearly. How can the contemporary critic, a product of his own time and of the very forces he seeks to objectify, manage to cross the hermeneutic horizon separating him from the historical moment of his subject? Many theorists contend that the full or objective recovery of the meaning of texts or objects from the past (and the city is a complex of both) is virtually impossible; at best, we can be cognizant of the way in which contemporary experience shapes our views. As a result, those studying the city of even the most recent past have resorted to metaphors of sight, such as "see clearly," "get a perspective on," or "view without obstruction." They have also used archaeological metaphors, which seem particularly suited to older cities: one "digs through layers of meaning" and "excavates the truth" about Troy or Rome. In a related image, that of the palimpsest, one sees the city as a compound of succeeding layers of building or "writing," where previous strata of cultural coding underlie the present surface, and each waits to be uncovered and "read." Any theoretical definition of the modern city must allow for the inevitable metaphoric displacement that past readings and the nature of critical language enforce.

II. Morphology and Metaphor: Three Phases in the Life of the Modern City

The modern city can be said to have undergone three phases of development since the early nineteenth century.[18] The first of these was marked by population growth on an unprecedented scale and by the emergence of industrial capitalism. The massing of the rural population in urban areas and the establishing of new class relations (for which the factory became a symbol) laid the basis for the classic nineteenth-century city. From a geographical standpoint, its distinguishing features were a relatively concentrated area of settlement and a higher degree of segregation of work, residence, class, occupation, and ethnicity than had existed in early modern cities or colonial towns.[19]

While the modern city began entering its second phase as early as the mid-nineteenth century, not until the opening decades of the twentieth century was its new character fully realized.[20] Sam Bass Warner, Jr., contends that in Philadelphia during the 1930s, "intense segregation based on income, race, foreign birth, and class rose to preeminence as the organizing principle of the metropolis."[21] This pattern took the form of a center city surrounded by dependent suburbs. As better paid and more highly skilled members of the working and middle classes moved out to the suburbs, they left behind them the poor, unskilled inhabitants of the older wards. This trend was intensified by the widespread use of automobiles and by the decentralization of businesses following World War II. In the United States, one result of these developments has been the now familiar pattern of black inner cities encircled by white suburbs.[22]

The outlines of the city in its third phase are only now becoming apparent. In 1970, planner Anthony Downs described two "urban frontiers." One was the "Frontier of Deterioration in older central cities and suburbs, especially in ghetto areas." The other was the "Frontier of Growth on the periphery of built-up portions of our metropolitan areas."[23] As Eric Lampard notes, professional urbanists began observing in the early seventies that

> the population was relentlessly spreading out *via* superhighways and freeways into "defensible," low density, residential space . . . graded by socioeconomic class, age, and affinity. Between these extensive and more exclusive residence turfs were placed the "metrocenters," or intervening clusters of common facilities containing shopping plazas, motels, cinemas, automobile service stations and repair shops, apartment blocks, gallery-museums, multi-purpose health spas, and schools of continuing education, etc. These multi-centered "urban fields" or

William Sharpe and Leonard Wallock

"urbanized regions" into which metropolitan and urbanized areas devolved were characterized as "plug-in cities"—from 50 to 100 miles across—where residences were connected "to an intricate . . . and efficiently managed network of freeways, telephones, radio and television outlets, and electric energy and water supply systems."[24]

This portrayal of the modern city in its third phase gained further credibility when, in 1983, the Federal Committee on Metropolitan Statistical Areas concluded a six-year study with the observation that "sprawling urban areas with no clearly defined center are the trend."[25] Evidence gathered in the last few years has reinforced the perception that American cities are becoming distended and decentered, thereby altering their very nature. In 1986, *New York Times* correspondent John Herbers argued, in a study entitled *The New American Heartland,* that the "once-mighty cities have come apart, and, in effect, pieces of them are marching out across the countryside without a center or direction."[26]

The three phases of the modern city—concentrated settlement, center city with suburban ring, decentered urban field—amount to a fundamental transformation of the physical and social environment, which in turn has inspired a conception of the urban no longer synonymous with locale. Traditionally, the idea of the city has been tied to the idea of place. According to Melvin Webber, this conception is "probably as old as urbanization itself."[27] Yet, as Webber contends, the widespread adoption of telecommunication and information-processing technology now means that "urbanity is no longer the exclusive trait of the city dweller; the suburbanite and the exurbanite are among the most urbane of men."[28] Similarly, geographer B. J. L. Berry observed in 1980 that the time-eliminating and space-spanning properties of the new communication technologies were creating "an urban civilization without cities."[29]

As the semantic paradox of the last quotation suggests, each phase in the life of the modern city poses a linguistic challenge. Indeed, it is possible to distinguish three major periods of metaphoric reevaluation and changing terminology that correspond roughly to the three phases of urban growth outlined above. Each of these periods has ultimately produced its own classic literature attempting to assimilate and clarify the metamorphosis taking place. The first outpouring of modern urban literature resulted from the industrial revolution and the sudden shift from a rural to an urban society in the early decades of the nineteenth century. Pioneering observers like Dickens, Mayhew, and Engels attempted to portray an unprecedented urban environment. What Dickens wrote in *Dombey and Son* about the coming of the railway stands not only for the building of the new "Great Towns," but also for the revolution in social conditions and consciousness brought about by the powerful centripetal forces of urbanization:

> The first shock of a great earthquake had, just at that period, rent the whole neighbourhood to its centre. Traces of its course were visible on every side. . . . Everywhere were bridges that led nowhere; thoroughfares that were wholly impassable; Babel towers of chimneys . . . carcasses of ragged tenements, and fragments of unfinished walls and arches, and piles of scaffolding, and wildernesses of bricks, and giant forms of cranes, and tripods straddling above nothing. There were a hundred thousand shapes and substances of incompleteness, wildly mingled out of their places, upside down, burrowing in the earth, aspiring in the air, mouldering in the water, and unintelligible as any dream.[30]

Using the physical landscape of London to symbolize the psychological effects of city life, Dickens perceived that the radical discontinuities of the built environment had a parallel in new forms of thought and social organization. This complementary relationship was also observed by other writers. In the "Great Towns" chapter of *The Condition of the Working Class,* Engels notes that "the disintegration of society into individuals, each guided by his private principles and each pursuing his own aims, has been pushed to its furthest limits in London. Here indeed human society has been split into its component atoms."[31]

The task was not merely one of describing a new world but also of finding new words and ways in which to do so. Steven Marcus comments that in portraying the squalor of Manchester's slums, Engels "has run out of superlatives before he has barely begun; the language itself is giving out on him."[32] Engels, Marcus goes on to show, confronts the dilemma of an inadequate vocabulary by specifying these dire conditions without employing any of the loftier conventions of nineteenth-century prose. In Dickens, on the other hand, the sordid realities of Victorian city life are mitigated by his comic genius for depicting the eccentricities of human nature shaped by the urban environment. Between the approaches of the novelist and those of the critic there is a third means of expressing the condition of modern life. Henry Mayhew combines the insights of the artist with those of the social scientist. He animates his empirical investigations of London's poor with dramatic monologues that convey as vividly as Dickens the "intricate, dense, eccentric texture of Victorian London." As John D. Rosenberg observes, Mayhew "does not distort, but he edits, shapes and intensifies, until we are stunned by the strange beauty and inventiveness of the spoken voices he recreates. His years of editorial experience, his nose for animal effluvia, his ear for quirks of speech, his novelist's eye for significant detail . . . all found the richest possible field for exercise" in London.[33]

For Engels, Dickens, Mayhew, and their contemporaries, the city formed a strange new world that had not yet become the entire world, although metaphorically the one might stand for the other. But in the city's second stage, the context of modern life became an urban one, and modern consciousness an urban consciousness. In *The Country and the City*, Raymond Williams explains that "city experience was now becoming so widespread, and writers, disproportionately, were so deeply involved in it, that there seemed little reality in any other mode of life; all sources of perception seemed to begin and end in the city, and if there was anything beyond it, it was also beyond life."[34] The rural mentality that had remained one of the crucial ways of defining the city mind, in terms of what it was not, now appeared an aspect of the past, not a characteristic of the present. The city and the country were thought of as separate places, but even in the country an urban consciousness became inescapable. As the horizon of the city expands, observed Georg Simmel, "the economic, personal, and intellectual relations of the citizenry, the sphere of intellectual predominance of the city over its hinterland, grow as in geometrical progression. . . . The most significant characteristic of the metropolis is this functional extension beyond its physical boundaries."[35]

Thus, in this era a modernist, metropolitan sensibility pervades both the celebrated representations of city life—Apollinaire's *Zone,* Biely's *St. Petersburg,* Stella's *Brooklyn Bridge,* or Léger's paintings of the Eiffel Tower—and key works that are nonurban in topic, such as Picasso's *Les Demoiselles d'Avignon* and Pound's *Cantos.* The age-old boundaries of city and country still obtain, but the distinction between the two in the nonmaterial artistic and mental realms is eroding.

The difficulties of language faced by writers in the first phase of urbanization recur in the second, with the emphasis turning to the psychological, internalized landscape of the city and its effect on human consciousness. What Raymond Williams remarked of *Ulysses* begins to hold true for all urban perception: "This is the profound alteration. The forces of the action have become internalized, and in a way there is no longer a city, there is only a man walking through it."[36] James Joyce's solution to the problem of representing the city within was the stream of consciousness interior monologue, a linguistic tour-de-force that sought to reproduce the various perceptions and recollections that cross the mind during the course of a day. On the other hand, in *The Waste Land,* T. S. Eliot made the "unreal" hallucinatory city a catchword of urban experience, turning the poverty of language into an authoritative strategy for discussing the modern condition.

The third phase of urban development includes the present day, though one might point to its beginnings during the past few decades. Urban experience is now in a sense universal. The city seems less and less a discrete locale, and therein lie many of our latest problems of definition. To an unprecedented degree, today's city involves not just place, but the goods, services, and relationships that have changed the texture of life there and that also affect the steadily declining portion of the population that lives outside metropolitan areas. The transfer of basic urban functions from a central

William Sharpe and Leonard Wallock

city, first to the suburbs, and then to the still larger decentralized "urban field" has required the visual vocabulary of the nineteenth-century city to change. With this transformation, once-significant urban emblems have been deformed, submerged, erased, or dislocated as the city has grown. It is usually claimed that the sheer physical expansion of the nineteenth- and twentieth-century city has led to our present inability to comprehend its intricate systems of exchange and influence. Thus, we nostalgically speak of Dickens as "the last man really to know London" or nod appreciatively at the sentiment expressed in the title of Thomas Wolfe's famous short story, "Only the Dead Know Brooklyn." As Wolfe's narrator categorically states in the opening lines, "Dere's no guy livin' dat knows Brooklyn t'roo an' t'roo, because it'd take a guy a lifetime just to find his way aroun' duh f —— town."[37]

But the reason the present-day city seems to us unknowable may instead lie in the decentralization that we have been tracing. In "Structure, Sign and Play in the Discourse of the Human Sciences" (1966), Jacques Derrida argued that

> if totalization no longer has any meaning it is not because the infinity of a field cannot be covered by a finite glance or a finite discourse, but because the nature of the field—that is, language and a finite language—excludes totalization . . . instead of being too large, there is something missing from [the field]: a center which arrests and founds the freeplay of substitutions.[38]

Like language, the city is a system of signification dependent on certain fixed relations and shared values for its comprehensibility or "interpretation." But if the traditional functions of the city are displaced to other parts of a more homogeneously urbanized environment, then the effect will resemble the loss of semiotic apprehensibility that Derrida describes. And, in fact, the instantly legible and easily visible emblems of urban power and centrality—the capitol building, the clock tower, the central post office, the main square—have increasingly been obscured and overlaid by building and demolition, freeway construction, densely packed high-rises and skyscrapers, one-way traffic patterns, and by vast indoor malls where clocks and exterior views are deliberately excluded from a carefully contrived environment. Indeed, Derrida's "missing center," which organizes a "field" of meaning, has already become an accepted part of urban theory. Eric Lampard, for example, addresses himself at length to the problems of elaborating the "decentered urban field."

There is little doubt that since the industrial revolution we have gradually constructed an urban vocabulary, based on concepts of space and concentration, that is rapidly becoming outmoded. We need to devise new terms and images that will allow us to trace the mutation of older urban shapes into new ones and to read the encoding of older forms retrospectively. The task might be seen as one of translation. However, before this can be done, the city must first be both "read" and "named," a circular process in which perception and language inevitably precede and prejudice one another. But in thinking of the city as a text, we must bear in mind that it is a text full of metaphors—including the linguistic metaphor itself—which need to be read and reread with vigilance.

III. Reading the City

One of the most useful ways of studying the city envisions the urban landscape as a form analogous to that of a literary composition. A decade ago Steven Marcus argued that the young Friedrich Engels had successfully completed such an analysis in *The Condition of the Working Class*. According to Marcus, Engels managed the difficult task of "reading the illegible" nineteenth-century city by revealing that its "apparently unsystematic and possibly incoherent" form could actually be "perceived as a total intellectual and imaginative structure."[39] In his essay in this book, Professor Marcus continues his assessment of representations of the modern city by again attempting to read the illegible, speaking this time of Saul Bellow, Thomas Pynchon, and the contemporary city. Indeed a cumulative accomplishment of the essays collected here is to make us realize how much the desire and quest for urban legibility has been an ongoing aspect of modern urban studies.

Moreover, examining how such exemplary nineteenth-century urbanists as Baudelaire, Mayhew, and Dickens attempted to come to terms with their cities provides us with a perspective on our own problems of metaphorization and representation. Baudelaire sought to elaborate an aesthetic of the transitory and the bizarre appropriate to the pace and style of modern life; Mayhew explored London slums as if they were as culturally remote as "darkest Africa"; and Dickens conceived of cities as welded together by networks at once symbolic and economic—railways in *Dombey and Son,* dust heaps in *Our Mutual Friend,* prisons in *Little Dorrit.* Reading these authors, we are led to question how our own visions of the city are acquired and represented. Like a literary text, the city has as many interpretations as it has readers; and while some analyses may gain a preponderance of support and the aura of authority, changes in the city and in its representation will ensure that our visions or readings of it continue to be plural.

The quest for urban legibility, born of the desire to read or make human sense out of an immense and seemingly inhuman structure, has a long history. Juvenal, Horace, and Martial depict the pandemonium of ancient Rome; in *The Dunciad,* Pope anatomizes the senseless Babel of London; and more than half a century later Wordsworth, in *The Prelude,* finds that same city nothing but "blank confusion." In *Bleak House,* Dickens goes a step further and refers to London as an "unintelligible mess" of reading and writing.[40] As for modern critics, several decades ago, in *The Culture of Cities,* Lewis Mumford complained about the "non-plan of the non-city" in industrial times.[41] The best-known recent application of literary metaphors to the urban landscape may be found in Kevin Lynch's *The Image of the City* (1960), which maintains that legibility is a vital component of all cities. His aim, Lynch says, is to

concentrate especially on one particular visual quality: the apparent clarity or "legibility" of the cityscape. By this we mean the ease with which its parts can be recognized and can be organized into a coherent pattern. Just as this printed page, if it is legible, can be visually grasped as a relational pattern of recognizable symbols, so a legible city would be one whose districts or landmarks or pathways are easily identifiable and are easily grouped into an over-all pattern. . . .

Although clarity or legibility is by no means the only important property of a beautiful city, it is of special importance when considering environments at this scale of size, time, and complexity.[42]

Proceeding even further with this literary metaphor, Lynch focuses on the "imageability" of the city—what makes it appear "well-formed, distinct, remarkable"; that is, legible "in a heightened sense." It is as if we are moving from simple prose (the merely *legible* city) to a kind of poetry (the "heightened" sensation of the imageable city), which can itself be further analyzed, like a poem, in terms of its "identity, structure, and meaning."[43]

It is commonly thought that the cities of the past were more legible than recent ones, that the movement from temple- or cathedral-centered ancient or medieval cities to the unplanned jumble of the industrial city and the contemporary urban field has been a gradual motion away from "an environment communicating to us in a language that we know."[44] Instead of the divinely ordered New Jerusalem that St. John "read" in his revelation, we are much more likely to confront an urban landscape that "reads" like subway graffiti or the calligraphy that defaces our public buildings and monuments. This last phrase itself exemplifies the perception that the city has become opaque—the city once had a face that we could see and comprehend, but now it is hidden from all but the specialist, whether writer, historian, or planner.

Trying to read the city is a continuing, historical effort, which subsumes other metaphors similar to that of legibility. The rapid increase in population, size, and density of the city in the nineteenth century, for example, suggested to many observers the metaphor of exploration, not in any mundane sense, but in terms appealing to the popular imagination: safaris in Africa, quests for the source of the Congo or the Nile. In her essay in this volume, "The Social Explorer as Anthropologist: Victorian Travellers among the Urban Poor," Deborah Epstein Nord shows how Mayhew used the analogy of London's East End to "darkest Africa" to reveal London as a

William Sharpe and Leonard Wallock

world in microcosm. An initiator of the "discovery of poverty" in London, Mayhew sympathetically charted the depths of an urban underworld that often seemed as foreign in dress, speech, and customs as the ends of the Empire, and was even less likely to be visited by the middle class. Yet Mayhew, even as he expertly guided his audience through London's "heart of darkness," would perhaps have refused to read the East End completely, even if he could. Mayhew sought to reveal how similar the poor were to the middle classes in human terms, despite their social differences due to environment. Thus he needed to insist upon a certain illegibility in his city. As Professor Nord writes, "He had to convince his public that the people of whom he wrote were *of* English society though separate from it, *related* to the middle class but a 'race' apart from it, fellow inhabitants of the same city but members of a different tribe."

This outcast London, mysterious even in the works of Dickens and enigmatic in the ever-receding tenement perspectives of Gustave Doré, has generally been claimed as the premiere modern city. Theodore Reff, however, arguing from an aesthetic point of view, would give the title to the Paris of Haussmann, Baudelaire, and Manet. Like Mayhew, the Frenchmen saw two worlds, rich and poor, in one city; but while Baudelaire and Manet sought not so much to explore as to express this divided life, Haussmann tried to suppress and conceal it. Haussmann did not entirely succeed in his efforts to raze the slums and politically radical neighborhoods of the city and to insulate the bourgeois from the remaining poor with grand boulevards and facades (the same technique of segregation Engels had noticed in Manchester). Haussmann's well-planned urban upheaval brought the homeless poor even more to light. As Professor Reff has shown elsewhere,[45] the leveling of Petite Pologne, one of the worst slums, drew to Manet's attention several of the characters he used in *The Old Musician,* elements of a displaced urban population, whose estranged spatial arrangement on the canvas reflects their alienation from each other. Challenging representation and iconography, but still working within their established confines, Manet at this time began to depict contemporary scenes from the socially ordered, self-possessed world of the Second Empire. *The Old Musician,* done during the same year as his first painting of modern Paris, *Concert in the Tuileries,* might seem incongruous with his new interest in modern subjects. But by tracking down Manet's artistic quotations and models, as Professor Reff does, one can decipher the vestiges of an earlier city encoded in Manet's canvas.

The foremost poet and art critic of the modern city, Charles Baudelaire, perceived in Manet "a decided taste for modern reality."[46] Indeed, Baudelaire's writings played a part in Manet's evolution toward an aesthetic of modern life. But in the "Tableaux parisiens" section of *Les Fleurs du mal* (1861), Baudelaire himself became the "painter of modern life" that his art criticism had demanded, one who was sensitive to the melancholy, fleeting, and subjective beauties born of the modern age. In the *Petits Poèmes en prose* of the early 1860s, he went on to develop the prose poem, a new artistic form that would be able to convey the intense, bizarre flights of fancy that the great city inspired. "Which of us," he wrote, "in his ambitious days has not dreamt of the miracle of a poetic prose, musical without rhythm or rhyme, supple and resistant enough to adapt itself to the lyric movements of the soul, to the undulations of reverie, to the shocks of conscience? It is above all from the frequentation of giant cities, from the interlacing of their innumerable networks, that this obsessive ideal is born."[47]

As Michele Hannoosh shows, Baudelaire saw that nature provided the Romantics "a vast dictionary," a source of symbolic materials by which the poet or painter could communicate his subjective imaginings to the rest of the world. Realizing that the urban environment was an equally rich repository of signs, Baudelaire transferred "all the aesthetic implications of the term 'nature' to modern city life." Hannoosh concludes that his search for a means of translating the artist's personal perceptions into conventions that would successfully render contemporary urban experience anticipates a similar quest by the Impressionists. Dissatisfied with the received language of painting, the Impressionists "reformed the language and revised the conventional procedures of technique." In this way

William Sharpe and Leonard Wallock

they sought to make the new Parisian world legible to others without compromising the integrity of their subjective visions of the city.

The translation that Dickens effected in London is no less exemplary, but what is perhaps most remarkable about the Dickensian portrait of what Baudelaire called the *"fourmillante cité"* is its accuracy and particularity. While the vast interlocking symbol-systems of prisons and railways, law courts and dust heaps given an unsurpassed poetic density to his representations of Victorian London, Dickens wrote with such an eye for detail and social organization that on many subjects he remains our best and most reliable urban historian of the period. Although almost all of his contemporaries were sensitive to Dickens' talent for caricature and broad comedy, the critic Walter Bagehot paid him an insightful back-handed compliment when he remarked that reading Dickens was like reading the newspaper. Not only in the great range of incidents, individuals, and issues faithfully covered, but also in their almost surreal juxtaposition and apparent randomness, Dickens' vast panoramas boldly revealed the labyrinths of the new urban world. Philip Collins captures the essence of Dickens' achievement when he focuses on how the phrase "a fanciful photograph" so aptly describes the combination of imagination and verisimilitude on every page. Like Baudelaire, Dickens reads his contemporary city so memorably that we feel we know it—and its author—intimately. But the fancy at the heart of these texts opens them to endless interpretation. To our delight, such literary cities are infinitely readable but never fully read.

The skyscraper architects of New York adopted another strategy for legibility, trying to make their new buildings instantly intelligible by casting them in historically familiar forms. While some architectural historians have criticized the New York of 1880–1930 as exemplifying an unwillingness to shed a mercantile classicism for the purer modernist lines of building found in Chicago, Thomas Bender and William Taylor make a strong countercase for the city's exhibiting a more urbanistic *ensemble* style of building based on the Beaux Arts tradition and the Chicago Exposition of 1893. Not simply "behind the times," New York architects wanted to apply a horizontally oriented historicism to the new verticality, in order to stress traditional civic values. Despite their great size, buildings like Grand Central Station, the Metropolitan Life Building, the old Madison Square Garden, and the Municipal Building are testaments to a concern for vista, street-level accessibility, and the semiotics of civic pride, a desire to make the city and its major foci rational, centered, and immediately apprehendable. They stress the horizontal lines of the Greco-Roman temple or the haughty composure of the Italian block-and-campanile (where the tower is of secondary, not primary value) over the vertical modernism of Louis Sullivan ("it must be tall, every inch of it tall") and the Chicago School.[48]

In short, the priority New Yorkers assigned to the concept of a legible city resulted in a cultural resistance to verticality, even as the world's tallest buildings were being erected in Manhattan. In one sense, the slow assimilation of the vertical aesthetic may indicate a natural resistance to change. New York planning and building, however, has historically emphasized surface legibility, from the original grid plan and the respect shown for it, even by multiblock structures like Grand Central and the Municipal Building, to the names of subway stations, which are street- rather than place-oriented. It is as if earlier generations were already anticipating the fear, now a commonplace in postmodern New York, of the city becoming once and for all illegible.

We find a far more extreme approach to the discontinuities of urban life in the Japanese view of the city presented by Paul Anderer in "Tokyo and the Borders of Modern Japanese Fiction." According to Anderer, for the modern Japanese writer the city is not a place per se, to be explored, confronted, and mastered, as in Western writing. Rather it comprises innumerable private spaces, well-known corners of a neighborhood, small areas as familiar as one's room at home. Not even modern by Baudelaire's definition, these cautious writers share with the Victorian poets of the nineteenth century (and with much American antiurban literature from Cooper to Hemingway) a conservative aesthetic that values the traditional, the private, and the natural over the new, the public, and the artificial. The English painter Samuel Palmer's epithet of 1862, "The Past for Poets, the Present for Pigs"[49] neatly sums up the Victorian reluctance to deal with urban subject matter; and, while the Japanese might formulate their aesthetic prescriptions more discreetly, the general effect is similar. A well-proportioned work of art cannot include urban disorder; indeed, in the nineteenth century, only "loose, baggy monsters,"[50] as Henry James dubbed the three-volume novels of Dickens, seemed adequate to the task of conveying—and being willingly deformed by—modern urban experience.

Yet in a deeper sense the Japanese may be the most modern of all, recognizing that within even their narrow limits lies a reality that can never be fully expressed. Is there any difference ultimately, they seem to imply, between the disconnected patches of decentered urban field and the domestic interior of a Tokyo suburb? In either case the big picture, the "total intellectual and imaginative structure" that Engels sought, now seems beyond our scope. For if any general attitude toward the representation of the contemporary city has been emerging, it is that the now-explicable nineteenth-century city has given way to the still elusive "nonplace urban realm" of the twentieth. As the purview of this collection of essays moves westward and forward in place and time, from the Paris and London of 1850 to the New York, Los Angeles, and Tokyo of the present day, the legibility of the urban object appears to decrease until writers seriously question whether it can be read any longer.

Such, apparently, is the gradual evolution of Saul Bellow's vision of the city over the four decades since his first novel appeared in 1944. Steven Marcus finds that from an initial skepticism about a classic vision of the city "that could make out the analogy between city and people without diminishing or reducing one into the other," Bellow has increasingly depicted a city ready "to collapse away from meaning . . . into incognizability and chaos." While Engels succeeded in revealing and reading vast, complex structures of social organization, Bellow seems to despair of making even the simplest interpersonal communication: "Every other man spoke a language entirely his own, which he had figured out by private thinking. If you wanted to talk about a glass of water, you had to start back with God creating the heavens and earth. . . . You were lucky even then to make yourself understood."

Nevertheless, Engels' meditation on whether the "deep structure" of Manchester results from accident or design anticipates Thomas Pynchon's doubts about whether the contemporary city has any underlying logic at all. As Engels had noted in regard to the systematic concealment of working-class Manchester from the middle classes, the arrangement appeared too spontaneous, too deeply embedded in the city's structure to seem intentional, and yet it was also impossible to view it as merely accidental or innocent.[51] Similarly the New York of *V* and especially the Los Angeles of *The Crying of Lot 49* ("less an indentifiable city than a grouping of concepts") continually show themselves to be devious fictions, assemblages of interpretive categories validated by history but ultimately as arbitrary and mystifying as a Manhattan subway map or the L.A. Interchange. In the final analysis, writes Pynchon, "behind the hieroglyphic streets there would be either a transcendental meaning . . . the orbiting ecstasy of true paranoia" (which so many of his characters feel), or there would be no meaning whatsoever. In describing Los Angeles as a "printed circuit," Pynchon seems to delight in precisely this dilemma: which is worse, he asks, the perpetual self-conscious paranoia of multiple misguided readings of the "hieroglyphic streets" or the possible discovery that his ultimate urban plot is real, and we are all its victims? We can never know the true status of the city or, consequently, how this knowledge would affect us. Both Bellow and Pynchon announce the death of the city as a signifying system, but for the former it is the "collapse of civilization . . . Sodom and Gomorrah, the end of the world," while for the latter it is a kind of delirious entropy, an overdetermined semiotic mesh endlessly indicating its own fictionality.

Yet, as the examples of Manchester and other nineteenth-century cities show, what looks chaotic at first may in time come to appear coherently organized. Such is the case already with the literary cities of *Ulysses, The Waste Land,* and *Paterson,* where the images of Dublin, London, and Paterson (New Jersey) that baffled early readers are now regularly mapped by critics. So far there is no common language for, or agreement upon, the nature of the contemporary city. The dilemma facing writers and urbanists today is that our spatially oriented vocabulary prevents us from discussing the interaction of space, time, and process except in negations and dialectical oppositions. But we will no doubt fashion a new vocabulary for the postindustrial city, just as writers of the nineteenth century created the language of the industrial city that we now take for granted and find hard to transcend.

IV. Naming the City

What direction is the quest for a new vocabulary of urban experience taking, and what challenges face the writers and urbanists who seek to name the modern city in its latest phase? In answering these questions, we focus on current examples from the United States. Depictions of New York in recent fiction suggest that there are two major approaches to the characterization of the city in the mid-eighties. The most prominent group of novels affirms the urban experience of young, upwardly mobile, white, middle-class, college-educated professionals ("yuppies"),[52] and as such exemplifies what might be called "literary gentrification."[53] This term is based on an analogy between a spruced-up city and a slicked-up city fiction. The literary city has undergone an "upgrading" of its rundown post–World War II image (associated with Bellow, Malamud, and others) that is comparable to the process of gentrification experienced by the actual city. However, as in life, in literature this gentrification has been only partial, leaving untouched a terrain of devastation that forms the subject matter for a second strain of contemporary writing, the novels of decay.

As the recent wave of hip, street-wise books such as Jay McInerney's *Bright Lights, Big City* (1984), Paul Rudnick's *Social Disease* (1986), and Tama Janowitz's *Slaves of New York* (1986) attests, in city fiction there has been a pronounced change in the sense of place.[54] From the classic works of the nineteenth century through the 1950s and 1960s, cities were made up of strongly defined neighborhoods and streets, with a thickly textured communal experience that shaped the lives of their inhabitants.[55] But current fiction, as epitomized by McInerney, Rudnick, and Janowitz, or by Louis Auchincloss' *Diary of a Yuppie* (1986), presents a largely delocalized city, where residence and workplace serve merely as background to the milieu in which people socialize. Midnight transformations of slums into after-hours meccas, bizarre interiors of all-night clubs, and a continual succession of hot spots in which to be seen—these replace the particular settings (mom and pop stores, traffic islands, streetcorners, local parks) that were once the staple of urban fiction and existence. Everything is so implicitly urban in the gentrified style that the city as an imaginative or emotional focus, or even just a physical factor, has practically ceased to exist.[56]

This waning sense of city as place is intimately linked to the inability to say what the city might mean. Whereas writers from Balzac to Bellow anatomized personal and class relations through the arrangement of the city or the layout of a boarding house, the social relations of recent books, like the images used to depict them, are decontextualized.[57] The casual inconclusiveness of this new strategy of urban representation, in which the nightclub scene, galleries, and loft living[58] are evoked in a quick-cut, video style, belies an uncertainty about the significance of the very things being shown. As the panorama gives way to the zoom shot, the descriptions of locales that filled New York fiction of the past have been supplanted by passing references to totemic bits of mass culture. For her thirtieth birthday one of Tama Janowitz's characters in *Slaves of New York* receives a Godzilla cigarette lighter, a "cassette tape of Teenage Jesus and the Jerks," a book about wrestling, and "a Statue of Liberty hat—a spikey helmet of flexible foam." Janowitz's narrator comments:"I know that this assortment of gifts means something specific and symbolic about people my age who live in New York and who are involved in the arts. . . . But what the gifts actually represent, I have no idea."[59] As the city recedes in contemporary urban fiction, its

William Sharpe and Leonard Wallock

deracinated inhabitants lose their ability to interpret themselves or the world around them.[60] In this new form of urban
illegibility, even those who speak the language may not know
what it means.

By contrast, the second major group of novels depicts an
urban decay in which such cryptic tribal discourse ceases altogether. Although a sense of place remains, the struggle to
decipher the city is far more desperate. Works such as Don
DeLillo's *Great Jones Street* (1973), Madison Smartt Bell's *Waiting for the End of the World* (1985), and Paul Auster's *City of Glass*
(1985) extend to the margins of society the concerns of earlier
writers, such as Bellow and Baldwin, over the deterioration of
the environment and the loss of a sense of common decency.[61]
But they do not speak of neighborhood life, rather they treat
in detailed fascination only the near-abandoned sites of once-
thriving communities, where half-crazed derelicts and condemned buildings wait in torment for final demolition. The
sordid eloquence of such locales only partially offsets the gib-
berish and brooding silence of their denizens. Such works display how gentrification has not extended into adjacent areas,
or fully reversed the effects of postwar blight.

These novels of urban apocalypse rely on imagery drawn as
much from biblical accounts of Babylon, Sodom and Gomorrah, and the New Jerusalem as from the actual topography of
their settings. In *Waiting for the End of the World,* Larkin, the
epileptic, alcoholic protagonist, haunts devastated landscapes
in Williamsburg and the Bowery that keep him maddeningly
in touch with both heaven and hell:

> On Bedford Avenue a pathway of blue hyphens had been
> painted down the street, as guidance to whom or what Larkin
> didn't know. . . . From his rooftop the blue dashes seemed a
> perforation, as if the whole botched neighborhood was pre-
> pared to be torn off and discarded by some almighty hand, a
> power discontented with its imperfection. . . .
>
> But Larkin had no use for walking on a line; his walks curled
> through the neighborhood like the slow process of decay.
> Buildings crumbled before and behind him; sometimes rumor
> gave out that lives had been lost too. Returning to his own cor-
> ner, Larkin could stand and see the shimmering towers of the

World Trade Center framed by the crumpled buildings farther down the block, the bright towers not just across the river but clearly in some other, hallucinatory world.[62]

Unable to endure his vision of these extremes, Larkin succumbs to demonic voices before confronting the mysteries of the Apocalypse. The biblical frame of reference that informs most nineteenth- and early twentieth-century treatments of the city persists, but now it is for a community of one. Even the most widely shared emblems of urban destiny have become symbols of private alienation, personal fate.

The two strains in contemporary urban writing emphasize either the prefabricated vocabulary of the yuppie or the otherworldly revelations of the dispossessed. Yet in both of these genres, the newest images of the city seem ultimately to belong to the oldest of urban archetypes, as the white noise of media hype and the howl of bag-peoples' personal demons confound both the with-it and the out-of-it. For this reason the detective protagonist of Auster's *City of Glass* is unnerved but not finally surprised by the discovery that his suspect has paced out the words T-O-W-E-R O-F B-A-B-E-L, a letter a day, through the streets of the Upper West Side. Cornered, the suspect confesses:

> I have come to New York because it is the most forlorn of places, the most abject. The brokenness is everywhere, the disarray universal. You have only to open your eyes to see it. The broken people, the broken things, the broken thoughts. The whole city is a junk heap. . . . I find the streets an endless source of material, an inexhaustible storehouse of shattered things.[63]

Shortly afterwards, Auster's detective loses even this baffling trail, and he withdraws into solitude, living in an alleyway and speaking to no one for several months.[64] Like other characters in the novels of DeLillo and Bell, the detective slips into a silence so profound that it is deafening. In the novels of gentrification the language of pop culture is spoken easily but has ceased to communicate, but in the novels of urban decay language has ceased to be spoken at all. Despite its widely divergent views of the contemporary urban landscape, the most recent fiction appears to offer a consensus: functioning amid the fallout from the Tower of Babel is still the city dweller's foremost challenge.

If literature has been attempting to wrest meaning from the city's junkyard of broken images, in the social sciences the struggle to put a name to the shape of the modern city has been even more pronounced. It has, in fact, provoked a crisis of language. In their attempts to characterize the most recent patterns of metropolitan growth, demographers, geographers, landscape architects, and planners have amply illustrated the problem of attempting to define an unknown phenomenon by using awkward variations on familiar terms. For example, to express the idea that accessibility rather than propinquity is the main feature of the new metropolitan areas, Webber has coined the term *nonplace urban realm*.[65] Each realm consists of "heterogeneous groups of people communicating with each other through space."[66] The extent of each realm is "ambiguous, shifting instantaneously as participants in the realm's many interest-communities make new contacts, trade with different customers, socialize with different friends, or read different publications." Postulating an entire hierarchy of such realms, Webber maintains that "in some degree, then, probably best conceived as the proportion of manhours devoted to playing out roles associated with the affairs of each realm, each settlement is the partial locus of realms at many levels in the hierarchy."[67] He then proceeds to calculate the "Hubits" (human hours $\times$ amount of information received) of realm participants in one interest-community across the United States.[68] Only through the use of paradoxical (nonplace) or imaginary (Hubits) terms does Webber feel he can depict the convergence of space and time evident in the new metropolitan areas.

In 1970, Anthony Downs also sought to propose what would become an acceptable framework for discussing urban growth. He, too, soon confronted formidable problems of definition. After selecting the relevant variables, he outlined five alternative forms: redevelopment, peripheral sprawl, planned peripheral growth, satellite growth, and nonmetropolitan growth. Still, the increasingly common phenomenon of dispersed settlement beyond the metropolitan areas was not covered by the terms *peripheral sprawl* or *satellite growth*. He explains that his second form of growth, called *peripheral sprawl*,

> includes another form that might be more logically called *satellite sprawl*. It is not on the edge of existing cities (hence peripheral) but away from the edge (hence satellite). Yet the term *satellite* implies a cluster of some type, rather than more scattered development. Moreover, *peripheral sprawl* is used by many observers to refer to *all* scattered development outside existing built-up areas, both on the edge and farther out but within commuting range. Thus, I have adopted this dual definition.[69]

Satellite sprawl is not only a dual definition; it is also a mixed and highly revealing metaphor. The term combines the space-age symbol of high-technology and frontier exploration with the Victorian vision of disorderly and unplanned growth. In satellite sprawl we encounter a peculiar mixture of past and present to express an otherwise indescribable future.

By the late 1970s the problem of identifying urban growth patterns had become so serious that a federal interagency committee was established to study and redefine what constitutes a metropolitan area. The convening of the Federal Committee on Metropolitan Statistical Areas "marked a recognition that old areas were expanding and new ones were being born at a rapid pace as the population, industry and other institutions dispersed into nonurban areas that had been declining for decades."[70] Observing the transformation of these rural areas into metropolitan ones, committee member Calvin L. Beale, chief demographer for the Department of Agriculture, noted that "they are simply dispersed in a way that does not support the usual urban living patterns."[71] The committee's revised boundaries and definitions, which covered more than three hundred areas, were said to be "the most far-reaching ones since the Government began designating metropolitan areas in 1910."[72]

Originally the Census Bureau used mainly population size to distinguish between urban and rural areas.[73] It did not try to specify the relationship and interaction between the areas being defined and, thus, to include the criteria of accessibility

William Sharpe and Leonard Wallock

proposed by Anthony Downs. Gradually the Census Bureau's definition of *urban* began to reflect a broader conception of the urban as place. As early as 1910, "metropolitan districts" were introduced. These included cities of 200,000 or more inhabitants along with those sections of the adjacent territory considered urban in character.[74] In 1949, a standard definition of *metropolitan* was employed by the Census Bureau for cities with populations of 50,000 or more that were functioning as "integrated economic unit[s] with a large volume of daily travel and communication between the central city and outlying parts of the area."[75] The most recent report, *Metropolitan Statistical Areas, 1983*, identifies its subject matter as a "geographical area with a large population nucleus together with adjacent communities which have a high degree of economic and social integration with that nucleus."[76] Recognizing widespread population growth outside of incorporated cities and towns, the federal committee responsible for this report also "repealed the longstanding requirement that a community must have a population of 50,000 to qualify as a central city within a metropolitan area."[77] Once again, problems of definition became formidable. In the absence of a minimum size requirement for the population of a central city, that designation was determined "by other qualities, such as whether a city is a work center surrounded by bedroom communities."[78]

Despite their different emphases, these attempts to define the modern city in its third phase agree on several points. They recognize that metropolitan areas are extending outward over large expanses and that cities and suburbs are being subsumed in urban fields. They also share a belief that the new areas of population concentration need not exhibit the traditional features of city life in order to be considered urban. As B. J. L. Berry wrote in 1980, "today's urban systems appear to be multinodal, multiconnected social systems sharing in national growth and offering a variety of life styles."[79]

In many ways *urban field* seems a useful designation for the expanding metropolitan areas. But, even as we employ the term, we should be aware that it contains paradoxes and connotations that distort our understanding of the entity being named.[80] In its broadest sense the word *field* is geographical, referring to a rural stretch of open land (*Oxford English Dictionary*). Thus, *urban field* summons up the age-old dichotomy of city and country and suggests a physical setting that is both built-up and yet undeveloped. Further, it connotes an undifferentiated extension whose uniformity contrasts sharply with the dense physical and social variety associated with the word *urban*. From this perspective, *urban field* suggests an unending repetition and eventual obliteration of the city's distinctive character. Finally, *field* implies a decentered set of relations and thus contradicts the oldest and most basic idea of the city, its sense of place.

The semantic imprecision of the term is demonstrated in its practical application. The developing urban fields are by no means as uniform or homogeneous as their name suggests. In the case of the United States, the 1980 census revealed that major cities of the South and the West were doing significantly better than large cities of the North in terms of income, employment, and opportunities for racial minorities. The major population shift from the Northeast and the Middle West to the South and the West that occurred between 1970 and 1980 attested to the greater opportunities of the Sunbelt. The 1980 census also identified "widening disparities between the residents of central cities in metropolitan areas and those of their surrounding suburbs, not only in income but also in employment, housing, living arrangements, and family structure."[81] So striking were these disparities that, even more than in 1970, the cities and suburbs had become "two different worlds."[82]

Moreover, the changes in urban fields since the 1970s have caused urbanists to reconsider the relationship *between* fields and the relationship of areas *within* each field. The condition of urban fields in the United States is influenced by their regional location. Because the regions developed at different rates and in different ways, until quite recently the critical divide between fields separated those of the Northeast and the Middle West from those of the South and the West. During the late seventies and early eighties, the economic prospects of the Sunbelt seemed to many observers far brighter than

William Sharpe and Leonard Wallock

those of the Frostbelt. However, over the last few years, the rapid population growth and economic expansion of the South and the West have slowed, while the population losses and economic decline of the Northeast appear to have been reversed. In 1985, a *Wall Street Journal* article captured these trends succinctly, observing, "Many parts of the Frost Belt are returning to prosperity, while the Sun Belt has collapsed into only a few 'sunspots.' "[83] Only over the long term will the question of an economic convergence or divergence between these regions (and thereby the contingent fate of individual fields) be resolved.

The ultimate relationship of areas within each urban field has been no less a matter of conjecture. During the early 1970s, some urbanists argued that the energy crisis would limit the spread of metropolitan areas and would precipitate a "recentralization" of the urban field.[84] This forecast was based on several questionable assumptions, not the least of which was that many businesses would begin moving back to the central city. In fact, just the opposite has occurred. New technologies that permit dispersal of workplaces in addition to the disadvantages of operating within central cities have prompted a continuing exodus of businesses from the city to the suburbs.[85] For example, whereas in 1970 fully 75 percent of the nation's offices were located in urban central business districts, by 1983 just 59 percent were found there. The decentralization of business is one of the principal reasons why, in recent years, the suburbs have boomed and prospered— growing by more than 5.8 million people (to 105, 247,000) between 1980 and 1984.[86]

During the 1970s, there were other reasons why a rebirth of cities appeared likely. Most cities "experienced a downtown economic revival and construction boom along with restoration of old housing by the middle class."[87] In the early 1980s the proliferation of urban, high-skill service industries and the spread of gentrification, from Boston's Back Bay to San Francisco's Haight-Ashbury, sustained the hope of an urban renaissance.[88] However, the impact of these developments upon the city's economic and residential base has not been as strong as anticipated. The new growth industries, which employ young urban professionals, have not created sufficient jobs to compensate for declines in manufacturing. Moreover, as John D. Kasarda explains, "there is a widening gap between urban job opportunity structures and the skill levels of disadvantaged residents," which is contributing to "high rates of structural unemployment . . . and rising levels of urban poverty and welfare dependency."[89] While gentrification has taken place in many cities, its extent has been limited, creating little more than what Berry calls "Islands of Renewal in Seas of Decay."[90] Thus, it seems that downtown renewal and gentrification will not succeed in reversing urban decay.[91]

If a recentralization of the urban field appears unlikely, new "metrocenters" are already emerging that offer quite a few of the amenities traditionally associated with life in the big city. Therefore, the recentering of the urban field may take the form not of a downtown renaissance but of a multinodal development.[92] Such an outcome is suggested by the recent burgeoning of Phoenix, Arizona, which extends over 360 square miles and is still spreading. According to the city's planning director, Richard F. Counts, in Phoenix the problem of sprawl is being addressed by creating "new incentives to build self-contained 'villages' within the city, each with jobs, housing and lower density than the city has known in the past."[93] Some new urban centers may develop along the lines of Phoenix's "low-slung, far-flung" metropolitan villages.[94] Others may retain something of their rural appearance and character, such as, Visalia, Tulare, and Porterville, cities in California's San Joaquin Valley between Bakersville and Fresno.[95] Still others, like White Plains, New York, may develop into what architecture critic Paul Goldberger called "a new kind of urban form—a subsidiary downtown offering a mix of suburban convenience and urban amenity."[96] Yet, regardless of the great variety in their forms, functions, and characteristics, all these centers are part of the larger communication and information field that defines them as urban.

Given the new and much less direct relation between spatial propinquity and information exchange, we can only speculate about how the urban center, suburb, and field will take shape in the future. During the 1970s, it was often projected that

William Sharpe and Leonard Wallock

"new technologies would allow everyone to live in cabins in the country and communicate electronically." However, as Donald C. Dahmann of the Census Bureau's population division recently observed, such speculations "failed to reckon with human desires to live together and deal directly with one another."[97] Moreover, corporate headquarters continue to locate in central business districts because their activities "demand a rapid response by corporate financial managers, and this in turn depends on having close and immediate contact with a battery of professional, administrative and other support systems, as well as with . . . competitors."[98] Finally, the fact that cities offer proximity not only to other human beings but to cultural amenities as well may give them an appeal that cannot be reproduced elsewhere. Robert Vaughan persuasively argued this last point more than a hundred years ago in *The Age of Great Cities*.[99] If, as these arguments suggest, certain social, economic, and cultural advantages are unique to the city, then the thrust of future development may be toward a proliferation of new centers rather than toward a homogeneous urban field.

V. The Politics of Urban Metaphor

The evolution of the multifunctional, nested hierarchy of activity centers has given rise to a new form of spatial organization—the polycentric ecological field—which has replaced the technologically antiquated primate structure of the monocentered industrial metropolis.

—John D. Kasarda[100]

The sometimes desperate effort to name the city returns us once again to the metaphoric properties of thought and language that inescapably structure our perceptions of the urban environment.[101] Perhaps the most notable feature of current urban studies has been the persistent use of spatial metaphors to describe the city. In the nineteenth century, the most important metaphor was the organism; the city as a sort of giant human being haunted the writing of poets as diverse as Wordsworth, Baudelaire, and Whitman, while social observers imaged the city as a wen, a cancer, a polyp, a beast, and so on. Today, the Metropolitan Statistical Areas definition relies on the atom—a nuclear city and "orbiting" electron-suburbs—thereby combining connotations of both space and energy. The shift from the organism to the atomic particle, from biology to physics, from something familiar and instantly apprehendable to a structure that we have probably seen only in diagram and that represents lines of force—all this is indicative of our increasingly complex and insecure sense of the contemporary city.

Organic metaphors express a conception of the city as a functioning whole that was common among nineteenth-century observers.[102] From Wordsworth to Baudelaire and beyond, the city seen in its entirety, from a distance or above, has been compared to a body or some other natural object. Now that even an aerial view may not reveal the extent or outline of the metropolis, we rely more and more on diagrammatic metaphors (such as atoms, satellites, doughnuts, and tiers) to represent its contours.[103] The use of such metaphors is likely to continue as long as the urban environment appears unintelligible, for they satisfy a deeply felt need to comprehend the city in visual terms. That a number of recent critics have stressed the importance of "mapping" the contemporary city is indicative of a nostalgia for urban legibility.[104]

Not only do these two varieties of metaphors serve different needs, they operate in different ways. Organic metaphors have been used to concretize functional relations—how the city *works*—whereas diagrammatic metaphors generally attempt to describe spatial relations—how the city *looks*. Both bodies and diagrams can indicate how the city has evolved, but they will not characterize growth in precisely the same ways because they possess different descriptive properties. The organic metaphor treats urban development as if it were natural and inevitable—fluctuations in size are an inherent part of its conception—while the spatial diagram depicts the current shape of the city without specifying the logic of its development. Thus, the diagram must be redrawn in order to encompass change: atoms, solar systems, and tiered wedding cakes normally remain the same in size and configuration. It is

William Sharpe and Leonard Wallock

probably for this reason that we have only one or two extremely versatile and enduring organic metaphors (the body, the plant) while we have many versions of the spatial metaphor.[105]

This fundamental shift in the use of metaphors reflects not only the city's evolution, but also the varying concerns of its observers, for language is intimately bound up with ideology.[106] The way in which we use metaphors indicates our political perspective, since our choice of terms is inseparable from the way we view the world. We must bear in mind, however, that metaphors may be employed in a variety of ways, and in fact the same one is often used by competing parties for different purposes. As Graeme Davison has shown, the organic metaphor was a powerful tool for Victorian public health reformers seeking to cure a diseased urban body; at the same time, it supported the position of conservatives endeavoring to establish the naturalness and immutability of the prevailing systems of political economy. Meanwhile, Engels and other radical reformers, realizing that organicism prevented a genuine consideration of economic alternatives, were eager to debunk the idea of laissez-faire capitalism as natural and inevitable.[107]

In "Politics and the English Language" (1946), George Orwell extends this analysis of organicism's inherently conservative nature to language itself, commenting: "It is generally assumed that we cannot by conscious action do anything about [the words we use]. . . . Underneath this lies the half-conscious belief that language is a natural growth and not an instrument which we shape for our own purposes."[108] Like Engels, Orwell recognized that metaphors affect our view of whether the thing being described is subject to change. Both saw that the way in which language is used can facilitate or impede political action. For this reason, we must constantly test our language against the social reality it describes. Reconsidering our terms allows us to think differently about, and perhaps alter, the status quo.

The current language reveals a series of assumptions which prejudice our analysis of the city and limit our view of its future. Perhaps the most popular term that urbanists have used to characterize the look of postwar American cities has been *doughnut complex*. According to George Sternlieb and James W. Hughes, "in many places the hole in the doughnut is a decaying central city and the ring is a prosperous and growing suburban and exurban region."[109] This terminology juxtaposes a rich, sweet morsel with an empty area that gives the pastry its shape and worth. But Sternlieb and Hughes then reverse the doughnut metaphor to account for cities such as New York, where "the hole is a core area of the city that is being revitalized and the ring is a surrounding part of the city that is becoming increasingly blighted." Unable to fit these opposing patterns of urban development into their metaphor, they turn the doughnut inside out and violate its logic. In either usage, this metaphor creates the impression that the affluent, white, middle-class areas are the only desirable portions of the metropolis, and that the areas populated by largely poor, largely minority groups are worthless and nonexistent. Moreover, *doughnut complex* shares the properties of other spatial metaphors in being ahistorical and in giving the impression of fixity. Taken individually, spatial metaphors make no reference either to past or to future and make no provision at all for change. For this reason their effect is like that of the organic metaphor of the nineteenth century: both suggest that little can be done to alter the current state of affairs.[110]

Today the challenge to urbanists is to develop a vocabulary that can speak to the ongoing process of urban development rather than its spatial contours at any given moment. Similarly, we need terms that will emphasize the new patterns of economic and social interaction that our long-standing preoccupation with proximity and place has obscured. In short, as urban geographers have long maintained, we need to address the temporal as well as the spatial dimensions of the modern city. Doing so will require us to move from definition by negation (decentered city, non-place urban realm, doughnut) to a new set of positive terms. Whether the new language will be derived from the computer, systems engineering, or some other space-age, "high-tech" field is hard to say. Whatever words we employ, field or atom or something as yet unnamed,

William Sharpe and Leonard Wallock

they will help shape our city, for the kind of metaphors we choose will influence the kind of city we see. As the examples of Engels and Orwell show, learning how to read the city is a necessary part of learning how to change it.

NOTES

1. "The Modern City as a Field of Historical Study," in *The Historian and the City*, ed. Oscar Handlin and John Burchard (Cambridge, Mass., 1963), p. 25.

2. "Letter 3," in *Selected Writings*, ed. Robert Creeley (New York, 1966), p. 225.

3. For an overview of the causes of urbanization, see Eric E. Lampard, "The Nature of Urbanization," reprinted in this volume.

4. Melvin M. Webber, "The Urban Place and the Nonplace Urban Realm," in *Explorations in Urban Structure*, ed. Melvin M. Webber *et al.* (Philadelphia, 1964), p. 79.

5. *An Anthology of New York Poets*, ed. Ron Padgett and David Shapiro (New York, 1970), p. xxxv.

6. Friedrich Engels, *The Condition of the Working Class in England*, trans. and ed. W. O. Henderson and W. H. Chaloner (Stanford, 1958); Henry Mayhew, *London Labour and the London Poor*, Introduction by John D. Rosenberg, 4 vols. (New York, 1968); and Charles Booth, *On the City: Physical Pattern and Social Structure*, ed. Harold W. Pfautz (Chicago, 1967). Another important contributor to the classic literature on the nineteenth-century city was Adna Ferrin Weber, who carried out a comprehensive analysis of the causes and consequences of population growth in *The Growth of Cities in the Nineteenth Century: A Study in Statistics* (New York, 1899).

7. Booth, pp. 18, 22.

8. See Steven Marcus, "Reading the Illegible," in *The Victorian City: Images and Realities*, ed. H. J. Dyos and Michael Wolff (London, 1973), I, 257–58, and *passim;* see also the opening pages of his essay in this volume.

9. Max Weber, *The City*, trans. and ed. Don Martindale and Gertrud Neuwirth (New York, 1958); Georg Simmel, "The Metropolis and Mental Life," in *Classic Essays on the Culture of Cities*, ed. Richard Sennett (Englewood Cliffs, N.J., 1969); and Booth, p. 85.

10. Simmel, p. 59.

11. Robert E. Park and Ernest W. Burgess, *The City*, Introduction by Morris Janowitz (Chicago, 1967), p. 1.

12. Park and Burgess, p. 4.

13. *Classic Essays on the Culture of Cities*, ed. Richard Sennett (Englewood Cliffs, N.J., 1969), p. 16.

14. Malcolm Bradbury, "The Cities of Modernism," in *Modernism*, ed. Malcolm Bradbury and James McFarlane (New York, 1976), pp. 96, 98–99.

15. "The Idea of the City in European Thought: Voltaire to Spengler," in Handlin and Burchard, pp. 95–114.

16. See Leslie Fiedler, "Mythicizing the City," and Leo Marx, "The Puzzle of Anti-Urbanism," in *Literature and the Urban Experience*, ed. Michael C. Jaye and Ann Chalmers Watts (New Brunswick, N.J., 1981), pp. 113–21 and 64–79, respectively. See also Morton White, "Two Stages in the Critique of the American City," in Handlin and Burchard, p. 87.

17. Henry David Thoreau, *Walden* (1854; rpt. New York, 1964), p. 260.

18. Historians have usually emphasized the transition from the medieval town to the early modern and modern city in Europe, and from the colonial town to the nineteenth- and twentieth-century city in the United States. Two outstanding examples are Oscar Handlin, "The Modern City as a Field of Historical Study," in Handlin and Burchard, pp. 1–26, and Sam Bass Warner, Jr., "If All the World Were Philadelphia: A Scaffolding for Urban History, 1774–1930," *American Historical Review* 74 (October 1968): 26–43. Although the three phases in the development of the modern city described in this essay have not been widely adopted, they have been well documented by historians and social scientists. It should be noted that this process of development did not occur in all large cities at the same time, to the same degree, or in the same way. Moreover, no attempt has been made here to differentiate between the various types of cities that existed during each developmental phase.

19. On the first phase of the modern city, see Asa Briggs, *Victorian Cities* (London, 1963); H. J. Dyos and Michael Wolff, eds., *The Victorian City: Images and Realities*, 2 vols. (London, 1973); Donald J. Olsen, *The Growth of Victorian London* (New York, 1976); David H. Pinkney, *Napoleon III and the Rebuilding of Paris* (Princeton, 1958); Howard Saalman, *Haussmann: Paris Transformed* (New York, 1971); Oscar Handlin, *Boston's Immigrants, 1790–1865: A Study in Acculturation* (Cambridge, Mass., 1941); Robert G. Albion, *The Rise of New York Port, 1815–1860* (New York, 1939); and Sam Bass Warner, Jr., *The*

William Sharpe and Leonard Wallock

Private City: Philadelphia in Three Periods of Its Growth (Philadelphia, 1968).

20. David Ward, *Cities and Immigrants: A Geography of Change in Nineteenth-Century America* (New York, 1971), pp. 125–45; Kenneth T. Jackson, "Urban Deconcentration in the Nineteenth Century: A Statistical Inquiry," in *The New Urban History*, ed. Leo F. Schnore (Princeton, 1975), pp. 110–42.

21. Warner, "If All the World Were Philadelphia," p. 35.

22. On the second phase of the modern city, see Alan A. Jackson, *Semi-Detached London: Suburban Development, Life and Transport, 1900–1939* (London, 1973); S. G. Checkland, *The Upas Tree: Glasgow, 1875–1975: A Study in Growth and Contraction* (Glasgow, 1976); Anthony Sutcliffe, *The Autumn of Central Paris: The Defeat of Town Planning, 1850–1970* (London, 1970); Norma Evenson, *Paris: A Century of Change, 1878–1978* (New Haven, 1979); Sam Bass Warner, Jr., *Streetcar Suburbs: The Process of Growth in Boston, 1870–1900* (Cambridge, Mass., 1962); Robert Fogelson, *The Fragmented Metropolis: Los Angeles, 1850–1930* (Cambridge, Mass., 1967); and James Marston Fitch, *American Building: The Historical Forces That Shaped It*, 2nd ed., rev. and enl. (New York, 1973).

23. Anthony Downs, "Alternative Forms of Future Urban Growth in the United States," *Journal of the American Institute of Planners* 36 (January 1970): 5.

24. Eric Lampard, "The Nature of Urbanization," reprinted in this volume.

25. *New York Times*, July 8, 1983.

26. *New York Times*, September 28, 1986. In *The Twentieth-Century American City: Problem, Promise, and Reality*, Jon C. Teaford concludes similarly that "Americans opted for the dissolution of the city and . . . created the dispersed and fragmented metropolitan world of the late twentieth century" (Baltimore, 1986, p. 156). See also Barry Edmonston and Thomas M. Guterbock, "Is Suburbanization Slowing Down? Recent Trends in Population Deconcentration in U.S. Metropolitan Areas," *Social Forces* 62 (Winter 1984): 905–25; Michael H. Ebner, "Re-Reading Suburban America: Urban Population Deconcentration, 1810–1980," *American Quarterly* 37 (1985): 368–81; and Barry Checkoway and Carl V. Patton, eds., *The Metropolitan Midwest: Policy Problems and Prospects for Change* (Urbana, Ill., 1985), pp. 2–3.

27. Webber, p. 81.

28. Webber, p. 89.

29. Brian J. L. Berry, "The Urban Problem," in *The Farm and the City: Rivals or Allies?* (Englewood Cliffs, N.J., 1980), p. 52.

30. Charles Dickens, *Dombey and Son* (1848; rpt. New York, 1970), pp. 120–21.

31. Engels, p. 31.

32. Marcus, "Reading the Illegible," in *The Victorian City,* p. 265.

33. Rosenberg, p. vii.

34. Raymond Williams, *The Country and the City* (New York, 1973), p. 235.

35. Simmel, p. 56.

36. Williams, p. 243.

37. Collected in Thomas Wolfe, *From Death to Morning* (New York, 1935), p. 91.

38. Reprinted in *The Structuralist Controversy,* ed. Richard Macksey and Eugenio Donato (Baltimore, 1972), p. 260.

39. Marcus, "Reading the Illegible," in *The Victorian City,* p. 258.

40. Wordsworth, *The Prelude* (1805) VII, 695; Charles Dickens, *Bleak House* (1853), chapter 52.

41. Lewis Mumford, *The Culture of Cities* (New York, 1938; rpt. 1970), pp. 183–90.

42. Kevin Lynch, *The Image of the City* (Cambridge, Mass., 1960), pp. 2–3.

43. Lynch, pp. 9–10.

44. Marcus, "Reading the Illegible," in *The Victorian City,* p. 257.

45. See *Manet and Modern Paris* (Washington, D.C., 1982), pp. 171–99.

46. Charles Baudelaire, *Oeuvres Complètes,* ed. Y.-G. Le Dantec and Claude Pichois (Paris, 1961), p. 1146.

47. Charles Baudelaire, preface to *Petits Poèmes en prose (Le Spleen de Paris)* (1863; rpt. Paris, 1967), p. 32.

48. Louis Sullivan, *Kindergarten Chats and Other Essays,* ed. Isabella Athey (New York, 1947), p. 206.

49. Cited in Peter Conrad, *The Victorian Treasure House* (London, 1973), p. 195.

50. Cited in Conrad, p. 9.

51. Engels, p. 56.

52. See Brian J. L. Berry, "Islands of Renewal in Seas of Decay," in *The New Urban Reality*, ed. Paul E. Peterson (Washington, D.C., 1985), pp. 69–96. Berry's study confirms what he calls "the gentrification hypothesis": that the key role in the rehabilitation of decaying homes and the restoration of blighted neighborhoods is being played by [mainly white,] relatively affluent, childless two-worker families—"yuppies" (83). In the typical gentrification scenario, visible physical improvements are soon followed by media attention, investment capital, high-priced shops and services, and a new set of well-to-do residents who "displace most of the remaining indigenous residents" (79).

53. The concept of literary gentrification, which was developed together by the co-editors of this volume, was first presented in a paper by William Sharpe entitled "Muck, Decay, and Literary Gentrification: New York in Literature since 1945," delivered at the Modern Language Association convention in New York, December 1986.

54. Literary gentrification has its counterpart in films such as *Desperately Seeking Susan* (1984) and *After Hours* (1985).

55. This is very clearly the case for black and Jewish ethnic writing of the postwar era: Ann Petry's *The Street* (1946) portrays the brutalizing environment of Harlem at 116th Street and Seventh Avenue; Paule Marshall's *Brown Girl, Brownstones* (1959) reveals the aspirations of the West Indian community in the area around Chauncey Street in Brooklyn; Bernard Malamud's *The Assistant* (1957) chronicles the marginal existence of a poor shopkeeper on the fringes of Eastern Parkway in Brooklyn; and Saul Bellow's *Seize the Day* (1956), *Herzog* (1964), and *Mr. Sammler's Planet* (1970) focus on middle-class despair at the deterioration of the Upper West Side of Manhattan. Among the many other works of the postwar period marked by a strong sense of geography and community are James Baldwin's *Go Tell It on the Mountain* (1953) and Ralph Ellison's *Invisible Man* (1952), which describe Harlem in the forties; Chaim Potok's *The Chosen* (1967) and *The Promise* (1969), which depict Hassidic life in Williamsburg, Brooklyn; Betty Smith's *A Tree Grows in Brooklyn* (1943), which affectionately recalls Irish family life in the Williamsburg section decades earlier; and Hubert Selby, Jr.'s, *Last Exit to Brooklyn* (1964), which details the violent and degraded life of Red Hook and the vicinity of the Brooklyn Army Terminal.

56. Whether treating the wealthy legal world of Louis Auchincloss's *Diary of a Yuppie* (1986) or the wackily narcissistic East Village nightlife spoofed in Paul Rudnick's *Social Disease* (1986), the gentrified novel eschews description of urban exteriors in favor of party scenes, dia-

logue, and ruminations about the morality of mergers and credit cards. Even Paul Auster's *New York Trilogy,* whose reliance on the conventions of the hard-boiled detective story promises a more sustained engagement with the city's environment, reduces the mimetic city to a minimum: "The address is unimportant. But let's say Brooklyn Heights, for the sake of argument. Some quiet, rarely traveled street not far from the bridge—Orange Street, perhaps. Walt Whitman handset the first edition of Leaves of Grass on this street in 1855, and it was here that Henry Ward Beecher railed against slavery from the pulpit of his red-brick church. So much for local color" (*Ghosts* [New York, 1986], p. 10).

57. For a consideration of the ways in which current New York fiction is deficient in "social ecology" and lacking in class analysis, see Lewis Cole, "City Limits," *Manhattan, Inc.* (December 1986): 189–92.

58. On the creation of a "Loft Lifestyle" see Sharon Zukin, *Loft Living: Culture and Capital in Urban Change* (Baltimore, 1982), pp. 58–81.

59. Tama Janowitz, "Spells," *Slaves of New York* (New York, 1986), p. 154.

60. Similarly, because he deals in distancing stereotypes, the insecure hero of *Bright Lights, Big City* cannot communicate with anybody. The second person singular narrative technique that gives the book its colloquial immediacy also dramatically highlights the extent to which the protagonist-narrator is talking to himself.

61. In *Portrait of an American City: The Novelists' New York,* literary critic Joan Zlotnick analyzes the images of New York in fiction from the Second World War through the mid-seventies, finding that the images most commonly employed are of bleakness, despair, anomie, violence, filth, decay, poverty, and crime (Port Washington, N.Y., 1982, pp. 165–221). Authors such as Saul Bellow, Bernard Malamud, James Baldwin, J. D. Salinger, and Sue Kaufman characterize the city's environment as hostile and inhospitable to both the artist and the ordinary resident. Their negative images suggest that the pessimistic portrayal of New York may correspond to the postwar crisis in urban affairs and the flight from the city that began in the sixties. Zlotnick concludes her survey with the remark that very few of these writers can "reassure us that there is more to New York than a crime-infested, polluted metropolis whose residents live in constant fear for their lives and sanity" (216).

62. Madison Smartt Bell, *Waiting for the End of the World* (New York, 1985), pp. 19–20.

63. Paul Auster, *City of Glass,* vol. 1 of *The New York Trilogy* (New York, 1985), p. 123.

64. A similar fate meets the detective hero of the second volume of *The New York Trilogy, Ghosts* (New York, 1986): A disguised writer hires the detective to do nothing but surreptitiously watch the writer over a period of years. The detective breaks off all contacts with the world at large as he becomes increasingly obsessed with his inability to make the words of his reports reflect the experience of his incomprehensible stake-out.

65. Webber, p. 79.

66. Webber, p. 116.

67. Webber, p. 118.

68. Webber, pp. 128–29.

69. Downs, p. 11.

70. *New York Times,* July 8, 1983. Though it was not yet apparent, according to census figures a reversal had already occurred in which metropolitan rather than nonmetropolitan areas were again leading the nation's population growth. Whether this was an actual trend or a mere artifact of changing census definitions was unclear. This further demonstrates the obsolescence of the terms "metropolitan" and "nonmetropolitan." See Richard A. Engels and Richard L. Forstall, "Metropolitan Areas Dominate Growth Again," *American Demographics* 7 (April 1985): 23–25, 45; *New York Times,* April 13, 1986.

71. *New York Times,* July 8, 1983.

72. *New York Times,* July 8, 1983.

73. "Account has also been taken of the political organization of the places in question and urban classification has been given for the most part only to those places which were incorporated as cities, towns, boroughs, or villages, and which in addition had the required number of inhabitants. This requirement of the status of municipal incorporation was perhaps not really an additional factor, though, but rather a recognition of the fact that separate counts of the compact population were made only for areas which were separate political entities and therefore had definite boundaries which could be followed by the enumerator." Leon F. Truesdell, "The Development of the Urban-Rural Classification in the United States Census," *Current Population Reports,* Series P-23, No. 1 (Washington, D.C., 1949), p. 2.

74. U.S. Bureau of the Census, "Thirteenth Census of the United States Taken in the Year 1910," *Population 1910,* vol. 1 (Washington, D.C., 1913), p. 73.

75. U.S. Bureau of the Budget, "Standard Metropolitan Area Definitions," (Washington, D.C., 1950), p. 1; see also Appendix II, "Metropolitan Area Concepts and Components," in U.S. Bureau of the Census, *Statistical Abstracts of the United States, 1982–1983* (Washington, D.C., 1982), pp. 895–96.

76. U.S. Office of Management and Budget, *Metropolitan Statistical Areas, 1983* (Washington, D.C., 1983), p. 2.

77. *New York Times,* July 8, 1983.

78. *New York Times,* July 8, 1983.

79. Berry, "The Urban Problem," p. 52.

80. In the 1960s a number of different terms, such as *megalopolis* and *spread city,* were proposed to describe urban expansion. See Mark Gottdiener, *Planned Sprawl: Private and Public Interests in Suburbia* (Beverly Hills, Calif., 1977), pp. 15, 28. The term *urban field* was coined by John Friedmann and John Miller in 1965 to signify "the older established centers, together with the intermetropolitan peripheries that envelop them." They anticipated that such fields would "constitute the new ecological unit of America's post-industrial society," replacing "traditional concepts of the city and metropolis." Their expectation that this "ecological" term would describe "the constantly widening patterns of interaction in an urbanizing world" and would address the "space-time continuum" of the modern city, went unfulfilled. As observers sought to characterize more precisely the types of development within the urban field, spatial models predominated and temporal images receded. What coiners of the term failed to reckon with was the primarily spatial connotation and appeal of the metaphor. Even the scientific connotations of *urban field* (magnetic field, particle field) carry a primarily spatial emphasis. "The Urban Field," *Journal of the American Institute of Planners* 31 (November 1965): 312–13, 319.

81. *New York Times,* February 27 and 28, 1983. On the urban problems of northeastern cities, see Katharine L. Bradbury, Anthony Downs, and Kenneth A. Small, *Urban Decline and the Future of American Cities* (Washington, D.C., 1982), p. 48; Katherine L. Bradbury, "Urban Decline and Distress: An Update," *New England Economic Review,* July–August 1984, p. 45.

82. *New York Times,* February 27, 1983.

83. *Wall Street Journal,* November 19, 1985; see also Peter A. Rogerson and David A. Plane, "Monitoring Migration Trends," *American Demographics* 7 (February 1985): 27–28, 47; *New York Times,* May 5, August 21, and December 30, 1985; January 19, April 21, June 8, and

August 24, 1986; Alexander Ganz, "Where Has the Urban Crisis Gone: How Boston and Other Large Cities Have Stemmed Economic Decline," in *Cities in Distress: A New Look at the Urban Crisis*, ed. M. Gottdiener (Beverly Hills, Calif., 1985), pp. 39–58. On the future of the Frostbelt and Sunbelt, see David C. Perry and Alfred J. Watkins, *The Rise of the Sunbelt Cities* (Beverly Hills, Calif., 1977); Carl Abbott, *The New Urban America: Growth and Politics in Sunbelt Cities* (Chapel Hill, N.C., 1981); Richard M. Bernard and Bradley R. Rice, eds., *Sunbelt Cities: Politics and Growth since World War II* (Austin, Tex., 1983); Barry Checkoway and Carl V. Patton, eds., *The Metropolitan Midwest: Policy Problems and Prospects for Change* (Urbana, Ill., 1985); and George Sternlieb and James W. Hughes, "Frost over the Sunbelt," in *Patterns of Development*, ed. George Sternlieb (New Brunswick, N.J., 1986), pp. 211–20.

84. Allan C. Ornstein, of Loyola University in Chicago, explains that, "after two decades of watching helplessly while their middle-class citizens pulled up stakes and headed for the suburbs, mayors and educators took heart in the 1970s over a projected 'return to the cities.' According to this hopeful scenario, a combination of commuting costs, condomania and urban renaissance would reverse the flight of the white middle class. With their return to the American city would come new jobs and new housing, an integrated city as well as integrated schools, an improved tax base and general prosperity. It didn't happen." Quoted in the *New York Times*, February 27, 1983.

85. In his essay that appears in this volume, Eric Lampard concludes similarly that "with the prospect of low-energy telecommunications, cable computerization, automated back offices and other database management systems coming 'in place,' the demand for space in centralized, energy expensive, business districts will in all probability be reduced in the 1980s." See also *New York Times*, May 13, 1984 and December 2, 1986; "Why Many Firms Return to Smaller Cities," *U.S. News & World Report*, April 2, 1984, pp. 76–77; Manuel Castells, "High Technology, Economic Restructuring, and the Urban-Regional Process in the United States," in *High Technology, Space, and Society*, ed. Manuel Castells (Beverly Hills, Calif., 1985), pp. 11–40.

86. "A Return to the Suburbs," *Newsweek*, July 21, 1986, p. 52; "America's Suburbs Still Alive and Doing Fine," *U.S. News & World Report*, March 12, 1984, pp. 59–62; Kenneth T. Jackson, *Crabgrass Frontier: The Suburbanization of the United States* (New York, 1985).

87. *New York Times*, February 27, 1983.

88. "The Year of the Yuppie," *Newsweek*, December 31, 1984, pp. 14–31. See also *Wall Street Journal*, August 21, 1984; *International Herald Tribune*, April 11, 1985.

89. John D. Kasarda, "Urban Change and Minority Opportunities," in Peterson, p. 34; George Sternlieb and James H. Hughes, "The Changing Demography of the Central City," *Scientific American* 243 (August 1980): 48–53.

90. Berry, "Islands of Renewal in Seas of Decay," in Peterson, pp. 69–96. See also Neil Smith, "Toward a Theory of Gentrification: A Back to the City Movement by Capital Not People," *Journal of the American Planning Association* 45 (October 1979): 538–48; H. Briavel Holcomb and Robert A. Beauregard, *Revitalizing Cities* (Washington, D.C., 1981); J. John Palen and Bruce London, eds., *Gentrification, Displacement and Neighborhood Revitalization* (Albany, N.Y., 1984); Richard Schaffer and Neil Smith, "The Gentrification of Harlem?" *Annals of the American Association of Geographers* 76 no. 3 (1986): 347–65; Neil Smith and Peter Williams, eds., *The Gentrification of the City* (Boston, 1986).

91. This conclusion was reached as early as 1980 by Richard Nathan in a study for the Brookings Institution (*New York Times*, February 27, 1983). See also John D. Kasarda, "The Implications of Contemporary Distribution Trends for National Urban Policy," *Social Science Quarterly* 61 (December 1980): 387–89; George Sternlieb and James W. Hughes, "Back to the Central City: Myths and Realities," in *America's Housing: Prospects and Problems*, ed. George Sternlieb and James W. Hughes (New Brunswick, N.J., 1980), pp. 153–75.

92. Kasarda, "The Implications of Contemporary Distribution Trends," pp. 390–91.

93. *New York Times*, February 28, 1983.

94. Berry, "The Urban Problem," p. 50.

95. These examples illustrate how urban fields are extending beyond the metropolitan fringe and engulfing even rural locales. J. C. Doherty labelled the new areas of low-density development "countrified cities," while others have chosen the term "citified country" to depict this phenomenon. According to John Herbers, such areas "cannot be classified as rural, suburban, or urban in the way most people think of those terms; they are a mixture of all three" and constitute what is "in essence a new form of American community." *New York Times*, March 23, 1980, and September 28, 1986. See also Larry Long and Diana DeAre, "The Slowing of Urbanization in the U.S." *Scientific American* 249 (July 1983): 33–41; Engels and Forstall, p. 23; and *New York Times*, January 16, 1986.

96. *New York Times*, July 12, 1983.

97. *New York Times*, April 13, 1986.

98. See Smith, "Gentrification, the Frontier, and the Restructuring of Urban Space," in Smith and Williams, p. 28.

99. *The Age of Great Cities: Modern Society Viewed in Its Relation to Intelligence, Morals and Religion* (London, 1843).

100. Kasarda, "The Implications of Contemporary Distribution Trends," pp. 390–91.

101. Portions of this section were originally presented by the authors in two papers: "'The Words that Describe It': Metaphors of Urban Culture in the Postmodern Era," at a conference entitled "The City and Culture: New York and Paris, 1945–1985," Reid Hall, Paris, June 1986; and "Imaging the Modern City," at the Society of Fellows in the Humanities' Symposium, "Begetting Images," Columbia University, March 1987.

102. Engels and those who saw themselves as trying to read an illegible city did not use the organic metaphor—or if they did, they challenged, qualified, or undercut it. Thus, in *The Condition of the Working Class in England,* Engels stresses the artificial or labyrinthine qualities of Manchester (see Davison, below) and in *Bleak House* Dickens subverts the organic unity of London (see William Sharpe, "Time, Tense and Organicism in the Victorian City," delivered at the MLA convention, New York, 1986).

103. Although other metaphors have taken precedence, the organic metaphor continues to be used. For example, several of the standard works on gentrification use the same word, "revitalization," to describe the recent history of the city (see above, note 90).

104. See, for example Frederic Jameson's call for a "cognitive mapping" of contemporary urban culture. Basing his strategy on Kevin Lynch's *The Image of the City,* Jameson notes that "we are here in the presence of something like a mutation in built space itself," and he turns to the metaphor of cartography as a means of endowing "the individual subject with some new heightened sense of its place in the global system." Frederic Jameson, "The Cultural Logic of Late Capitalism," *New Left Review* 146 (July–August 1984): 80, 92.

105. The contemporary preoccupation with spatial urban imagery expresses itself somewhat differently in the work of writers and artists. Although they employ similar diagrammatic metaphors (atoms, printed circuits, grids), their emphasis is likely to be on how these organizing structures have been confused, overlaid, or undermined. Hence the numerous references to Babylon and the Apocalypse, to contemporary towers of Babel, to centerless labyrinths and urban hieroglyphics for which we have no key. Thus, in *Paterson,*

William Carlos Williams compares the sprawling city to the radioactive element of uranium: "that complex / atom, always breaking down" (New York, 1963, p. 178).

106. As Paul de Man notes in his essay "The Resistance to Theory," sensitivity to language is a necessary component of any sophisticated political analysis: "what we call ideology is precisely the confusion of linguistic with natural reality, of reference with phenomenalism. It follows that, more than any other mode of inquiry, including economics, the linguistics of literariness is a powerful and indispensable tool in the unmasking of ideological aberrations, as well as a determining factor in accounting for their occurrence" (*Yale French Studies* 63 [1982], p. 11). On the political character of metaphor, see also George Lakoff and Mark Johnson, *Metaphors We Live By* (Chicago, 1980), pp. 236–37; and Dwight Bolinger, *Language—The Loaded Weapon: The Use and Abuse of Language Today* (London, 1980). For a theoretical examination of the role of metaphor, see Sheldon Sacks, ed., *On Metaphor* (Chicago, 1979).

107. Graeme Davison, "The City as Natural System: Theories of Urban Society in Early Nineteenth-Century Britain," *The Pursuit of Urban History,* ed. Derek Fraser and Anthony Sutcliffe (London, 1983), pp. 349–70. According to Davison, Engels' "Great Towns" chapter is "a devastating, if largely implicit, attack on the idea of the city as a social system. His favourite metaphors are of disorder . . . and of artificiality" (368). Davison also quotes the Owenite reformer James Hole's rejoinder to organicist claims that laissez-faire capitalism was the natural, God-given state of human affairs: "The selection of London as proof that the unconscious working of 'the natural laws' of wealth are vastly superior to any *arrangements* of wisdom and benevolence shows how much the influence of . . . a preconceived theory can impair the perception of the strongest minds. . . . So 'excellently' do the natural laws adjust the material relations of man, that while the productive labourers . . . are perpetually kept at the verge of starvation, those who *produce* no wealth . . . appropriate the lion's share" (367).

108. "Politics and the English Language," in *The Norton Anthology of English Literature,* Vol. 2, ed. M. H. Abrams *et al.,* 5th ed. (New York, 1986), p. 2260.

109. Sternlieb and Hughes, "The Changing Demography of the Central City," p. 48.

110. For an analysis of the political implications of other current terms such as "renaissance" and "revival," see Peter Williams and Neil Smith, "From 'Renaissance' to Restructuring: The Dynamics of Contemporary Urban Development," in Smith and Williams, pp. 204–24.

William Sharpe and Leonard Wallock

The Nature of Urbanization

Eric E. Lampard

. . . indeed Human Ecology would be a good alternative name for
this new history as I conceive it.
—H. G. Wells, *Experiment in Autobiography*, 1931

This paper serves as an introductory "back to basics" in
the study of urbanization. It reviews the course of modern
urbanization and moves from what is known, or thought to
be known, about the process toward speculation. The concern
here is with certain general tendencies of society which, in
concert, may ultimately effect its transformation: (1) *the growth
and concentration of population since the eighteenth century* and
their association in time and place with *industrialization of productive activities,* and (2) the apparent *dissociation* of these phenomena during the present century in some of the older
industrial-urban countries leading to some deconcentration
of population and a partial de-capitalization of the urban core.
Finally, the paper confronts the possibility that capitalized
social change now renders the inherited morphology of urban
society obsolete much as "progress" outmoded small-town rural society across wide areas of Europe and North America
during the late-nineteenth and early-twentieth centuries. An

This essay represents a shortened version of "The Nature of Urbanization"
in *The Pursuit of Urban History,* ed. Derek Fraser and Anthony Sutcliffe
(London: Edward Arnold, 1983); © Edward Arnold, reprinted with permission. The occasion for these reflections was a correspondence between
H. J. Dyos and the author in 1978 concerning a projected conference "on
the whole ethos and method of urban history." At that time Dyos remarked,
"I am thinking that it would help to clarify the forces producing urbanization in the past if we could extrapolate a little and take account, among
other things, of technological change in the present and future in order
to see the historical discreteness of the process at full stretch." The statistical
bases for arguments presented in this essay are given in the original volume.

exploration of these issues may perhaps throw some light upon questions regarding the abatement or possible reversal of the urban trend.

The Course of Urbanization

Almost 90 years ago a young American economist, Adna F. Weber, contrasted the demographic situation in the rapidly developing country of Australia *c.* 1890, with a third or more of its settler population already resident in cities of 10,000 or more residents, and that of the United States a century earlier, *c.* 1790, with approximately the same number of people of broadly similar culture and resources, but with little more than 3 percent resident in such concentrations. "The vital fact" explaining the difference Weber asserted, was that "Australia is of the nineteenth century, rather than the eighteenth century." He was merely echoing a consensus among many late-nineteenth-century observers that "the most remarkable social phenomenon" of the age was "the concentration of population in cities."[1] Meanwhile, of course, parts of North America and other continents had also experienced "the nineteenth century" such that, by Weber's measure of concentration, the population of the United States *c.* 1890 was 28 percent and the Dominion of Canada almost 18 percent "urbanized." Less than a century before, only the Netherlands and the United Kingdom among countries anywhere in the world had attained such levels of concentration but by 1890 Belgium, Germany, France, Uruguay, and Argentina had fallen into line behind the United Kingdom and the others with a quarter to one half of their growing populations dwelling in towns with 10,000 or more residents.

By "nineteenth century" as explanation, Weber meant to epitomize that prodigious adaptation of physical and social environments whereby humans were bringing about a reversal of the proportions in which historically they had distributed their numbers between town and country. As recently as the close of the eighteenth century from 80 to 95 percent

Eric E. Lampard

of populations everywhere had still lived and worked in small towns and rural communities with fewer than 10,000 inhabitants but, as the nineteenth century waned, in certain countries only 50 to 60 percent of much larger numbers dwelt in such villages and countrysides. By Weber's measure of concentration, nevertheless, fewer than a dozen countries were yet fully participating in the remarkable adaptation of that century.

Certainly Weber was aware that cities inordinately large in population or built area had existed at one time or another since remote antiquity. The peculiar nineteenth-century achievement, however, was population concentration. For many of his contemporaries, perhaps, concentration meant no more than growth of urban population and increases in the incidence of great cities *but it is clear* that Weber meant the tendency for "city" populations in the aggregate to increase *relatively*, or even absolutely, faster than "rural" or "noncity" populations. Like other pundits of the day, he sought to understand "the forces" that were producing "such a shifting population," whether they were likely to persist into the twentieth century, and what "the economic, moral, political, and social consequences of redistribution" would be in areas where those forces appeared likely to empty the countrysides of people within a matter of decades—in certain localities rural depopulation was already a fact.

Deconcentration or, at least, local decentralization was also a late-Victorian interest, although it was not generally identified with either depopulation or decay. Many saw it hopefully, with Charles Horton Cooley in the early 1890s, as fostering *détente* in an otherwise "permanent conflict between the needs of industry and the needs of humanity." By means of "the city railways," it had become possible to reconcile the industrial requirement of aggregation with the human and domestic need for space.[2] Commenting in 1909 on a marked reduction in statutory "overcrowding" in the towns of England and Wales over the last decade of the century, Arthur Shadwell, a prominent epidemiologist and "efficiency expert," emphasized that the achievement was not simply a statistical illusion resulting from "the extension of boundaries" but an "actual decrease of overcrowded persons." "Tramways have made the outskirts accessible," Shadwell concluded, "and builders have utilized the opportunity." Similar relief was afforded German towns where the recent growth and concentration of population and manufactures had produced the most acute housing problem in Europe. During the 1890s the proportion of all Germans resident in large cities had more than doubled but "increasing wealth and a rising standard of living" had led to improved dwellings with larger numbers of rooms and, as a consequence of "cheap locomotive facilities," the "reduction of the population in old insanitary quarters." Since the "bulk of urban Germany"—according to accounts given the International Housing Congress in London in 1907— was of recent construction, it was principally from new and rehabilitated structures, rather than demolition, that the betterment had stemmed: all under a system of benevolent local controls, "particularly the principle of town planning, coupled with the purchase of neighbouring ground with a view to future expansion."[3]

By the early-twentieth century, larger numbers and proportions of townspeople in leading industrial countries could be found living in residential suburbs either within or beyond their city's municipal bounds. Since the area on the city's perimeter increased as the square of the distance from its center, the faster speeds of public transport appeared to be solving the nineteenth-century "city problem" insofar, at least, as it was rooted in overcrowding and congestion.

By and large decentralization has been the prevailing tendency in the more urbanized, high-income countries of this century. Weberian optimism and liberal prescription regarding the benign morphology of city growth seemed to be borne out (at least until the early-twentieth-century solutions were recycled during the interwar years as the emergent "problems of the automobile age"). To be sure, we have vastly enlarged "the data base" for comparative study and many points in the economic and demographic analyses of population growth and redistribution have been greatly refined since Weber's day, but the core of his remarkable understanding of nineteenth-century concentration seems as valid today as when

Eric E. Lampard

published 80-odd years ago. We can amend him in historical particulars, re-do his arithmetic in places, update him on some of the issues, and narrow or widen the scope of his conclusions somewhat in the light of accumulated experience but, in the main, his work on the conditions for population concentration has not been superseded. Even the turn-of-the-century confidence that a market society could find answers to "the Social Question" without recourse to costly and imperfect bureaucratic remedies is paralleled by today's enthusiasm for private sector therapy reborn since World War II in conjunction with the positivist pronouncements of the policy scientists and the editors of *The Economist*. Yet, as Weber would surely have reminded us, *we are of the twentieth century:* we cannot reinstate the nineteenth century even with computers. We must take account of the further unfolding of human ecology since 1900 in order to assess the historical discreteness of the urbanization process "at full stretch."

However, to consider urbanization over its full course, we should first go back to its beginnings at the latter half of the eighteenth century. We need not go back further, since at that time no more than 2.4 percent of an estimated world population *c.* 900 millions resided in concentrations of 20,000 or more inhabitants, while at the close of Weber's nineteenth century about 9.2 percent of some 1,600 millions dwelt in such places. As recently as 1800 there were only 44 agglomerations with ≥ 100,000 residents compared with some 270 by 1900. By 1960 more than a *quarter* of the nearly 3,000 million humans resided in concentrations ≥ 20,000 (over one *third* by the various national census definitions of "urban"), with the possibility of nearly 40 percent of 6,000 millions in such concentrations around the year 2000. Some 3,090 million town residents by the latter year would then constitute an aggregate larger than the entire human race *c.* 1960. Given late-twentieth-century rates of rural-to-urban shift, the prospect of a global "full stretch" need not be put later than the third quarter of the twenty-first century, little more than a hundred years or so after the first national "full stretch" had been reached in Britain during the second quarter of this century.

Although public attention has understandably been riveted

on the phenomenal growth of human population in pessimistic or optimistic response to well-advertised Malthusian themes, of more telling interest perhaps is the fact that people have been concentrating in towns at much faster rates than they have been reproducing themselves. The widening disparity between the two rates since *c.* 1800, moreover, is not a phenomenon that can be explained by differences in net reproduction rates between two residential categories: urban and rural. Allowing for what we know of declining mortality in towns and of peripheral extension of cities by political annexation, the observed rate of increase of town population over the past two centuries can only be understood as the outcome of unprecedented net migration whereby many people born in the countrysides and villages came to settle permanently in one or other of the growing number of towns.

In this world perspective, the singular urbanization of Europe and its overseas settlements stands out in bolder relief. Until the eighteenth century, a majority of the world's small numbers of townspeople appears to have lived in the larger rather than the smaller centers and even at that century's close well over *half* lived in the 44 large cities (almost half in five or six agglomerations ≥ 500,000.) No single city jurisdiction anywhere yet contained a million residents, although the populations concentrated in the vicinities of Edo (Tokyo), Peking, and London may well have exceeded that size before 1800. Europe with but 18 percent of world population and 21 large cities, ≥ 100,000, already contained 30 percent of all the world's large-city dwellers and had attained a degree of urbanization 76.5 percent above the prevailing world level. Asia, with 19 large cities and some 63 percent of the world's large-city population, was the second most urbanized continental region but fell far below Europe in this respect, although the latter had no more than 3 percent of its population actually resident in large cities, and at most 6 or 7 percent altogether in its 154 concentrations, ≥ 20,000.[4] Possibly even greater shares of the world's urbanites had dwelt in large cities *c.* 1750 or 1700. Only during the middle decades of the eighteenth century had smaller centers with fewer than 100,000, or even ≤ 20,000, residents begun to grow rapidly—notably in parts of Europe

Eric E. Lampard

and North America. Over the first half of the nineteenth century, in fact, incremental town population continued to accrue in greater measure to places with from 5,000 to 19,999 residents and, to a slightly lesser extent, towns 20,000 to 99,999, rather than to large cities with 100,000 or more inhabitants. Between 1800 and 1850 the numbers of European large cities doubled (42) but, according to Paul Meuriot, their share of that continent's expanding population had increased by a mere 0.8 percentage points[5] which, nevertheless, sufficed to raise the level of European urbanization to 152 percent above the mid-century world level.

For all Europe's priority with respect to urbanization, the vast majority of Europeans in 1800 or 1850 were not town-dwellers. Concentration was not only a highly selective experience on the world stage, but hardly less so within Europe itself. Only five European countries had more than one person in every ten resident in towns, $\geq$ 10,000, in 1850 (eight if Scotland, Saxony, and Prussia are treated as national entities). Nevertheless, given Europe's precocity in this regard, its distinctive accomplishment was not to have produced populous cities nor elaborate networks of administrative or commercial central places but rather to have generated social systems which could propel rising proportions—eventually majorities—of growing national populations into town life *and livelihood* on a sustained basis: in short, to have transmuted themselves into urbanized societies.[6]

As recently as the end of the sixteenth century in Europe only the Low Countries and northern provinces of Italy had as much as 15 to 20 percent of their populations resident in agglomerations of 20,000 or more inhabitants. Elsewhere in Europe the level of concentration at the time nowhere surpassed 6 or 7 percent. When most people still lived and worked on the land, hunger and intermittent famine were common facts of life. What could not be grown locally was for all practical purposes not there; the cupboard was bare. Among the most urgent tasks of nation state governments, as of earlier city commonwealths, was the assurance of a food supply in town *and* country; even rich townspeople could not always rely upon "the market" for their own provisions.

Nowhere was there "demand" enough to call forth agricultural production and distribution on a scale to cover the normal needs of a nation, let alone cope with emergencies. For cultivators to devote more of their time and energies to enlarging the output of foods and fibers commercially, it was necessary for the numbers of people engaged in nonagricultural productions to increase. For this, the rural populations had to produce not foods and materials alone, but most of the nonagricultural workforce as well. Countryfolk would have to surrender more of that plurality of processing and fabricating tasks which, in conjunction with extractive industries, had composed their seasonal round *(cumul)* in Europe and elsewhere time out of mind. Greater specialization of *function* by place, as it were, had to supersede the lesser specializations of *time* in place. Such a consummation had never been accomplished by the symbiotic transactions of town and country in the past, except on a limited local basis, although the two or three most urbanized provinces and populations of medieval Europe had been heavily involved in interregional (intercity) and even intercontinental dealings in the period of their greatest prosperity. Several centuries were required, however, to solve this riddle and the *urbanization of nonagricultural activities,* while never absolute, proved to be a key.

Creation of a working world *apart* from the countryside took even longer than the concomitant "agricultural revolution." Neither the persistence of great cities (as on the Italian peninsula) nor the maintenance of historically high levels of urbanization for 300 years (as in the Low Countries) had generated a transactional "kick" or other impetus sufficient to set off an open-ended process of social development that through innovation and its reinforcement—essentially a "learning by doing" experience at that time—would amplify behavioral and institutional departures from prevailing patterns in the direction of sustained concentration.

On both sides of the Atlantic Ocean, the association between development of industrial manufactures and the clustering of the workforce in villages and small towns was marked at various times in the late-eighteenth and early-nineteenth

Eric E. Lampard

centuries. Improved water wheels, mechanical spinning, and other devices were among the first entrepreneurial responses to their perceptions of greater market potentials. Not before the adaptation of fuel-burning engines to generate, and mechanisms to utilize, steam power—an effort extending over more than a century before James Watt and across territories from Naples to Glasgow—was it possible, however, to enlarge and diversify the entire populations' work performance on a greatly increased scale. Only then would more than 15 to 20 percent of growing national populations become permanently resident in towns or much larger proportions of working people committed to *full-time* activity away from agriculture (and its related tasks). This shift in work and, increasingly, in residential settings gathered momentum locally when entrepreneurs were able to organize the novel technological means to undersell existing markets for more or less commonplace products such as textiles. Its subsequent unfolding and transformative outcome were conditional on developing more extensive markets for both familiar and wholly novel goods and services, ultimately upon *the creation and profitable diffusion* of items unnecessary or unknown to earlier generations in country or town.

Political economists had little difficulty in "explaining" urbanization as a consequence of economic progress. Already by the second quarter of the nineteenth century most informed observers took it for granted that the unprecedented growth of towns was intimately bound up with the expansion of industry and that their conjoint outcome had been a marked increase in national wealth. The primacy and automaticity of "rational market forces" accounted for advances in the state of the arts, movements in residence, and other related changes including the order in which such events occurred. In the perceptive words of an American economist, "the proportion between the rural and town population" was an important index of a country's "capacity for manufactures, the extent of its commerce and the amount of its wealth." "Populous cities," he concluded, "are the result to which all countries that are at once fertile, free, and intelligent inevitably tend."[7] Within nations, rural-agricultural regions were commonly less prosperous than their more industrial counterparts, while the "gap" between richer "urban-industrial" and poorer "rural-agricultural" countries in Europe tended to widen over the middle decades of the nineteenth century. Hence the dominant patterns of migration among people who were "free" to move from the more rural to the more urbanized regions, from country to town.

Already by the beginning of the nineteenth century, the proportion of Great Britain's working people engaged more or less full-time *away from agriculture* and related pursuits had risen almost to two-thirds. The share of national income (in current prices) at that time was likewise about two-thirds. Over the first half of the century the workforce in agriculture, although larger in absolute size, fell from about a third to no more than a fifth of the whole, *c.* 1850, with the farm share of national income shrinking in approximately the same degree. Thereafter even the absolute numbers engaged in agriculture fell rapidly such that by the time of Queen Victoria's death in 1901, only about 8.7 percent of the workforce and 6.0 percent of national income were contributed by the agricultural sector. Meanwhile, over the same half-century intervals, real national product per capita increased respectively by 83.7 and 121.5 percent. Britain had grown faster and further away from rural life and economy than any other country down through the third quarter of the century. Despite the greater velocities of latecomers, moreover, Britain (including Ireland) managed to exceed all Europe in statistical levels of urbanization and per capita product down until World War I. By the 1880s, however, Germany, Switzerland, and Denmark were reducing Britain's lead in per capita incomes even faster than they were closing in levels of urbanization.

One of the first countries outside of Europe to experience rapid population concentration was Britain's close trading partner, the United States (particularly its New England region). By the 1840s per capita product in the United States roughly equaled that in Britain and exceeded that in France. Within the United States, the per capita product of workers outside agriculture already averaged twice as much (in cur-

Eric E. Lampard

rent dollar value) as that of workers on farms (including the output of slaves in the lucrative cotton culture). Nonagricultural employment, to be sure, was by no means coextensive with "urban" employment either then or at any other time; nevertheless the urbanizing United States and, later, the Dominion of Canada pulled ahead of Britain in per capita income terms at notably lower levels of urbanization countrywide.[8]

The contemporary experience of countries as diverse in size of population, area, and resource endowments as Great Britain, Belgium, and the United States over the first half of the nineteenth century broadly confirmed the expectations of liberal-minded economists and the manufacturers. More detailed evidence from the latter half of the century suggests that countries that moved later and more rapidly toward a redistribution of their populations between countryside and town generally achieved the highest percentage gains in per capita product at the time: e.g., the German Empire and Switzerland in the decades before 1890, Sweden and France by the early-twentieth century. While there appears to be no significant correlation between rates of national population growth and of gross national product per capita (Bairoch's figures), the association between urban increases and per capita product is close from the second and third quarters of the century.

Among higher-income countries that underwent rapid surges of urbanization in the late-nineteenth or early-twentieth centuries there was, of course, no uniformity in their commitment of resources among the several nonagricultural sectors. From the early-twentieth century, more palpably in the interwar years, furthermore, the strong association between urbanization and income increases *weakened,* although concentration and income levels continued moving in the same directions; compression of the agricultural work force, for example, was particularly abrupt in continental countries during the postwar investment revivals of the 1950s or 1960s (notwithstanding the import of so-called guest workers from abroad). Throughout earlier phases of the association, nevertheless, demands originating among the growing numbers of townspeople in different countries helped shape the composition and volume of business activities and, in that sense, the momentum of population concentration reinforced the profitability and ascendancy of the nineteenth-century market realm. Additional and novel demands were met by technical and organizational initiatives of entrepreneurs responding to their perceptions of "opportunities" in the urbanized setting. Where the inducements did not suffice, however, energies commonly flagged and innovation had to wait on such promptings as moved philanthropic or governmental agencies to action (according to criteria other than those obtaining in the marketplace). Thus, increases in the numbers and proportions of urban populations under nineteenth-century conditions were not simply equilibrating responses to short-run variations in income opportunities between agricultural and nonagricultural activities but themselves among major endogenous *determinants* of such differentials and variations over the long period.[9] The unfolding of late-nineteenth and early-twentieth-century urban life was consequently both product *and* producer of the larger mutation of the human eco-system: a self-transforming process of open-ended development (with no evident tendency to entropy).

In almost all countries where population concentration and per capita income increases were sustained, real national product and income were being enlarged relatively more from value added by nonfarm commodity production and commerce than from rising value added on the land. The composition of product indicates, moreover, that as family incomes rose, a larger share of purchases went on the available assortment of nonfarm goods and services, such as they were, without any absolute reductions in per capita consumption of basic farm products (except perhaps among the periodic or permanent urban poor). Had such differential productivities and income elasticities not prevailed, population concentration would have faltered as the average productivity and income advantage of relatively faster growing industries were eroded, and as incentives to work off the land were correspondingly reduced. In the event, the more en-

Eric E. Lampard

terprising residents in urban settings learned *new ways* of doing things (processes) and discovered *new things* to do (products and services). Almost always commercial and technical intelligences were more readily available to those in a position to exploit them at the nodes of transactional systems (as the addresses of successful patent applicants attest regardless of their actual birthplaces). Within the city's spaces, meanwhile, competition would foster a more intensive specialization of functions and land uses according to their relative yields (as given by markets).[10] Uses of nearby farmlands likewise were subject to the same capitalizing exigency—the need to match the rising "value" of their peripheral sites by increased returns from crops. Of course, such differentials within towns, as between town and country, were periodically diminished by fluctuations in business or other social dislocations but continuous, if irregular, improvements in communications and transport allowed resurgent gains from further specialization, integration, or agglomeration by those in a position once again—with access to information and finance—to capitalize them. The long-run capital-widening effects of population concentration yielded "externalities" both to industries and localities in which settings the capital-deepening effects of technical or other innovations might accrue "internally" to the more enterprising firms almost without regard to size. Hence the energies of growing populations, augmented by their adaptations of mechanical powers, were increasingly taken up in fitting out their members for town life and livelihood and, somewhat belatedly perhaps, in outfitting the towns for their enlarged populations.

The peopling, building, and servicing of towns on the scale of the nineteenth and early-twentieth centuries were in themselves major propellants of the "self-transforming" social process. The larger and more numerous towns formed social settings in which the aggregate transactions of residents increasingly determined future modes of living, and from which stemmed effective demands that selectively determined the priorities of "development" in a global market. Expenditure shifts were not of course confined to more varied categories of private household consumption: food, clothing, furnishings, housing, transport, medicine, and other services. The mounting scale of more specialized production and marketing organizations entailing a heavier absolute burden of fixed costs—under highly competitive conditions—called for still further adaptations and improvements in transport and communications, financial and accounting controls, legal, insurance and promotional services, etc., which were neither necessary nor economical in the conduct of smaller enterprises serving more localized markets either then or in the past.[11]

While we have thus far characterized the urbanization of population and its effects as trends and tendencies modulated only by fluctuations of the business cycle, a closer examination suggests that population concentration and associated changes in the volume and content of output (and final consumption) were geared to other long-run movements in demographic and economic variables. Simon Kuznets has indicated such linkages in the historical record of virtually all countries whose industrializing experiences overlapped the nineteenth century from Britain through the U.S. and continental European countries to Japan and the more recently settled British overseas dominions at the close of the century. By attenuating the influence of short-period cycles on pertinent statistical series through one or another smoothing device—five-, seven-, or ten-year moving averages—the process of "industrialization" or, more specifically, "economic growth" can be shown to have proceeded in *alternating* surges and slackenings in rates of growth of both product and population. The duration of these "long swings" in activities differs widely in time and place but all generally start "upward" (accelerate) in periods of comparative unemployment among labor and excess capacity in plant and equipment. They are sustained in ascent by rising average levels of investment, the most prominent features of which are long waves in the construction of transport and communications facilities, in residential building, public utilities, and other urban installations. The booms in construction are broadly coincident with waves of rural-to-urban and international migration and, not surprisingly, parallel movements of capital.[12]

Eric E. Lampard

The earliest of these identifiable "swings" in the United States, for example, was inaugurated by relatively high rates of capital formation in transport undertakings (inland waterways and steam railroads), urban building, and related construction. Its progress involved the migration of countryfolk to the port cities of the Atlantic and Gulf coasts and the new manufacturing towns of the northeastern states (supplemented from the late 1840s by the first massive influx of foreign born), as well as collateral thrusts of western land occupancy. This investment boom (like its successors later in the nineteenth and early-twentieth centuries) was maintained by a highly elastic labor supply, the accessibility of material resources, increased manufacturing capacity and, not least, by the accompanying growth of aggregate demand at prices that sustained certain types of business and household spending and appeared, for a while at least, to justify further increases in capacity. While population movements in the U.S. were led by changes in producer durable goods industries and capital stock in manufactures, other thrusts—in residential building, public utilities, and what R. A. Easterlin has called "urban household demand"—seem to have followed on "a gradually tightening labor market" that induced further concentration of population.[13]

Commitment of productive resources to such time-lagged, concentration-sensitive, modes of capitalizing the environment served to maintain expenditures and their multipliers over terms *longer* than those indicated by actual business cycles. These outlays continued while their impetus lasted to have buoyant impacts on certain job sectors and output, as well as on the population's demographic performance, despite the depressant effects of trade recession. The expectation of rising incomes fostered concentration which, in turn, heightened the population's propensity to technical and organizational innovation which, *via* capital embodiment, further enhanced profits and wages such that urbanization gradually took on the attributes of *a learning and locomotive experience,* self-sustaining (if not actually self-generating) behavior within successive alternations of faster and slower rates of increase in income and product. City-building activity manifested a population's acquired faculty for capitalizing a particular site in the course of integrating its transactions over a widening social space.[14] Urbanization, or relative preponderance of city-building, was thus the ecological condition of certain nineteenth-century populations institutionalizing their adaptive capability to conserve and augment the net (balance) of their numbers and "goods."

The term "industrial" in this institutionalizing context is used with reference to increasing ratios of material to human capital and, in particular, to the profitable substitution of modes of embodied capital (practical arts, knowledge, etc.) for given amounts of labor or natural resources in any output. Lower unit labor costs registered the greater "efficiency" with which capital assets were employed by their owners and, as labor "saving," released hands or heads for undertaking novel or additional lines of work—until their further displacement when capital substitutes might again enhance the measured productivity of all resources in accomplishing these particular tasks. Insofar as labor eventually "shared" directly (after capital) in productivity gains from technological and organizational innovation by higher wages or, indirectly, from lowered prices, labor-service as well as property incomes would rise on average and buttress the twin process of capital substitution and labor displacement, augmenting thereby the endowment of capital per unit of paid labor time.[15] Under the competitive market auspices of the nineteenth century, therefore, "industrial" cities were powerful engines of economic growth through *development.* An urbanized area or "city" was a multifaceted node of more or less fixed location, variable size (in population and built area) and, depending on the resourcefulness of its inhabitants, of more or less open-ended accomplishment. The growing weight of the urbanized populations in the whole and the differentiation of their urban environments alike were joint products of the unfolding profit regimen and the logic of its "industrial" behavior.

As majorities of growing national populations came to live and work in urban environments, the momentum of concentration (as given by the rate of increase in a population's urban share) slackened in the wake of secular fertility decline

Eric E. Lampard

and, in countries of European settlement, reduced immigration. Not only was the reservoir of rural population slowly running out but the productivity gains accruing from its transfer to more highly capitalized urban settings evidently was running down. By the 1920s in the United States, considerably earlier in Britain (1890s), increases in per capita personal incomes and in rates of patenting mechanical or other inventions were increasingly *independent* of increments to urban population. Further concentration of people and productive activity in leading industrial countries no longer constituted movement, as it were, along an ever-descending learning cost curve. Certain indicators of the "long swings" hitherto prevailing in rates of growth and concentration of resources, moreover, became obscured by the shocks of twentieth-century wars and depression; and the consequent resort to "managed" economies.[16] The cognitive reinterpretation of the environment which sustains creative innovation and profitable capitalization, therefore, has come to depend not, as in Durkheim's day, on the informal *densité dynamique* inherent in population concentration and the contagion of competition, but on formalized investments in research and development activity and on access to elaborate "information processing" and communications networks which have emancipated many of their users from any particular stake in physical contact or place.

The Morphology of Urban Areas in the Course of Urbanization

The implosion of human and mechanical energies represented by the increases in numbers and sizes of population concentrations only gradually affected the inherited forms and structures of towns. Very considerable increases in "central" *densities* took place in the late-eighteenth and early-nineteenth centuries wherever people and properties were crowded into the comparatively undifferentiated microspaces of urban districts old and new.[17] Under the impacts of crowding and capital gains, there followed a substantial, albeit irregular and piecemeal, *extension of the built area:* even before a public transportation service was improvised in the form of horse-drawn short stages and omnibuses to supplement the essentially pedestrian mode of town circulation. Through countless decisions of mostly small proprietors and individual households, estate developers and building contractors, the extension of towns went forward in a variety of building arrangements and cadastral patterns.[18] The official territories of larger towns typically doubled in size over the first half of the nineteenth century in a number of countries—from two or three to seven or eight square miles and more—while commercial and residential building development almost always proceeded beyond the local authorities' extended reach.

Like the formative process of urbanization, the morphological changes in towns were wrought in the marketplace. While improvements in intraurban service, notably street railways and tramways after 1850, facilitated an enlarged territorial scale and greatly articulated the structure of urbanized space (already marked in some localities by the intrusion of steam railways), the critical factor throughout was *the competitive sorting of land uses* by a highly speculative land market according to their ability to pay. When "push" became "shove," the commercial and occasional manufacturing uses rose to dominance in the most accessible central districts (with a civic hub in many instances) inasmuch as increasing returns to specialization induced a clustering of like and complementary functions on particular streets, blocks, or neighborhoods. Competition for sites among numerous categories of users prompted further *differentiation* of the larger town mosaic along lines of internally specialized, if spatially interspersed, residential and nonresidential areas linked into a larger labyrinth by the public streets, transport, and other common facilities.

New modes of manufacture and doing business, together with the accretion of a multiplicity of wholesaling and retail functions, heightened pressure for place in the core of towns. The districts adjacent to harbors, river and canal docks took on a greater import for town livelihood than older market or public squares. In rapidly growing new towns such "dis-

Eric E. Lampard

tricting" tended to happen even more precipitately than in older and larger places still cluttered with the past. Meanwhile, residential quarters—ranging from the cramped households of proprietors to the congested "slums" of the very poor—remained tenaciously intermixed with other uses insofar as walking access to the workplace was a *sine qua non* for most towndwellers long after the advent of cheaper local transport. But, for all the built compactness of urban space at the time, the civic boundaries of large agglomerations in Britain and, to a lesser degree, in France, Germany, or the Low Countries, were extended over wider areas during the first half of the nineteenth century than in the previous 400 years. The areas of Anglo-American colonial-ports incorporated as "boroughs" or "towns" by their founding companies or proprietors had, likewise, been of "medieval" dimensions before the rash of annexations in the second quarter of the nineteenth century.

There is no need to rehearse the consequences for cities of that remarkable engineering and organizational synthesis, the locomotive steam railway. For all its disputed economic impact on interregional transportation service, there is no doubt that steam trains were neither technically nor financially adapted to conditions of congested intraurban street travel. Firms using railway goods services for their long hauls of materials or products remained dependent—as did passenger movement—on horses and horse-drawn vehicles for local collection and delivery. Such firms might now, however, locate themselves on spur lines or sidings in close proximity to the mostly outlying terminals or goods yards in order to minimize both freight and site factors in their overall production costs. When constructed on cheaper peripheral lands, the railway stations of the second quarter of the nineteenth century furnished an additional focus for the accretion of manufactures, warehouses, and heavy materials-handling functions, supplementing and in some instances displacing riverside wharfage and harbor facilities and relieving some at least of the demands for space within the distended central business areas. The early horse-powered buses and tramcars often tied these newly differentiated clusters to the "old towns" *via* commercial and residential streets imparting thereby a novel arterial structure to the burgeoning urban space.[19]

Each subsequently developed source of energy or medium of transport in the nineteenth-century market setting added its own set of effort-conserving and output-enhancing potentials to those inherited from the past. Every new mode of energy conversion (coal gas, electricity, petroleum combustion, etc.) or communications device (electromagnetic telegraph and telephone, electronic wave or "wireless" telegraphy, etc.) augmented the means available for producing and distributing "values" over space and time and thus reduced physical and psychological barriers of distance. More costly than steampower to generate, electrical energy was nevertheless adapted for transmission with greater ease, in more variable amounts and, ultimately, over much longer distances and thus became cheaper by the unit for many types of commercial use. Applied to a vehicle on tramway, electro-motive power from a central station permitted quicker acceleration and more frequent stops at low measured cost compared with steam engines (albeit with vastly greater overhead requirements than a competing horse-car system).

Electric power allowed the introduction of comparatively *rapid* local transit service at street level for the first time. Its ready adaptation by franchised private or public monopolies between the 1890s and World War I extended the effective area of urbanized space by doubling the distance that might be traversed in any time over that attainable by horse-drawn vehicles. On an elevated, underground, or other limited-access railway much greater distances could be covered although the financial advantage over steam locomotion in this respect was less impressive. Withal, the combination of relatively flexible power supply to workplaces with rapid public transit service relaxed some of the *centripetal* attraction that had hitherto held work and residence to within a mile or so of each other for a majority of town workers and aggravated, thereby, the chronic congestion and pollution at most town centers.[20]

The irregular accession of municipal territory and administrative jurisdiction throughout the latter half of the nineteenth century was one consequence of this dilation of daily urban circulation. Another was the greater margin allowed for environmental self-determination at least among those towndwellers whose rising incomes afforded a degree of residential choice not open to their forebears in town or country. Cities of from 5 to 10 square miles in surface area at the mid century had typically extended their municipal authority over 20 to 50 square miles and their built areas even more by the 1890s. By that time, a reduction of pressures on the housing stock, commercial buildings, sewers and other infrastructural systems (excepting transport) had in many instances contributed a measure of environmental amelioration that raised public health standards and—in conjunction with better diet and high-pressure water supply—lowered urban mortality for virtually all age groups except infants and those over 65.[21]

The concentration of workshops, factories, warehouses, and transport facilities that comprised "the means" of industrial production—and, incidentally, the sinews of the growing towns—were a cumulative outcome of innumerable business decisions that lay almost wholly outside the purview of local authorities. Apart from dispensing poor relief, granting licenses, or managing corporation properties where they existed, only the immediate decisions affecting new street layouts or preserving old rights of way seem to have much exercised the local magistracies, special commissioners, or common council committees. Indeed such bodies were often acquiescent or moribund and the more serious obstacles to change were likely to be interposed by those other proprietors and corporations who for whatever reason, felt their own vested interests imperiled. Most residential structures, water works, transport, gas or other amenities, even street illumination in some instances, were also furnished by private investors: directly and by contract or franchise. When substantial classes of townspeople no longer appeared able to fend for themselves, let alone hire even perfunctory surrogates to fulfill their public obligations, then voluntary and charitable associations—usually with a sectarian inspiration—would have to step in with new "missions" to the city's poor or service the newly recognized "needs" of the destitute and downcast.

The symbiotic relation between local authorities and development interests became closer over the second and third quarters of the nineteenth century with respect to public health and order: two quintessential incidents of police power at all times. Under conditions of rapid population concentration, only "reformed" local governments could effectively manage "the preservation of the peace," while the burden of new or improved "public" functions necessarily committed those governments to an altogether higher order of public expenditures.[22] Regardless of whether the clamor for (or against) new public works originated with locally affected private interests, or from promptings of high and remote authority seeking to establish public "standards," matters of water supply, sewage disposal, the protection of property, or the provision of schooling became local, and ultimately supra-local, issues involving critical questions of *powers* and *finance*. Almost for the first time, municipalities in a number of countries were being driven to invest in the enhancement of their local tax base. Given the capital costs of new public works and the increasing rates and taxes levied to service the new order of local government debt (in addition to other outlays), it is not surprising that so many rudimentary services and other concerns were left to the initiatives and resources of charitable and voluntary societies: until such times as grants-in-aid from higher authorities became available on either discretionary or mandatory bases for public health, education, and poor relief, etc. Insofar as property was not only a primary beneficiary of "reform," but paid most of the taxes and assessments toward its implementation, the lesser property owners, shopkeepers, and householders were understandably persistent in demanding "retrenchment" as the necessary corollary of public largesse. But the conflicts and divisions within the body politic under nineteenth-century impulses toward democracy should not obscure the fact— even in the United States—that local governments were intrinsically preoccupied with the unwonted task of making the swollen cities "work," not with pioneering proto-welfare states.[23]

Cooperation between private financial and real-estate interests and public office-holders was vital to the process of peripheral expansion. The profitability of much private real-estate development was conditional on a growing public involvement by way of infrastructure, utilities, and services. By the late-nineteenth century, however, the incorporated territories of larger cities could rarely if ever keep pace with the centrifugal extension of their built areas—even in the German states where municipal land purchases beyond their immediate bounds had appeared to guarantee public control over *Stadterweiterung*. But within a decade or so of rapid transit's flowering in the early-twentieth century had come the adaptation of "cheap," petrol-fueled, internal-combustion engines as thermally efficient in fractional low "horse-powered" motors as in higher ones. Under the impact of the personalized horseless carriage (together with public and commercial motor vehicles) running on ordinary hard-surfaced or macadamized streets, the explosion of the built area was intensified not only along the axial and radial salients marked out by tramways and "commuter" rail lines since mid-century, but also in *lateral* directions where sectors of intervening land had hitherto remained largely "undeveloped." The incorporated areas of large cities were progressively extended by annexations or consolidations from 50 or 60 up to 100 or more square miles between the two World Wars but, in most cases, they formed a diminishing share of the contiguous urban landscape—the conurbations and metropolitan districts extending outwards over hundreds and eventually thousands of square miles. Long before that pass, of course, urban activities and demands had become too important in the life and well-being of industrial nations to be left in the hands (let alone pockets) of townspeople or their local governments.

The twentieth century witnessed an altogether unparalleled expansion and reorganization of macro-urban space. From its outset the "necessity" for, and "advantage" of, a *central* location for certain types of manufacture and selected classes of residence were being substantially reduced by improved transport and communications. Many businesses as well as households sought relief from the burden of local rates and property taxes in what William Ashworth once called "the social opportunism" of the suburbs. By the century's third quarter, the Standard Metropolitan Statistical Areas of the United States—particularly in urbanizing "sunbelt" regions of the south and southwest—typically sprawled over surfaces of 15 to 25 thousand square miles. Although political reformers and town planners often deplored the political and administrative *fragmentation* of the urbanized territory as compromising the fiscal soundness and efficient conduct of urban government, their apprehensions made no lasting impression on public opinion either in countries like Britain and France, where exchequer grants and other subvention of local authorities had long since become the accepted mode, or like the United States, where they had not.[24] Political division of the decentralizing urban structure has been, if anything, even more incidental to the urbanization process than was the partial unification of that structure in its earlier centralizing phase, since urban development—and ultimately urban morphology—in industrial nations remained throughout an essentially market phenomenon. During much of the decentralizing era, the market has increasingly looked, for its own reasons, to higher levels of government for its enabling framework and financial underpinning—even in the United States—while central regimes have come to treat local governments—even in federal systems—as administrative agencies or clients.

If technological mastery made the consummation of urban population possible, only financial capacity—the effective command over resources—could translate potential into actuality. Like any other set of industrial products, the nineteenth-century urban artifact was produced for profit and the "opportunity cost" of its accretion, repletion, or piecemeal replacement was always determined by going conditions of demand and supply of productive resources. All artifactual parts of cities were paid for out of the savings (or borrowings) of hundreds and thousands of punters and plungers in the course of everyday transactions. Their lots, structures, equip-

74

ment, stocks of goods, furnishings, leases, rights of way, etc., summed to the physical urban experience—supplemented and supported, to be sure, by the growing commitments of local and, in due course, higher levels of public authority. Each venture would have depended at any time on some enterpriser's expectation—more or less informed—of its *net* earnings potential as conventional accounting might disclose. In this sense, the profitable capitalization of the social environment became—even for the charities when they turned "scientific" and "professional" *c.* 1900—as much the end of city life as the means.

As the net accumulating product of innumerable private savings and investment decisions, the maintenance and enlargement of urban areas were always competing for resources by the returns they might offer *relative* to those from alternative courses undertaken outside the city milieu. The lowering of transport and other transactional costs continually raised the informational horizons of would-be lenders and spenders ("space-time convergence") and fostered thereby a more intensive specialization and integration of labor among localities and regions. The destabilizing impacts of recurrent market extensions, while never approaching the instantaneous adjustments posited at the margin by economists' textbooks, would nevertheless bring home to capitalists the measure in which their private returns still balanced their private costs. Meantime, those without assets to risk in the marketplace would have nothing to lose but their jobs and the brief respite afforded by their private parsimony while exercising their freedom to find another. Despite the "immense irresolution and inertia" which some nineteenth-century observers professed to see in humankind, the determined concentration of people and their cumulative effects must be seen in retrospect as an indispensable ecological constituent of those creative eruptions in national fortune that, until 1914–1918 at least, justified the late-Victorian faith in a progressive providence. There was little inclination, nor yet occasion, to conceive of alternative courses that, leading away from the city, might alter the structure and form of urbanized areas almost beyond recognition.

Urbanization at Full Stretch and
the Morphology of Space-Time Convergence

Economic and social changes have unfolded and intermittently accelerated in the more urbanized countries but with only slight relation to population concentration in the more recent decades. The energy-intensive pattern of decentralization in the form of peripheral or ring development has, indeed, sometimes taken place at the expense of the market's readiness to maintain the "inner city" or restore core land uses as profitable investments. Even before the collapse of the 1920s property boom, "blighted areas," "depressed zones," and other evidences of physical deterioration manifested the failure of the market to conserve or replace certain parts of older cities (and "one-industry" towns) where, without a steady influx of low-income workers and their dependents, even slums were no longer always profitable. In some United States cities, for example, manufacturers as well as residents were abandoning congested "downtown" districts and, as reported by President Hoover's Committee on Recent Social Trends in 1932, the general effect of this drift, combined with the more intensive uses of some sites brought on by ever larger steel-framed structural units, had been "to hasten the obsolescence of much of the older pattern of the city." Business and financial interests, which had continuously built and rebuilt sites in piecemeal fashion during the rapid concentration of the nineteenth century, could seldom afford to renew rundown central neighborhoods since, apart from large-unit office space, fancy apartment houses, or occasional luxury hotels, "these areas are always in competition with newer subdivisions which offer a more inviting field for private enterprise."[25]

With the reduced momentum of population concentration generally, and a coincident relaxation of centripetal inducements locally, the problem for business in many larger cities was (and is) to keep finding something profitable (or otherwise worthwhile) to do with urbanized land—particularly in the peak central spaces formed during the dynamic clustering of the last century. By the second quarter of this century, the

Eric E. Lampard

financial costs of renovating or replacing outmoded structures and land uses were in many places beginning to exceed the possibilities for remunerative current use. Even under the impact of economic depression in the early 1930s, land and property values could still not be deflated fast or far enough to make redevelopment of the core attractive to private capital. Notwithstanding the well-established precedent of central grants for public works and capital spending by local authorities, the depression enlarged areas of physical decay in major European manufacturing towns without altogether arresting the tendency to suburban sprawl—even in such "construction-conscious" states as Italy and Germany (where the percentage of GNP originating in building and construction fell off sharply again from the mid-1930s). The United States, on the other hand, was neither institutionally nor ideologically prepared for federal moneys to flow directly to the capital budgets of hard-pressed city governments. Despite hastily improvised federal-state programs for emergency public works in 1933 and Housing Acts in 1934 and 1937, the largely token housing provision was contained under such slogans as "slum clearance" and "greenbelt towns" (three small garden suburbs). Meanwhile, federal insurance schemes for private savings and loan associations, federal underwriting of home improvement loans and long-term, fixed interest, mortgages for new houses and rental accommodations (which met federal standards) not only took much of the risk out of private sector money lending but revived the process of peripheral subdivision. It was in the United States, nevertheless, that by 1940–41 the influence of "Keynesian" compensatory spending notions had led to proposals from private foundations and real-estate interests, as well as planners and academic economists, for federal funds to "free" land in blighted areas from "inflated" assessments and to launch large-scale urban redevelopment projects as "a vast stimulus to private enterprise."[26]

Neither in North America nor Europe were such funds forthcoming. From 1938 rearmament and war not only absorbed a growing part of savings and stretched the public credit but, if anything, reinforced the dispersal of population and plant from central cities. By 1940 Europe's cities were immediately vulnerable to aerial bombardment, and unplanned "slum clearance" and other demolition went forward over the ensuing five years with unprecedented popular support. Given the changing morphology of urban areas, however, it is not surprising that the surges of postwar urbanization in Europe and North America redounded as much to the advantage of suburbs or planned "new towns" as to the restoration or rebuilding of "inner cities." Even with governments regularly spending from 15 to 25 percent or more of peacetime national product—in accordance with the new consensus politics of economic growth—no lasting renewal of the urban economic base was accomplished nor the low-density urbanization of the countrysides much restrained. Given the now vast entailments of public and private overhead, how could central land uses be invented quickly enough and maintained profitably enough to preserve land values, ground rents, and improvements (alike major components of the tax base) in *competition* with peripheral extensions or new towns elsewhere?[27] Once the market had performed this feat—with but modest infrastructural and protective service demands upon the taxpayers—by replacing obsolete structures and noncompetitive uses in the course of enhancing the high-value central districts and capitalizing the low-density perimeters. Indeed, the development of accessible peripheral lands long served to moderate the bidding up of land values in the core.

Most of the social and environmental costs of the nineteenth-century industrial city-building enterprise went unremarked and uncompensated—except by sectarian and private philanthropies. Tensions arising among the population from the differential distribution of private (and social) gains and costs from specializations of function and place proved to be the rift in the social fabric that complicated the system's adjustments to cyclical and structural change. Only under the heightened consciousness of disaffected "classes" forming into more coherent labor and political organizations in the late-nineteenth and early-twentieth centuries were answers to "the Social Question" adapted in a widening array of publicly funded professional and bureaucratic "social services." During these "reform" upheavals, the governments of cities finally ceased to be self-governments in any recognizably corporate sense and the politics and public finance of urbanized areas became inseparable from the broader concerns of state or national authorities. More recently the private sector, notwithstanding the interim increases in national income and product, could no longer afford to play its preeminent role—even with tax abatements and outright subsidies—in maintaining and extending the older urbanized areas. It had moved on to more enticing courses that—under conditions of "high technology" and transnational organization—could be pursued almost without regard to place or social setting in, what one California planner aptly termed, "the nonplace urban realm."[28]

Cities can no longer be built and operated "on the cheap." They are not the natural nurseries of capitalizable inventions nor, under the waning momentum of population concentration, do they generate sufficient *net* saving to sustain themselves in the evolving social system. The enhanced productivity effects of capital widening are no longer attainable simply by concentrating workers from residual farming or other low-income rural pursuits—even in Third World countries—nor are the "externalities" which once underlay increasing returns to agglomeration from specialization for many small-scale producers anything like as decisive. Not only have employment opportunities in traditionally city-building manufactures contracted over recent decades but the much touted expansion of services to business and finance has lost much of its former buoyancy outside a handful of *transnational* centers in which the large-scale corporate intelligence and control functions are currently emplaced. With the advent of electronic telecommunications, video-cable networks and computerization, moreover, "the need" for physically processing and distributing printed information, for face-to-face transactions, and for centrally located office space is likely to diminish, thereby threatening the viability and valuation of the energy-inefficient mass of "down-town" improvements. Meantime, the city tax base has been overwhelmed by the gradual erosion of its productive population and wealth and by the deepening "problems" of the automobile age. Left to their own resources, local governments in urbanized areas and large conurbations would be unable to meet their mounting obligations but, even with massive grants from the center, many have recently avoided default only by running down sewers, streets, water systems, transport or other infrastructural facilities, schooling, and protective services on which the still city-bound private sectors must depend for their profitability.[29] Despite the planned "shrinkage" of certain core areas and land uses to ease the burden of public spending in time of inflation, urban managers look for a growing part of their current revenue (as well as capital) to the budgetary munificence of central administrations, themselves strained by legislative commitments to provide services and subsidies to ever-wider segments of business (including agriculture) and the voting public—in addition, in many instances, to maintaining or increasing vast armaments expenditures in peacetime.

In a few countries it is already possible to discern the historical discreteness of the urbanization process "at full stretch." According to national census measures in use *c.* 1960, the Netherlands, Great Britain, West (possibly East) Germany, Denmark, Sweden and Belgium, together with continental expanses such as Australia and perhaps the United States, had concentrated some 70 to 80 percent or more of their populations in variously defined "urban" areas. With the exception of Britain and the Low Countries, moreover, the high tide of this concentration had mostly come in over the past century with the momentum of residential shift slackening in each case when from half to two-thirds of national populations had become urbanized. Meanwhile, by 1960 only Great Britain had actually registered a net decrease of a few percentage points from peak levels reached before the mid century, although urban recruiting had come to a standstill almost everywhere outside the Soviet Union during the 1930s. Since 1960, however, net concentration appears to have been halted again, or reduced to a trickle, in three or four other countries despite the ease with which census "urban" defi-

Eric E. Lampard

nitions (even more than city boundaries) may at any time be stretched to recapture fugitive townsmen. Insofar as the *extreme reach* of concentration experienced by such diverse social-political aggregates as the Netherlands and Great Britain (front runners since the eighteenth century) or Australia (A.F. Weber's epitome of the nineteenth century) has never run much beyond 80 percent or so of population (60 to 70 percent by the standard $\geq$ 20,000 measure), urbanization "at full stretch" may be expected to leave a residuum of from 15 to 20 percent dwelling outside the officially designated urban territory. While movements of townspeople may continue to bring net shifts (1) among urban areas of different population size or (2) between urban areas in different regions, the process of concentration in a national territory appears to have run its course when about four in every five persons reside in urbanized areas.[30]

Enough has been said to indicate that urbanized areas in countries that have more or less completed the transformation from rural to urban distributions are very different in function and form from the late-nineteenth-century cities they displaced. Inasmuch as most modes of manufacture and many business services no longer require a core, or even central-city, location, such activities have been more freely distributed with respect, say, to critical inputs, cheaper "back office" space, or enhanced access to transport, communications or amenities. They can be found out along the specialized motorways or clustered in the vicinity of peripheral airports. Actual deconcentration, however, may simply be a further instalment of the *selective* decentralization of residences and work that—in a context of local population increase and novel modes of transport and communication—has been characteristic of the agglomerative process under market auspices since at least the middle decades of the nineteenth century. If so, then this process has by now gone so far that it has not only altered the social morphology of larger conurbations—the West Midlands, New York–New Jersey Metropolitan Region, the Ruhrgebiet, and their like—but also progressively reduced the advantage and attraction of many erstwhile urban nuclei as the primary locus of corporate in-

vestment. Hence the physical deterioration or localized abandonment of plant, housing, and other facilities in inner cities
across North America and Europe from St. Louis and Detroit
to Glasgow, Liège, Naples, and numerous points between.
Although profitable speculation in "development" values and
large-unit real estate in the "bright light" districts continues—
with varying degrees of public inducement and subsidy—only
the taxpayer can nowadays afford to underwrite the quasi-
philanthropic enterprise of conserving inner cities. But, as
relatively fewer taxpayers reside, or do business, in central
districts, and as still more jobs and homes gravitate to outer
cities and beyond, the priority which politicians and planners
have hitherto attached to maintaining and extending central-
city functions and facilities in the wake of capitalist withdrawal
may itself go by default.[31]

The metropolitanization of urban morphology had deep
roots in nineteenth-century American cities but its rapid extension nationally since the 1920s was largely a function of
rising incomes and energy consumption. The professional
urbanologists generated by universities and private "think
tanks" in response to "the exploding metropolis" of the 1950s
and "the Urban Crisis" of the 1960s generally attributed these
twin ills of society to the automobile, affluence, and racism.
By 1970 they found that the population was relentlessly
spreading out *via* superhighways and freeways into "defen-
sible," low density, residential space (< 1,000 persons per
square mile), graded by socioeconomic class, age, and affinity.
Between these extensive and more exclusive residence turfs
were placed the "metrocenters," or intervening clusters of
common facilities containing shopping plazas, motels, cine-
mas, automobile service stations and repair shops, apartment
blocks, gallery-museums, multi-purpose health spas, and
schools of continuing education, etc. These multi-centered
"urban fields" or "urbanized regions" into which metropolitan and urbanized areas devolved were characterized as "plug-
in cities"—from 50 to 100 miles across—where residences
were connected "to an intricate . . . and efficiently managed
network of freeways, telephones, radio and television outlets,
and electric energy and water supply systems.[32] With the rapid

Eric E. Lampard

automobilization of society outside the United States after mid-century, populations in other highly urbanized countries were also reported by itinerant American urbanologists to be "substituting mobility for place."[33] With local variations, to be sure, western European countries and countries of European settlement overseas were seen to be following the American way—"Today California," as it were, "and tomorrow. . . ." The first reaction among planners then was to view the unanticipated rise in fuel costs in almost all countries after 1973 as putting an end to this dislodgement of urban jobs and households. Some urban romantics went so far as to forecast "the renaissance of the city" but, with the prospect of low-energy telecommunications, cable computerization, automated back offices, and other database management systems coming "in place," the demand for space in centralized, energy-expensive, business districts will in all probability be further reduced in the 1980s. Somewhat paradoxically, perhaps, the full stretch of urbanization in this age of costly energy and low distance frictions is unlikely to proceed as far—either in density or degree—as it did in that already remote era when the frictions of distance were high and energy—inanimate and human—still cheap.

Thus conditions of technology and organization in this new age may not exact the degree of agglomerative response required of populations in very different environmental circumstances as recently as 1900. Changes in relative prices resulting from technical substitutions and energy conservation—as well as from secular tendencies in the composition of output and workforce—may permit a larger share of slow-growing populations in future to distribute themselves advantageously with respect both to energy and ecosystem over a more extensive, low-density, urban field than that envisioned before 1973.[34] In countries with fast-growing populations, it may still prove advantageous to move people off the land in the interests of raising agricultural productivity and food supply, but the capital-widening effect of crowding people into hastily improvised cities may not prove as pronounced or profitable as it was for so long under the low budget conditions of the nineteenth century. Other things being equal (which, of course, they never are outside of textbooks and laboratories), countries which have only experienced rapid and unremitting urbanization over the last four or five decades might, nonetheless, expect to avoid some of the heavy social costs entailed when concentrating labor under the conditions which prevailed in Europe, say, a century and more ago. Those who would learn from history, however, are not only condemned to paying pretty much the full cost of avoiding its repetition (at today's prices) but also to incur, under tutelage of the latest policy science, a whole gamut of unperceived and possibly more injurious costs peculiar to our own time.

If the urbanization of the nation under untrammeled market guidance led to the "nationalization" of the urbanized areas, the greater powers and resources disposed by the modern state did not arrest the city's penchant to follow "such a process of dissection and diffusion as to amount almost to obliteration." As H. G. Wells had so graphically forecast at the turn of the century, the functional and morphological fragmentation of "railway begotten 'great cities' " would mean that "coming cities will not be, in the old sense, cities at all."[35] As the older social fabric of town and country unraveled in the course of this transformation, the functional interdependence of more specialized parts—no longer embedded in ties of affinity and community—was rewoven as an integral design at higher and more abstract levels of authority; urbanization changed the nature of the modern state in its civic aspect and altered the domestic "outputs" of government at all levels. Politics was translated from activities and interests primarily rooted in the concerns of localities into media-based movements and coalitions affecting "the national interest."

But the fate of urbanized areas, like that of cities, is always determined in *interaction* with the world around. The widening scope and intensity of national administrative responsibility for urban areas and populations in the twentieth century again was part of a more comprehensive corporate effort to sustain the urbanized industrial state in which periodic fluctuations in private business (even more than its structural shifts) were becoming incompatible either with

Eric E. Lampard

managing the heavy fixed costs of large-scale enterprises or with securing continued consent to inequalities of income and wealth (and related social class divisions) that had been aggravated in the course of urbanization. During the third quarter of this century, nevertheless, the tentative accommodations of earlier "welfare states" fashioned in depression and war gave way before a bold consensus politics of economic growth and social mobility that reinstated the priorities and, in lesser degree, prescriptions of an otherwise faltering market system and, not surprisingly, propelled the automobile-distended conurbations into the even more extended urban field: not, in any historic sense, a city at all.

Long before the early-twentieth-century city and suburbs gave place to the urban field, the great rural-to-urban displacement was subsiding and the proportion of population remaining in the countrysides had become correspondingly small (and specialized around agriculture). Two currents of migration have accordingly assumed a larger significance in highly urbanized countries than net concentration itself: (1) *local redistribution* in conurbations and metropolitan areas toward the multi-centered urban field (containing growing numbers of *rural* nonfarm residents again) and (2) *general redistribution* within the city size structure commonly, but by no means, uniformly, toward middle-sized centers in recently developing regions. Neither of these currents in itself is peculiar to highly urbanized societies or to this age. The populations of cities were growing incrementally *extra muros,* as well as at their cores, centuries before the steam railway affected compact settlements. Many inner precincts of urban centers had experienced substantial loss of residents decades before decentralization became prevalent with the horse trams and electrified railways of the late-nineteenth century. The growth of towns in newly developing regions, likewise, was commonplace in parts of medieval Europe and in areas of European settlement in the Americas long before the industrial revolution of the late-eighteenth and early-nineteenth centuries. Both redistributive movements of the late twentieth century, nevertheless, suggest continuing social and economic changes within urbanized societies affecting people's choice of residence. Such positional mobility among urban areas in different regions or among the different areas of an urban field may register rising average levels of personal income and hence a more widely distributed power of environmental self-determination centering on size of household, amenity, or personal life course development—the media's "alternate life styles." Either movement could be indicative of significant changes in society—especially if the postwar era of managed economic growth and *embourgeoisement* almost literally ran out of "gas" in the 1970s—but neither is likely to attain the relative magnitude or momentum of the historic concentration process that first accomplished the great reversal between rural and urban residence during the nineteenth century.

The end of urbanization is no sign of the imminent end of the world. It offers little comfort to the eco-doomster or latter-day millenarian dismayed by the character of present-day material advance. The city-and-suburb of the late-nineteenth century have merely been submerged in the uncentered urban field, much as H. G. Wells had anticipated, although the inertia of the older mode has proven far more expensive to overcome than the early regional planners had supposed. The historic city of Europe or early America may be quite dead but its successors, by whatever name, are not yet Patrick Geddes's "Necropolis." Passing generations still wax nostalgic for the half-recollected "cities" of their youth, while new crops of realists continually arise to insist upon the inevitability of progress. The further shrinkage of the core populations of older centers—planned or otherwise—is taking place even as "spread cities" of newly developing regions (including the clogged "cities" of many Third World countries) go through the brief allotment of their "boom town" years.

Urbanization at full stretch means that increases in urban population, if any, will not be as potent in bolstering output or shaping consumption as they were in the past. Other agencies and incitements will have to offset their absence from capitalism's perennial contest with diminishing returns. Changes in the composition and distribution of urbanized populations will, nevertheless, continue to have social and

Eric E. Lampard

economic consequences irrespective of their overall rates of growth or decline. Similarly, future cohorts born into existing cultural and social environments will be moulded by technological and organizational change to life courses that increasingly diverge from those of their parents and grandparents. Already the impact of transnational competition in the 1970s has shaken the built-in public stabilizers and oligopolistic divisions that underpinned the remarkable political economy of "growth" in the urbanized countries since Bretton Woods and Hiroshima. Perhaps the only critical question, from an ecological standpoint, is whether such changes— the unanticipated ones as well as wholly exogenous shocks— unfold at rates that will allow humans in their various institutions and settings to cope. If so, then urban history may be usefully pursued *via* some "plug-in" gallery-museum over the efficiently managed networks of one's own nonplace urban field.

NOTES

1. Adna F. Weber, *The Growth of Cities in the Nineteenth Century: A Study in Statistics* (New York, 1899), p. 1. The citations from Weber in the following pages are drawn principally from chapters 1 and 3.

2. Charles Horton Cooley, "The Social Significance of Street Railways," American Economic Association *Publications* 6 (1891), pp. 71-73.

3. A. Shadwell, *Industrial Efficiency: A Comparative Study of Industrial Life in England, Germany and America* (London, 1906), chapter 11. *International Housing Congress, Proceedings* (London: National Housing Reform Council, 1907). T. C. Horsfall, *The Improvement of the Dwellings and Surroundings of the People: The Example of Germany* (Manchester, 1904). But if German housing conditions had been greatly improved by *Stadterweiterung* since 1871—see the very different representations of Ernst Engel, *Die moderne Wohungsnoth* (Leipzig, 1873) and Friedrich Engels, *Die Wohnungsfrage* (1872) in Marx-Engels *Werke*, 5 (Berlin, 1959), pp. 210–87—expectations and standards had also risen, see A. Skalweit, "Die Wohnungszustände in den deutschen Grosstädten und die Möglichkeit ihrer Reform," *Städtebauliche Vorträge aus dem Seminar für Stadtleben*, ed. J. Brix and F. Genzmer, VI, No. 6 (Berlin, 1913).

4. E. E. Lampard, "Historical Aspects of Urbanization," in *The Study of*

Urbanization, ed. P. M. Hauser and L. F. Schnore (New York, 1965), Tables 2 and 3.

5. P. Meuriot, *Des Agglomérations urbaines dans l'Europe contemporaine; Essai sur les causes, les conditions, les conséquences de leur développement* (Paris, 1897), pp. 30–31.

6. On the priority of urbanization within nineteenth-century Europe and certain countries of European settlement overseas: E. E. Lampard, "The Urbanizing World," in *Victorian Cities: Images and Realities,* ed. H. J. Dyos and M. Wolff (London, 1973), p. 8. On the social role and productive performance of administrative and market centers in non-European systems from the seventeenth century, see Gilbert Rozman, *Urban Networks in Ch'ing China and Tokugawa Japan* (Princeton, 1974). Also his stimulating comparison of "urban networks of advanced pre-modern societies" in *Urban Networks in Russia, 1750–1780,* and *Pre-modern Periodization* (Princeton, 1976), pp. 220–75.

7. George Tucker, *Progress of the United States in Population and Wealth in Fifty Years* (Boston, 1843), p. 127.

8. E. E. Lampard, "Historical Contours of Contemporary Urban Society: A Comparative View," *Journal of Contemporary History* 4 (1969), pp. 10-25. P. Bairoch, "Europe's Gross National Product: 1800-1975," *Journal of European Economic History* 5 (1976), pp. 273-340, shows that inequality of income distribution among European nations increased between 1830 and 1913, as it did between per capita GNP of 19 European nations as a whole and that of so-called Third World countries. The economies of small countries which "followed a policy of complementarity" with the U.K. experienced slower economic growth than more urbanized small countries that "followed a policy of industrial competition." For the relation between urbanization and relative growth performance of U.S. regions 1870-1920, see Harvey S. Perloff *et al., Regions, Resources and Economic Growth* (Baltimore, 1960), pp. 109-221.

9. E. E. Lampard, "Urbanization and Social Change," Seventh International Economic History Congress, *Proceedings,* ed. Flinn, II, p. 534. W. Arthur Lewis, *The Evolution of the International Economic Order* (Princeton, 1978), pp. 38-46, has given urbanization (rate of growth of urban population) a key role in the determination of late-nineteenth-century international investment and economic growth. European lenders such as Britain, France, and later Germany loaned principally to already rich borrowers (whose per capita incomes were higher than their own): the U.S., Australia, Canada, Argentina. Lending countries whose urban populations were growing at from 1.0 to 2.5 percent per annum invested in borrowers whose urban

Eric E. Lampard

populations were growing at from 3.5 to 5.3 percent per annum. "Urbanization is a decisive factor," Lewis argues, "because it is so expensive." The difference between costs of urban and rural development is not the difference between investing in factories or farms which, in either case, comprises only "a small part of total investment. . . . The difference turns on infrastructure": urban residential building, water supply, schooling, hospitals and public health, public transport, etc. "The cause of these high rates of urbanization" at any time "has been rapid population growth." *Unless* cultivable land is accessible, a growing rural population has to send its excess (net increase) to the towns to work *if* work is available there. The "quantitative significance of this migration depends on two factors" (1) the rate of natural increase, and (2) the existing ratio of urban to total population. To absorb the whole increase, urban population has to grow—according to Lewis—at a rate which might be expressed $\frac{\Delta P/P}{U/P}$ (assuming no gain from net international migration). In the case of late-nineteenth-century Germany, this meant 1.2/48 = 2.5 percent per annum. In the Latin America of the 1970s: 3.0/50 = 6.0 percent per annum which means "rural population remains constant while all natural increase is accumulating in the towns." Neither Asia nor Africa can achieve the 12.5 percent annual rates of urban population growth which their rates of natural increase impose according to the Lewis formulation. Since industry cannot be spread out around the countryside, urbanization is "inevitable": (a) because people are prepared to move to towns and (b) because "industry is itself gregarious: most industrialists prefer to establish themselves in existing industrial centers" which have both "the requisite physical infrastructure" and "the network of institutions that binds industrial establishments together." According to the argument of this paper, moreover, it was this "gregariousness" inherent in population concentration that engendered the modes of economic growth (investment opportunities) at least into the early decades of the present century. The critical importance of capital investment in infrastructure, educational, and social services for development was stressed by E. E. Lampard and L. F. Schnore, "Urbanization Problems," *Research Needs for Development Assistance Programs* (Washington, DC: Brookings Institution, proc., 1961), LS1-63, but critics thought this policy emphasis would divert scarce resources away from "production" and smacked too much of "socialism."

10. I. Feller, "The Urban Location of U.S. Invention, 1860-1910" *Explorations in Economic History* 8 (1971), pp. 285-364. R. Higgs, "Urbanization and Inventiveness in the U.S., 1870-1920," in *The New Urban History,* ed. L. F. Schnore (Princeton, 1975), pp. 247-59. More

generally on innovation, B. T. Robson, *Urban Growth: An Approach* (London, 1973), pp. 131-85. Also, M. J. Bowden, "Growth of Central Districts in Large Cities," in *The New Urban History*, ed. Schnore, pp. 75-109. J. E. Vance, Jr., "Land Assignment in the Pre-Capitalist and Post-Capitalist City," *Economic Geography* 47 (1979), pp. 101-20.

11. E. E. Lampard, "Urbanization of the United States: The Capitalization and Decapitalization of Place," in *Villes en mutation XIXe et XXe siècles* (Brussells: 10e Colloque internationale, Crédit Communal de Belgique, 1982), Table 2, on changing farm real-estate values in the fringe areas of major U.S. cities, 1850-1959, and *passim*.

12. S. Kuznets, "Long Swings in the Growth of Population and in Related Economic Variables," *Proceedings of the American Philosophical Society* 102 (Feb. 1958), pp. 25-52. Idem, *Economic Growth of Nations, Total Output and Productive Structure* (Cambridge, Mass., 1971), pp. 34-50. Brinley Thomas, *Migration and Urban Development: A Reappraisal of British and American Long Cycles* (London, 1972), pp. 4-12, stresses the interdependence, and alternation, of expansive phases of "swings" in resources supply on the two sides of the Atlantic. Also, Walter Isard, "Transportation Development and Building Cycles," *Quarterly Journal of Economics* 57 (1942), pp. 90-112.

13. R. A. Easterlin, *Population, Labor Force, and Long Swings in Economic Growth: The American Experience* (New York, 1968), pp. 21-74. Idem, "What Will 1984 Be Like?" *Demography* 15 (1978), pp. 397-432. W. W. McCormick and C. M. Franks, "A Self-Generating Model of Long Swings for the American Economy, 1860-1940," *Journal of Economic History* 32 (1971), pp. 295-343, adds monetary and technological variables to enhance the "explanatory value" of Easterlin's model. For criticisms of the long-swing approach, see B. Klotz and L. Neal, "Spectral and Cross Spectral Analysis of the Long-Swing Hypothesis," *Review of Economics & Statistics*, 55 (1973), pp. 291-98, which is skeptical of the sequence of effects among variables posited in the model. Also, J. Soper, *The Long Swing in Historical Perspective: An Interpretive Study* (New York, 1978).

14. E. E. Lampard, "Urbanization," *Encyclopedia of American Economic History*, ed. G. Porter (New York, 1980), III, pp. 1028-57. Not all localities and regions, of course, conform to the growth pulses indicated for the nation as a whole. With the exception of New York–New Jersey, the earlier a metropolitan area developed in the nineteenth century—e.g., in the Northeast or Great Lakes regions—the less likely its growth phasing (with respect to population, labor force structure, or investment in producers' durables) will conform precisely with those of the nation after 1870. In short, the thrust of national growth takes place at any time in the economic base of particular localities.

15. The standard accounting method for determining the relative contributions of the factors of production to net national product (or change in total factor productivity) is wholly conventional. Thus, a 5 percent increase in labor input is said to increase output by 5 percent times (x) the elasticity of output with respect to labor: but only under strict *ceteris paribus* conditions. Since there are, in any case, no direct measures of factor elasticity, recourse is had to attributions made in accordance with the theory of marginal productivity distribution, i.e., the relative distributive share of income received by each of the several factors in the market place; thus, labor's actual earnings = the marginal product of labor (the same applies to capital or land). Under competitive assumptions, if labor receives 75 percent of output as payment for its contribution, the elasticity of output with respect to additional units of labor input = 0.75. Hence the relative contribution of labor to measured increase in output in this instance will be: 0.05 × 0.75. Yet there is nothing in the logic of marginalism which warrants such an identification. However helpful such presumption might be with regard to "decision making" under profit-maximizing constraints (assuming no changes in the relative prices of products), the method does not in fact tell which of the factors "produced" how much (this or that much) of incremental output. Nor does the share of the output not "explained" by the sum of output attributable to quantities of factor inputs in this manner represent "residual" productivity change.

16. The fact that rates of increase in average incomes or in patenting inventions have become increasingly *independent* of rates of urban population growth or of increases in the urban share of population does not mean that incomes or inventiveness are now unrelated to investment booms (such as characterized the accelerating phase of "long swings" in the nineteenth and early-twentieth centuries). Indeed, post World War II booms in certain European countries were partly sustained by the savings generated through rapidly rising incomes and by the availability of labor as indicated (a) by a shrinking low-wage agricultural sector and (b) by the influx of *Gastarbeiter:* see Moses Abramovitz, "Likenesses and Contrasts between Investment Booms of the Postwar Period and Earlier Periods in Relation to Long Swings in Economic Growth," in *Population, Factor Movements, and Economic Development,* ed. Hamish Richards (Cardiff, 1977), pp. 22-49. Notwithstanding rapid urbanization of population in parts of continental Europe since 1945 (cf. Tables 1.3 and 1.5), the timing and magnitudes of residential building, "urban household demand," and related infrastructural spending are no longer the buttress for waning investment incentives in other sectors, but rather a *competitor* with such (expanding) sectors for limited capital resources (as in the developing countries also). An important difference between the older urbanization, say, before the first World War and recent ur-

banization under post World War II conditions has been the critical role of *government* expenditures and capital budgeting in sustaining (inflating?) the revived "market" economies of western Europe and North America.

17. Towns in Europe before the industrial revolution were generally compact settlements but their population densities after *c.* 1500 do not appear to have been very high (even excluding their suburbs). Much as in the nineteenth century, densities per acre might vary from one part of town to another: e.g., Rome in 1526 (pop. 53,897) averaged 15.5 "mouths" per acre but the range over its vast surface, 5.27 sq. miles, ranged from 120–130 "mouths" in the two most crowded *rioni* to no more than 3 or 4 in the least crowded. Out of 125 (not necessarily representative) superficial densities for towns in France, the Low Countries, and central Europe between the sixteenth and eighteenth centuries, given in the sources cited by Roger Mols in his *Annexes (op. cit.,* III, Appendix Tables 1,2,3,4,) there are no more than half a dozen instances of average densities (over areas a quarter or a third the size of Rome in 1526) above 180-200 persons per acre. While densities were usually higher by the eighteenth century, the heavy crowding evidenced at times in Grenoble, Breslau, Bordeaux center or Leipzig was exceptional. Two-thirds of the small numbers of readings from the sixteenth century fell within the range of 30-60 persons per acre; 60-120 in the seventeenth century; between 70 and 180 for the more numerous eighteenth-century readings, and 90-190 persons per acre in the opening decades of the nineteenth century. Much the same can be said of numbers of persons per dwelling: 4-7 in the fifteenth and sixteenth centuries; 5-10 in the seventeenth century (Seville over 11); 7-10 in the eighteenth century, with Berlin (17), Paris (20). Geneva and Grenoble (upwards of 20) and Vienna (40). While town households were usually smaller than rural households, differences in numbers between wealthier farmers and the rural proletariat are clearly paralleled within many towns. The lowest residential densities sometimes occur in the "poorer quarters" which, contrary to conventional wisdom, are often centrally situated and report a greater incidence of unattached men and women, female heads of household, widows or women taxables than other parts of town. Ibid. II, pp. 156-64.

18. Patterns of land-holding differed considerably between regions and countries and affected the character and timing of urban land development (particularly on the peripheries). The conclusion of J. R. Kellett, *The Impact of Railways on Victorian Cities* (London, 1969), pp. 383-424, that "the ground plan formed by property titles" was "the key to explaining the whole course of development of certain types of urban area, and the emergence of characteristic residential and industrial zones" probably applies to most rapidly urbanizing areas

Eric E. Lampard

and, if one were to write "by property titles within the gridiron plan" even to most nineteenth-century town plantings and extensions in the U.S. See Michael P. Conzen, "The Morphology of Nineteenth-Century Cities in the U.S.," and G. A. Stelter, "Urban Planning and Development in Upper Canada," in *Urbanization in the Americas: The Background in Historical Perspective,* ed. W. Borah, J. Hardoy, and G. A. Stelter (Ottawa: National Museum of Man, 1980), pp. 119-41, 143-55. Also, J. E. Vance, Jr., *This Scene of Man: The Role and Structure of the City in the Geography of Western Civilization* (New York, 1977), pp. 24-26, 265-69.

19. R. E. Dickinson, *The West European City: A Geographical Interpretation* (London, 1951), pp. 461-71. Bowden, "Growth of Central Districts," in *The New Urban History,* ed. Schnore, pp. 75-109. D. Cannadine, "Victorian Cities: How Different?," *Social History* 4 (January, 1977), pp. 457-82. H. J. Dyos, "Railways and Housing in Victorian London," *Journal of Transport History* 2 (1955) pp. 11-21; idem, "The Slums of Victorian London," *Victorian Studies* 11 (1967), pp. 5-40. H. Matzerath, "Städtewachstum und Eingemeindungen im 19. Jahrhundert," *Die deutsche Stadt im Industriezeitalter,* ed. J. Reulecke, (Wuppertal, 2nd edn., 1980), pp. 67-89. E. E. Lampard, "Some Aspects of Urban Social Structure and Morphology in the Historical Development of Cities in the U.S.," *Cahiers Bruxellois* 22 (1978), pp. 73-115. Also, Hans Straub, *Die Geschichte der Bauingenieurkunst* (Basel, 1949), esp. chapter 8 on nineteenth-century civil engineering achievements.

20. S. J. Low, "The Rise of the Suburbs," *Contemporary Review* 50 (1891), pp. 545-58. T. C. Clarke, "Rapid Transit in Cities," *Scribner's Magazine* 11 (May 1892). G.W. Hilton, "Transport Technology and the Urban Pattern," *Journal of Contemporary History* 4 (1969), pp. 123-35. J. P. McKay, *Tramways and Trolleys: The Rise of Urban Mass Transport in Europe* (Princeton, 1976), estimates a roughly fourfold increase in per capita usage of public transport in Europe, 1886-1910, compared with a 50 percent increase in the U.S.: "Europe was on the verge of taking an indisputable lead in urban public transport." Pierre Pierrard, "Habitat ouvrier et démographie à Lille au XIXe siècle et particulièrement sous le Second Empire," *Annales de démographie historique,* 1975, pp. 37-48. D. Rebentisch, "Industrialisierung, Bevölkerungswachstum und Eingemeindungen: Das Beispiel Frankfurt am Main 1870-1914," *Die deutsche Stadt,* ed. Reulecke, pp. 90-113. David Ward, "A Comparative Historical Geography of Streetcar Suburbs in Boston, Mass. and Leeds, England," *Annals of the Association of American Geographers* 54 (1964), pp. 447-89. S. B. Warner, Jr., *Streetcar Suburbs: The Process of Growth in Boston, 1870-1900* (Cambridge, Mass. 1962), esp. pp. 1-66, 153-66. R.D. Simon, "The City Building Process: Housing and Services in New Milwaukee Neighborhoods, 1880-1910," *American Philosophical Society Transactions* 68 (1978). J. A. Tarr, *Trans-*

port Innovation and Changing Social Patterns: Pittsburgh, 1850-1950 (Pittsburgh, 1972). Only in Belgium did industrial workers take to the rails at an early date in any numbers for the "journey to work." From the 1860s the *chemins de fer vicinaux* permitted workers in towns to dwell in nearby rural districts.

21. See above the contemporary opinion of Adna F. Weber, Arthur Shadwell, Thomas C. Horsfall, and others on environmental improvements and decentralization around the turn of the century, E. E. Lampard, "Urbanizing World," in *Victorian City*, ed. Dyos and Wolff, pp. 10-27, in outlining the urban demographic transition, suggested that urban mortality peaked in England and Wales, roughly 1849-66, based on *Reports of the Registrar General* (the incomplete registration system probably underrepresented deaths before the 1860s). Thereafter crude mortality fell steadily to the low levels of *c.* 1905 at the time of the Board of Trade "Cost of Living of the Working Class," House of Commons, *Accounts and Papers*, 1908, Vol. 107. Infant mortality, with wide differences among towns to be sure, was generally rising until 1896-99, at 160-3/1,000. By 1905 it was 128 and in 1910, 105: "Report by the Medical Officers on Infant and Child Mortality," Local Government Board, *39th Annual Report*, House of Commons, *Accounts and Papers*, 1910, Vol. 39.

22. E. P. Hennock, *Fit and Proper Persons: Ideal and Reality in Nineteenth-Century Urban Government* (London, 1973), esp. pp. 295-307. W. H. Dawson, *Municipal Life and Government in Germany* (London, 1914), chapter 18, judges German city government to be effectively more "autonomous" than British local government. British town government had become "self-government by statutory delegation." German (more especially Prussian) city government was "self-government by prescriptive right, modified by administrative sanction," Albert Shaw, *Municipal Government in Continental Europe* (New York, 1895). H. Jacobi, *German Administration since Bismarck* (New Haven, 1963), p. 65. Giorgio Piccinato, "Ideologie und technisches Instrumentarium in der Stadtplanung, 1820-1914," *Stadtbauwelt* 24 (1980), pp. 1041-8. Marcel Smets, *L'Avènement de la cité-jardin en Belgique. Histoire de l'habitat social en Belgique de 1830 à 1930* (Liège, 1977), pp. 8-77. Thomas Logan, "The Americanization of American Zoning," *Journal of the American Institute of Planners* 42 (1976), pp. 377-85. F. Mancuso, *Le vicende dello zoning* (Milan, 1978), an insightful treatment of the development of legalized zoning practice in Germany and the U.S. E. E. Lampard, "City Making and Mending in the United States: On Capitalizing a Social Environment," *Urbanization in the Americas*, ed. Borah *et al.*, pp. 109-15.

23. Spending by local governments in England and Wales (including borrowing) rose almost sixfold (in current £) between the late 1860s

and 1914. Local indebtedness comprised almost a fifth of all local receipts at the earlier date and rose to a quarter by the early 1880s. A decade later it had fallen to about one-eighth but thereafter rose rapidly to more than a quarter by the early 1900s before shrinking again to little more than a tenth of receipts by 1913 (these debt ratios exclude school boards outside London, and debt incurred by the Metropolitan Water Board and the Port of London Authority). Grants from the Exchequer (under 1.0 percent of local revenue in the late 1860s) rose steadily from about 5.0 percent in the 1870s to 15.0 percent by 1907 before slipping to under 14.0 percent, 1911-13. Poor relief involved the largest single outlay until the mid-1870s when debt service assumed the first place. Expenditures on schooling also rose rapidly at that time but were exceeded by roads and bridges and police. Interest on debt remained the largest charge, 20-25 percent, on current expenditures over the balance of the period, with roads and bridges also overtaking poor relief in the late 1890s. By that date, outlays on schools probably exceeded both these categories, with expenditures on police, sewerage and water service, gas and other public utilities the next largest items. The *capital* spending by local governments more than doubled in the aggregate, 1883-1914, with sewers and water services, roads and bridges, schools, gas electricity, and transport forming the lion's share. Mitchell, *Abstract of British Historical Statistics*, Public Finance, Tables 9, 10, 11.

24. U.S. local governments in the aggregate raised over 90 percent of their current receipts before 1929 (about 80 percent from local, mainly property, taxes until the 1930s). The rapid growth of municipal indebtedness in the post-Civil War decades principally involved water works, debt service, streets and bridges, aid to railways and other utilities and, to a lesser extent, sewers and schools. On the urbanization of local government debt and private mortgage debt in the U.S. in the late-nineteenth century, see Lampard, "Urbanization of the U.S.," *Villes en mutation*, notes 33, 39. S. Andic and J. Veverka, "Growth of Government Expenditure in Germany since the Unification," *Finanzarchiv* (January 1964), esp. pp. 198-213.

25. R. D. McKenzie, "Rise of Metropolitan Communities," *Recent Social Trends in the U.S.* (New York, 1933), I, pp. 492-96. Once the general economic depression had taken hold, the question of "blighted" and "obsolete" areas within cities became overlaid by the experience of decline in entire industries and their regions—the "depressed areas" in Europe and North America. An incipient tendency to "disinvestment" asserting itself locally in older core districts was thus rapidly superseded by general economic and social crises reflected in excess capacity and rising unemployment in almost all sectors of commodity production, including building and construction.

26. In the U.S. the emphasis on "home" building and "home" ownership

as a national (political) interest, as well as a private (market) interest received priority over the broader issues of "urban blight" or "slum clearance": see Herbert Hoover's remarks opening the President's Conference on Home Building and Home Ownership in 1931, *Preliminary Reports*, "Housing Objectives and Programs," XL, pp. 1-4. This stance was in marked contrast to the housing, planning and other policy concerns of national and local governments in Europe inaugurated during earlier crises, as remarked by Edith E. Wood, *Recent Trends in American Housing* (New York, 1931), pp. 12-20. Both Hoover's and the more thoroughgoing New Deal Housing measures were designed to prop up the mortgage lending and construction industries and reduce the carrying costs of private homeownership (following major recommendations of the President's Conference: *Final Report of the Committee on Large Scale Operations* (Washington, DC, 1932), p. 24. The Resettlement Administration's "greenbelt town program" and the *public* housing provisions of the 1937 U.S. Housing Act were essentially "make work" programs and, for all their radical potential, closely circumscribed by the U.S. Congress at the time. The fact that many homeowners and a few slum dwellers may have benefited from federal programs does not alter the point that the purpose and form of such measures were essentially a response to the organized interests that lobbied for (or against) them: in this case, the mortgage, real estate and construction industries and, in the last instance, the established trade unions. Other beneficiaries were the housing officials and planning functionaries. The Executive branch's National Resources Committee, *Our Cities: Their Role in the National Economy* (Washington, DC, 1937) first stressed an affirmative (as distinct from an incidental) economic role for cities in national recovery, and the same Committee's *Urban Government* (1939) called for a "national urban policy" now that some 500 distinct services and relationships had developed between federal agencies and municipal authorities (in such matters as education, public health, local improvements, planning and zoning, public relief and housing). Potentially far-reaching proposals were made in the late 1930s and early 40s to use federal spending on the decaying cities to enliven "stagnant" private investment channels, see Guy Greer and Alvin Hansen, "Urban Redevelopment and Housing," National Planning Association *Pamphlet No. 10* (Washington, DC, 1941), pp. 7-18; idem, "Toward Full Use of Our Resources," *Fortune*, Nov. 1942. Urban Land Institute, *Decentralization: What Is It Doing to Our Cities?* (Chicago, 1940). National Resources Planning Board, *National Resources Development Report for 1942* (Washington, DC, 1943), p. 107. As late as 1946 Louis Justement, *New Cities for Old* (New York, 1946), pp. 33-38, argued that private enterprise could no longer afford to "recapitalize" central urban land values without the public being required "to foot the bill in one form or another." Only if the public came to

Eric E. Lampard

purchase urban land outright (in cities ⩾ 25,000), would it be possible to retain the rebuilding for private enterprise: Lampard, "City Making and Mending in the U.S.," *Urbanization in the Americas,* ed. Borah *et al.,* esp. pp. 110-15.

27. A penetrating account of these economic and political processes working out the fate of a great city is S. G. Checkland, *The Upas Tree: Glasgow, 1875-1975. A Study in Growth and Contraction* (Glasgow, 1976), pp. 46-100. R. B. Andrews, *Urban Land Economics and Public Policy* (New York, 1971) gives a description of "the life cycle" of residential and commercial properties from development through blight in the institutional setting of the U.S. The phases of deterioration and decline, tax delinquency and possible demolition facilitate the succession to growth and redevelopment. Abandonment of properties—widespread for several decades in parts of New York City, St. Louis, Chicago, Detroit, and other large cities—does not form part of the American real estate vision. It involves a succession to vacancy, vandalism, and arson. See R. P. Sangster, "Abandonment of Inner City Properties," *Federal Home Loan Board Journal,* Feb. 5, 1972. On the "negative reinforcement" aspect of urban deterioration of services as well as properties, W. J. Baumol, "The Dynamics of Urban Problems and Its Policy Implications," *Essays in Honour of Lord Robbins,* ed. M. Preston and B. Cory (London, 1972), pp. 380-93.

28. Melvin M. Webber, "The Urban Place and the Nonplace Urban Realm," *Explorations in Urban Structure,* Webber *et al.* (Philadelphia, 1964), pp. 79-153, proposed that recent technological advances permitted the spatial separation of closely interacting people "in community without propinquity." In light of the loss of urbanizing momentum and denaturing of the city over the past half century or so, it is ironic perhaps that the Reagan administration in the U.S. (like its Thatcher counterpart in the U.K.) proposes to legislate tax reductions and relaxation of environmental regulations for small businesses which will locate in "run-down" neighborhoods and employ local residents (at low wages under dubious conditions): *New York Times,* Nov. 23, 1980. This is rerunning the nineteenth century with a vengeance but once whole cities were "enterprise zones" with only modest infusions of public capital.

29. E. E. Lampard, "The Survival of Industrial Cities: Comment," in *Modern Industrial Cities: History, Policy, and Survival,* ed. Bruce Stave (Beverly Hills, Cal., 1981), pp. 268-82. But see B. J. L. Berry, "Inner City Futures. An American Dilemma Revisited," ibid., pp. 187-219, and Elizabeth Lichtenberger, "The Changing Nature of European Urbanization," in *Urbanization and Counterurbanization,* ed. B. J. L. Berry (Beverly Hills, Cal., 1976), pp. 81-107.

30. If the level of concentration peaks around 80-85 percent of popu-

lation, then the process of urbanization may well resolve into movements *within* the city-size distribution: E. E. Lampard, "Evolving System of Cities in the U.S.: Urbanization and Economic Development," in *Issues in Urban Economics,* ed. H. S. Perloff and L. Wingo (Baltimore, 1968), pp. 109, 138. The recent growth of medium-sized cities, for example, in West Germany, the United States, and Canada, together with the decline of large-city populations, may well indicate this course of succession rather than wholesale deurbanization. See Giorgio Piccinato, "The Survival of Industrial Cities: Comment," in *Modern Industrial Cities,* ed. Stave, pp. 282-85: "The future lies in the trend toward smaller cities, not the abandonment of the city *per se.* The growing amount of public investment in all European urban centers is very much a reflection of this trend."

31.   Some preliminary analyses of 1980 U.S. census tracts in close-in "blighted zones" of inner cities indicates that the much advertised private-public programs of "neighborhood preservation and renewal" have not yet arrested the loss of population from within a radius of two or three miles of central business districts. These programs encourage affluent persons to restore old structures for residential purposes in order "to stem the flight of the middle class" and buttress the municipality's eroding tax base. Public housing funds may also be used in certain instances to rehabilitate housing for large low-income families. Between 1968 and 1979, however, only 0.5 percent of 20 million dilapidated housing units nationwide were affected by "revitalization and restoration efforts.": U.S. Dept. of Housing and Urban Development, "Whither or Whether Urban Distress," Paper presented to Joint Economic Committee, U.S. Congress, March 20, 1979. Meanwhile the urban *proportion* of U.S. population increased by only 0.2 percentage points to 73.7 percent, 1970-80, in spite of a rise of 11.8 percent in actual numbers; the population of metropolitan areas (SMSAs) increased by 9.1 percent and that of nonmetropolitan areas by 15.4 percent. The central cities of the metropolitan areas, however, experienced a net loss of residents to their ring areas and to nonmetropolitan areas; a 15 percent gain in the black population of central cities did not offset the loss of some 7 percent of their white populations. But in sample tracts of neighborhood renewal and adjacent areas of large central cities, black population *declined* by 20 percent, while white population fell by a percentage greater than their city-wide loss (except in Philadelphia and Washington, DC where numbers of whites in neighborhood renewal areas increased). Such "gentrified" precincts tend to be populated by single persons, couples without children, and by childless married couples. Of the 26 largest U.S. cities only four (San Diego and San Jose, Cal., San Antonio, Tex., and Phoenix, Ariz.) gained census white population, 1970-80, while Philadelphia, San Francisco,

Eric E. Lampard

Washington, DC, Cleveland, and St. Louis registered a reduced number of blacks as well. Among northern cities only Detroit registered a substantial increase in black numbers (14.2 percent) to set against its loss of more than half (50.7 percent) its 1970 white population. The partial rebuilding of inner cities on a smaller (white) population base with a generally smaller (and blacker) city-wide population, is unlikely to stem the shift of political representation to "suburban" ring and nonmetropolitan areas.

32. John Friedmann, *The Future of Urban Habitat* (Los Angeles: School of Architecture and Urban Planning, UCLA, 1972), pp. 5-7: "The social costs of this accommodation are enormous, but substantial savings accrue from letting the core city run down." Anthony Downs, "Alternative Forms of Future Urban Growth in the U.S.," *Journal of the American Institute of Planners* 36 (1970), pp. 1-11. Also, Stephan Jonas, "Future Organization of the European Industrial City: 'Urban Alternatives,' " in *Modern Industrial Cities*, ed. Stave, pp. 221-48.

33. Wilfred Owen, *The Accessible City* (Washington, DC, 1972), pp. 15, 21, 65, 112, summarizes the evolution of British planning thought on "new towns" from Harlow (Mark I) to "new communities" of "the automobile age" (Mark III). But he notes: "Many who drive farther in order to live better find that too many others have had the same idea. The only recourse is to move again. . . . Sooner or later outward dispersal from one city will run into suburbs spreading from the opposite direction, and the escape routes will be closed." The motor highways built since the 1950s across the countries of the Common Market—that mausoleum for spent sovereignties—will certainly foster dispersion of the footloose production of "marketed" goods and services from the older cities at the same time as they serve, presumably, to enhance the European interregional division of labor. The motor highway serves the reverse role of those maritime "liquid roads" that, according to Fernand Braudel, contributed so much to the development of Mediterranean city civilization: *Civilisation matérielle et capitalisme* (Paris, 1967), chapter 8.

34. The "urban field" may gradually supersede the U.S. "metropolitan area" insofar as the latter is conventionally centered on "a large population nucleus," ≥ 50,000, whose contiguous counties maintain "a high degree of economic and social integration with that nucleus." It is precisely the *centralized* focus of circulation in the metropolitan area that makes it a high per capita energy mode of settlement and renders energy-intensive modes of information processing and "face to face" transactions in high-value central business districts an expensive luxury, given the possibilities for newer low-energy communications (e.g., electronic means of managing bank clearing house dealings). Thus the effort of the Real Estate Research corporation

to demonstrate the "relative cost effectiveness" of prototype high-density urban concentrations over low-density, spaced-out, "communities." *The Costs of Sprawl* (3 Vols.: Washington, DC, Government Printing Office, 1975), not only underestimated the high-cost public services and programs needed to make a late-twentieth-century U.S. city function (see D. R. Vining, Jr. "The President's National Urban Policy Report: Issues Skirted and Statistics Omitted," *Journal of Regional Science* 19 (1979), pp. 69-77, but neglected the full implication of low-energy communications and data-based management for the CBDs of "large population nuclei." The "face to face" communications advantage of the historic city, as argued by Richard L. Meier, *A Communications Theory of Urban Growth* (Cambridge, Mass., 1967) may finally be fading. Certainly U.S. social scientists are moving rapidly to embrace the "polycentric ecological field" in which a CBD is "just one specialized node in a multinodal, multi-connected ecological field of interdependent activity centers": J.D. Kasarda, "The Implications of Contemporary Redistribution Trends for National Urban Policy," *Social Science Quarterly* 61 (1980), pp. 374-400.

35. H. G. Wells, *Anticipations of the Reaction of Mechanical and Scientific Progress upon Human Life and Thought* (London, 1902). Wells's comments on this "new and entirely different phase of human distribution" originally appeared in *The Fortnightly Review* in 1900. Also, E. E. Lampard, "Figures in the Landscape: Some Historiographical Implications of Environmental Psychology," *Comparative Urban Research* 5 (1977), pp. 120-32.

Eric E. Lampard

Dickens and the City

Philip Collins

When Dickens was "a very queer small boy," living in Chatham (he recalled), it used to be a great treat to be taken for a walk past a substantial country house that had much caught his fancy, Gad's Hill Place: and his father used to say to him, "If you were to be very persevering, and were to work hard, you might some day come to live in it."[1] At the age of forty-five, he did so, and a few years later, in an *Uncommercial Traveller* essay, he told his public about this childhood ambition and its realization. Inevitably one is here reminded of *Culture and Anarchy,* written in the same decade, where Matthew Arnold refers to

> that beautiful sentence Sir Daniel Gooch quoted . . ., and which I treasure as Mrs. Gooch's Golden Rule, or the Divine Injunction "Be ye Perfect" done into British,—the sentence Sir Daniel Gooch's mother repeated to him every morning when he was a boy going to work: *"Ever remember, my dear Dan, that you should look forward to being some day manager of that concern."* (ch. 2)

Like Mrs. Gooch's dear Dan, Mr. Dickens' dear Charley had worked hard and succeeded, and now he used and advertised his success, in the traditional English way, by buying a country house—and he could never have succeeded so remarkably as an author (any more than could his contemporary Tennyson, then the most popular and rewarded poet, as Dickens was the most popular and rewarded novelist, Britain had ever known) had not he, like Tennyson, shared and embodied many of their society's most cherished values, such as Mrs. Gooch's Golden Rule. Tennyson indeed bought two country houses.

Tennyson, country-born, found his imagination nourished by country living; Dickens did not.[2] As one of his sons remarks, Dickens in later years, despite his daily feats of pedestrianism through the local countryside, never took to the country, "never acquired, or cared, I think, to acquire, the accurate knowledge of country sights and sounds . . . which comes . . . very rarely to the town-bred man who takes in middle age to the woods and fields."[3] He never shared Tennyson's interest in those rosy plumelets tufting the larch; more germane to his art and range as a novelist, he never acquired any feel for the social and economic life of the countryside. The significantly unnamed village where Pip grows up (in *Great Expectations,* written after his move to Gad's Hill) is no more "there" than David Copperfield's village birthplace, Blunderstone—as it would be convincingly "there" in a George Eliot or a Hardy novel. But happily Dickens as novelist dwells little more on the village or the woods and fields than Tennyson as poet concerns himself, unprofitably, with the city. These two authors, dominant and unprecedentedly popular in their respective kinds—*the* "two voices" of their age (to borrow the title of a Tennyson poem)—neatly typify the special concerns of mid-nineteenth-century English fiction and poetry. "God made the country, and man made the town," William Cowper had pronounced a quarter of a century before their births: and Victorian poetry was to specialize in God's territory, as Victorian fiction was more characteristically to concern itself with "what man has made of man" and has produced, environmentally and socially, in the man-made town.

So another of Dickens' childhood excursionary "treats" was to prove more fruitful for his creative imagination. At the age of ten, after those Gad's-Hill-viewing years at Chatham, he was living in London, with his family in precarious circumstances. To be taken out for a walk from the indigent Camden Town suburb into which the family had descended "into the real town," he told his friend and future biographer John Forster, "perfectly entranced him with pleasure"—"especially if it were anywhere about Covent Garden or the Strand." (Covent Garden, it should be interjected, was famous then not only for its great theatre and its market but also for the hordes of vagrants that haunted it, living partly off market scraps and odd-jobs.) "But, most of all," Forster continues,

> he had a profound attraction of repulsion to St. Giles's [then, to interject, a notorious criminal slum]. If he could only induce whomsoever took him out to take him through Seven-Dials [the

subject of an early essay], he was supremely happy. "Good Heaven," he would exclaim, "what wild visions of prodigies of wickedness, want and beggary arose in my mind out of that place!"[4]

It could hardly be more significant for the future novelist that his supreme happiness, at the age of ten, was produced by "wild visions" of prodigious metropolitan "wickedness, want and beggary." His was to be one of those "other pens" stigmatized, during his childhood, by Jane Austen in the frankest cop-out in English literature: "Let other pens dwell on guilt and misery: I quit such odious subjects as soon as I can . . ." (*Mansfield Park*, ch. 48). Significant too is that favorite phrase of Dickens', "the attraction of repulsion."[5] His imagination and verbal skills were manifestly stimulated by the repulsive, objectionable, ludicrous, and grotesque, not by God's handiwork in the woods and fields, which evoked at best his inertly pious aesthetic approval; God had of course got it all right, but rightness was not Dickens' literary territory. As a middle-class boy, albeit precariously middle-class, he had felt shocked by and superior to, though also thrilled by, those Covent Garden destitutes and the "dirty men, filthy women, squalid children" whom he had noticed in his "Seven Dials" essay (*Sketches by Boz*), written before he became a novelist, living in streets "of dirty, straggling houses, with now and then an unexpected court composed of buildings as ill-proportioned and deformed as the half-naked children that wallow in the kennels" (an early and simple example, this, of Dickens' imaginative habit of comparing and conflating buildings with their inhabitants). But, middle-class in origins and outlook though he was, at the crisis of his family's fortunes he became, as Forster says, or almost became, one of the "very poor and unprosperous, out of whose sufferings and strugglings . . . his not least splendid successes were wrought. . . . They were not his clients whose cause he pleaded . . . but in some sort his very self."[6]

Covent Garden, very suitably, became one of his main symbols of the metropolis. With London's other great historic theatre, Drury Lane, just over the way, it represented for him the nation's most exciting cultural center—but it was encompassed by destitution and beggary. Fittingly, the offices of his weekly magazine, where in his later years he kept a much-used *pied-à-terre*, lay a hundred yards or so to the south. "Within so many yards of this Covent-Garden lodging of mine," he writes in a late *Uncommercial Traveller* essay,

> as within so many yards of Westminster Abbey, St Paul's Cathedral, the Houses of Parliament, the Prisons, the Courts of Justice, all the Institutions that govern the land, I can find—*must* find, whether I will or no—in the open streets, shameful instances of neglect of children, intolerable toleration of the engenderment of paupers, idlers, thieves, races of wretched and destructive cripples both in body and mind, a misery to themselves, a misery to the community, a disgrace to civilization, and an outrage on Christianity.[7]

It is an observation often repeated, and dramatized, in the novels. In the early novel *Nicholas Nickleby*, when the hero returns to London, the narrator remarks—with scant relevance to the concerns of this novel—upon the "point and purpose" that may be discerned in the ironically disparate street-scene:

> the rags of the squalid ballad-seller fluttered in the rich light that showed the goldsmith's treasures; pale and pinched-up faces hovered about the [shop-]windows where was tempting food. . . . Life and death went hand in hand; wealth and poverty stood side by side; repletion and starvation laid them down together. (ch. 32)

In a more mature novel, *Bleak House* (in which the first word, the first sentence, indeed, appropriately is, "London"), the point is made more succinctly, fiercely, and relevantly: that politically tolerated sanitary hazard, the pestilential city graveyard where "our dear brother" Nemo lies buried, is, says the narrator mordantly, "a shameful testimony to future ages, how civilization and barbarism walked this boastful island together" (ch. 11). Dickens, who was to give his name to this age—for we still speak of "Dickens' England," whereas it would make little sense to talk of "Tennyson's England" or "George Eliot's England"—could be rightly conscious that his novels were offering "testimony to future ages," often "shameful" testimony, about the England and especially the London of his day. As Walter Bagehot was splendidly to remark in 1858, "He describes London like a special correspondent to posterity."[8]

Or, as Donald Olsen has lately put it, Dickens was "imposing his brilliant but perverse vision of London on the consciousness both of his contemporaries and of posterity"—a striking judgment, which unfortunately Professor Olsen does not argue or justify there nor, so far as I can find, elsewhere in his authoritative writings on urban history. But Olsen, in this essay on "Victorian London," makes a general point that relates significantly to the formation of Dickens' attitudes and to his representativeness. Between 1825 and 1837, Olsen argues, "London experienced a crisis of conscience," underwent a remarkably sudden psychological revolution:

> The ways in which people regarded London changed completely and permanently during the decade following 1825. London turned from being an object of pride to an object of shame, from a symbol of wealth to a symbol of poverty, from a vision of health to a vision of disease, from one of light to one of darkness.[9]

Olsen suggests reasons for this major shift in how London was viewed, and argues that this notion that London was conspicuously "dirty and deadly" was unjustified by the facts. So, by Olsen's account, Dickens' "brilliant but perverse vision of London" was not only influential but also widely shared. He supplied his special brilliance certainly; his "perversity," however, was not an idiosyncratic minority report but the reflection of a widely held if (as Olsen insists) a mistaken opinion. I have often argued that, politically, Dickens (born in 1812) was a man of 1832; I must now, under Olsen's instruction, learn to see him in his role as urban "special correspondent to posterity," as a man of this 1825–37 critical reaction. The Olsen dates fit Dickens' formative years well. He arrived in London from Chatham in 1823, and his first books are *Sketches by Boz* (1836) and *Pickwick Papers* (1836–37). On London, then, as on so much else, Dickens was not too unfairly nicknamed (in Trollope's *The Warden*) "Mr. Popular Sentiment."

This is evident, even without benefit of Olsen. Witness the rags-and-riches title of the novel by his friend and fellow-feeler, Douglas Jerrold, published a year before *Bleak House*, *St. Giles and St. James* (1851). Dickens, however, was the only literary genius of his day who had the experiences and memories, and the psychic impetus, to write greatly on this theme. (His manuscript note for the bottling-warehouse episode in *David Copperfield* states this with pained brevity: "What I know so well.") But, if "the very poor and unfortunate" were in some sort his own past self as well as "his clients," he did not ignore or scorn the pleasures that money can buy. In an important essay, "Where We Stopped Growing," about childhood experiences that remain part of his mental furniture, "the whole region about Covent Garden" is inevitably featured:

> We have not outgrown the two great Theatres. Ghosts of great names are always getting up the most extraordinary pantomimes in them, with scenery and machinery on a tremendous scale.[10]

Dickens had a lifelong passion for the theatre—had indeed nearly joined Covent Garden as a professional actor at the age of twenty—and the theatre is of course an essentially urban art. If Dickens is remembered as a compassionate observer, a reformer, an indignant denouncer of social evils, he is also the most genial and the most humorous of English novelists, and his presentation of the city includes aspects and attitudes corresponding to these various facets of his artistic personality.

London is overwhelmingly the main locale of his novels, every one of which except *Hard Times* has scenes there, and usually it is the predominant scene. His heroes such as Oliver Twist or Nicholas Nickleby or David Copperfield or Pip have often been born and raised in the country but, like their creator, they soon make their way to the metropolis. His characters make excursions from London: Mr. Pickwick goes to Kent, Suffolk, Bath, and elsewhere, Nicholas Nickleby travels North and then South, Martin Chuzzlewit gets to America, the Dorrit family use their newfound wealth to make a grand tour to Italy—and so on—but they all return to London where, in their absence, various other plot-lines have been proceeding. Only in *The Old Curiosity Shop* does the main action proceed from London into the provinces, where it concludes: but

Philip Collins

most of the other characters stay in Town and most of the action takes place there. Not an extensive or particularly adventurous traveller himself, Dickens wrote two travel books, which offer accounts of some cities overseas: Boston, New York, Washington, Baltimore, and the model factory town of Lowell, Massachusetts; and of Venice, Rome, Naples, and other Italian cities. Some of these locations appear again in his fiction. He was fond of Paris and spent much time there, but he wrote little about it except in his letters (though a bygone Paris appears of course in his historical novel *A Tale of Two Cities*). For the ancient cathedral cities of England he had little feeling; as a contemporary reviewer remarked, "In *Martin Chuzzlewit* our writer hurries from Salisbury to London, . . . and in *David Copperfield* is glad to escape from Canterbury to the more congenial climate of Doctors' Commons."[11] Canterbury, indeed, is hardly more described, in its historic picturesqueness, than is St. Alban's, through which the characters in *Bleak House* are continually passing on their way to and from John Jarndyce's house nearby (the narrator does once concede that St. Alban's possesses an old abbey). Dickens did not have much of an eye for the historic, though he was trying to do more with his rendering of the cathedral city of Cloisterham (he had Rochester in mind) in his final uncompleted novel, *Edwin Drood*. He made something, but not very much, of the resort towns, Bath and Brighton and Leamington, in various novels. Before I engage more fully with our main subject—Dickens' main urban subject—London, one other man-made environment deserves some comment: the industrial town.

London was of course, as it always has been, Britain's largest industrial city, but it was so many other things—the capital city, the social and financial and entertainment center, the port, and simply the largest city ever built—that Dickens, like most people, rarely thought of it in that way. Daniel Doyce's factory, in *Little Dorrit*, is the only industrial establishment in Dickens' London (and is thinly presented); the warehouse in which David Copperfield works is a preindustrial manual-labor workshop. But Dickens like other thoughtful contemporaries was fascinated by and concerned about the new-style towns then emerging, almost wholly given over to industry, sometimes to a single industry. How new and bewildering a phenomenon this was, Dickens expresses by a remarkable image, in *The Old Curiosity Shop,* when Little Nell and her grandfather find themselves in "a great manufacturing town" in the Black Country of the West Midlands: they

> ... stood, amid its din and tumult, and in the pouring rain, as strange, bewildered, and confused, as if they had lived a thousand years before, and were raised from the dead and placed there by miracle. (ch. 43)

Steven Marcus, who quotes this in his *Engels, Manchester and the Working Class,* argues that only the mature Dickens can stand beside or surpass Engels' representation of the industrial city, displaying "such an intimate, creative hold upon its living subject."[12] High praise indeed, for the industrial environment is neither a predominant nor a frequent topic for him. One novel, *Hard Times,* is devoted to the subject (but it is only a quarter of the standard length of his novels), and industrialism appears incidentally and sometimes very briefly in *Pickwick Papers, The Old Curiosity Shop, Dombey and Son,* and *Bleak House,* and in some short stories and letters, and many of his speeches were delivered in and related to Birmingham, Manchester, and other such cities. "All roads led to Manchester in the 1840s," remarks Asa Briggs in his *Victorian Cities,* though there was "an inevitable lag in imaginative response to the most interesting new phenomenon of the age."[13] Not only did Engels and other observers, foreign and native, troop to Manchester, but also in and around this decade there was a small vogue for "industrial novels," usually set in the North, and sometimes specifically in Manchester (Harriet Martineau's *A Manchester Strike* and Mrs. Gaskell's *Mary Barton: a Tale of Manchester Life*). Dickens had got in early, with that impressive episode in *The Old Curiosity Shop* (1840–41). He had even shown his ambitiousness by including, briefly and irrelevantly, a glimpse of "the great working town of Birmingham" in his first novel, *Pickwick Papers* (1836–37: ch. 50). There he was noncommittal except for his repeating the adjective "great"; he made no attempt to comprehend this city or to coordinate the positive and the negative impressions recorded. But to include this brief passage at all in the comic

Philip Collins

picaresque of *Pickwick* was an earnest indication of later intentions; and it may be relevant that Birmingham, the first and the last industrial city Dickens wrote and spoke about, was the one he knew much the best, returning there quite often and developing an affection for the place. For here I recall Asa Briggs's interesting speculation that

> If Engels had lived not in Manchester but in Birmingham, his conception of "class" and his theories of the role of class in history might have been very different. In this case Marx might have been not a communist but a currency reformer. The fact that Manchester was taken to be the symbol of the age in the 1840s and not Birmingham . . . was of central political importance in modern world history.[14]

Dickens' next presentation of industrialism was in *The Old Curiosity Shop*, where the stress is entirely on the phantasmagoric horror of this new way of life: the blasted and polluted landscape, the shrieks of the engines, "a hundred strange unearthly noises never heard elsewhere," the foundry-workers "moving like demons and . . . labouring like giants," the red-hot metal emitting "a dull, deep light like that which reddens in the eyes of savage beasts," strange engines that "spun and writhed like tortured creatures," and much more in similar vein (ch. 44). In an essay on this topic, I contrasted this passage with one from a late short story, "Mugby Junction" (1866), which contains a panegyric of a "great ingenious town" (unnamed, but Dickens meant Birmingham), where the depressed middle-aged hero, Mr. Jackson, takes a salutary walk:

> How the many toiling people lived, and loved and died; how wonderful it was to consider the various trainings of eye and hand, the nice distinctions of sight and touch, that separated them into classes of workers, and even into classes of workers at subdivisions of one complete whole which combined their many intelligences and forces, though of itself but some cheap object of use or ornament in common life; how good it was to know that such assembling in a multitude on their part, and such contribution of their several dexterities towards a civilising end, did not deteriorate them as it was the fashion of the supercilious Mayflies of humanity to pretend, but engendered among them a self-respect, and yet a modest desire to be much

wiser than they were (the first evinced in their well-balanced bearing and manner of speech when he stopped to ask a question; the second, in the announcements of their popular studies and amusements on the public walls); these considerations, and a host of such, made his walk a memorable one.[15]

Turgidly written, indeed, and quite lacking in the sensory quality of the *Old Curiosity Shop* episode, this passage is a reminder that Dickens often wrote best on his "repulsions" and worst on what he approved of; still, this passage is instructive in its welcoming acceptance of industrialism—and the more obviously if one recognizes in that reference to "the supercilious Mayflies of humanity" a hit at Ruskin and his recently renewed attack on the division of labor ("It is not, truly speaking, the labour that is divided, but the men— Divided into mere segments of men").[16]

I compared these two passages, not to suggest that the early Dickens was horrified by industrialism and the later Dickens enthusiastic about it: he had, I think, no consistent thought-out notions on the matter, nor did his attitude to it develop along a single line; on this as on other matters he was, as a colleague remarked, an ideological "wobbler." For me, this comparison illustrates three simple points. First, that Dickens is writing novels, not treatises aiming at comprehensiveness or objectivity; Little Nell needed a fearsome experience at that point in her narrative, Mr. Jackson needed a moral and emotional pick-me-up at that point in his, and Dickens accordingly and quite legitimately selected disparate elements from his experience and assessment of the industrial town for these purposes. Second, that both these fictional passages correspond to certain external realities: Manchester wasn't Birmingham, but the Wolverhampton area recalled in *The Old Curiosity Shop* wasn't Birmingham either; industrialism bore a different face in one area or industry from another. Third, that Dickens had the good sense to recognize that neither a sweeping rejection of nor an uncritical rejoicing in industrialism was reasonable (though it is his way to express this awareness by one black and one white passage rather than by deliberating about what shade of gray is most appropriate). Thus I am not puzzled or troubled by the fact

Philip Collins

that in *Hard Times* he is wholly hostile to the industrial society of Coketown whereas in the previous novel, *Bleak House*, the self-made ironmaster, Mr. Rouncewell, is applauded, almost idealized, and Dickens even pays industrial Yorkshire the compliment of sending his heroine and her bridegroom to live there at the end of the novel. One reason for this, though not the only reason, is that ironmasters were considered good employers and ironworkers were the industrial aristocracy, while millowners—as in *Hard Times,* where he has Lancashire in mind—had a bad reputation and conditions of employment in the cotton industry were notoriously bad.

Hard Times is the odd novel out in Dickens' fiction (much the shortest; no London scenes; no wedding-bells at the end), and it is exceptional too in its mode of writing. Usually Dickens' writing is full of detail, but not here—partly maybe because he was working on unfamiliar territory but also because a profusion of detail would militate against his major point about the industrial scene and ethos, that it is monotonous, a point famously enacted in what he explicitly calls a "keynote" passage about Coketown and its inhabitants ("people equally like one another, who all went in and out at the same hours, with the same sounds upon the same pavements, to do the same work, and to whom every day was the same as yesterday . . .": ch. 5). *Hard Times* is unlike the other industrial novels of its period, too. We hardly see inside the factories, there is little or nothing about unhealthy working or housing conditions, or unemployment, or child-labor; there is no strike or riot or arson or machine-breaking, no industrial violence or unrest. Instead Dickens concentrates on the intrinsically poor quality of industrial life, and the ideology which justifies it, rather than the isolable and readily curable evils of the system or the flashpoint crises such as strikes.

"He was a master in London; abroad he was only a workman," a colleague said of him:[17] and certainly *Hard Times* is not one of his richer books. He knew London much more intimately than the industrial north, and as the huge capital city of the world's greatest empire it gave him an ideal vantage-point from which to write about mid-nineteenth-century life. As a reviewer wrote in 1861:

> Dickens is the novelist and poet of great cities and of civil life,
> especially of London life. We do not know of whom beside we
> can say this. . . . This is the age of great cities, and Dickens is
> the painter of great cities . . . the epic poet of city life.[18]

This comparison of his renderings of urban life to painting
and poetry is appropriate and was often made. Here for
instance is Moncure Conway, an American coming to know
Dickens' London on foot, after reading the novels:

> Dickens was a wonder. The more I saw of London the more
> I loved and honoured the London Dante who had invested it
> with romance, and peopled its streets and alleys with spirits,
> so that the huge city could never more be seen without his
> types and shadows.[19]

Like Bagehot and Olsen, Conway here testifies to Dickens'
having imposed his vision of London on the international
consciousness. "Special correspondent to posterity," Bagehot
called him, and the journalistic image captures important
elements in his work, its on-the-spot up-to-dateness, but Conway's "London Dante" is suggestive too: Dickens' rendering
is not literal or merely journalistic, but highly imaginative
and moralized (with more *Inferno* than *Paradiso* depicted).
Dickens in a letter spoke of his mind's having taken " a fanciful
photograph" of an unfamiliar scene[20]—a paradoxical phrase
that neatly conflates the imaginative and the reportage elements in his vision.

Bagehot, continuing his journalistic image to explain why
London was specially advantageous to Dickens' genius, remarks that London—and Dickens' novels—were "like a newspaper. . . . Everything is there, and everything is
disconnected": the novels had episodes corresponding to the
newspaper's births, deaths, and marriages page, police-court
reports, Society news, leading-article, and so on. Dickens, we
have seen, was very conscious of the ironic juxtapositions of
wealth and poverty, power and degradation, so conspicuous
in the capital. Here is another such passage, an early one
from *Master Humphrey's Clock*, rather rhetorical in manner but
making this point with unusual completeness ("Master Humphrey, from His Clock-side in the Chimney-corner"):

It is night. Calm and unmoved amidst the scenes that darkness favours, the great heart of London throbs in its giant breast. Wealth and beggary, vice and virtue, guilt and innocence, repletion and the direst hunger, all treading on each other and crowding together, are gathered round it. Draw but a little circle above the clustering house-tops, and you shall have within its space, everything with its opposite extreme and contradiction, close beside.

There follows a series of contrasts, between birth and death, prosperous virtue and indigent crime, and then, with the arrival of dawn, life stirring in a medley of disparate environments:

Each of these places is a world, and has its own inhabitants; each is distinct from, and almost unconscious of the existence of any other. There are some few people well to do, who remember to have heard it said, that numbers of men and women—thousands, they think it was—get up in London every day, unknowing where to lay their heads at night; and that there are quarters of the town where misery and famine always are. They don't believe it quite—there may be some truth in it, but it is exaggerated, of course. So each of these thousand worlds goes on, intent upon itself, until night comes again—first with its lights and pleasures, and its cheerful streets; then with its guilt and darkness.

It belongs of course to Dickens' social mission, as well as to his imaginative inclination, to harp on these contrasts and to make the comfortable world of his readers "believe it quite." I shall return to that: but first I draw attention to the final words of this quotation, "until night comes again—first with its lights and pleasures, and its cheerful streets; then with its guilt and darkness." Night in the big city particularly attracted him, as man and author; he loved those lighted streets, with of course the dark patches around and beyond them, mysterious and threatening. But crime, misery, and destitution are far from being his only urban subjects: recall "night with its lights and *pleasures,* and its *cheerful* streets." His first book, *Sketches by Boz,* published almost on his twenty-fourth birthday, was almost wholly devoted to London, and after an essay "The Streets—Morning" he has a companion-piece, "The Streets—Night", which begins:

But the streets of London, to be beheld in the very height of their glory, should be seen on a dark, dull, murky winter's night, when there is just enough damp gently stealing down to make the pavement greasy, without cleansing it of any of its impurities; and when the heavy lazy mist, which hangs over every object, makes the gas-lamps look brighter, and the brilliantly-lighted shops more splendid, from the contrast they present to the darkness around.

Here one is reminded of such later set pieces as the shops on Christmas Eve in the *Carol*. And the pleasures and cheerfulness of London after dark appear prominently in *Sketches by Boz*, too: such essays as "Private Theatres," "London Recreations," "Astley's" [circus], "Public Dinners," even "Gin-Shops," where the relaxations of "Everyday Life and Everyday People" (to cite the subtitle of the book) are celebrated with zest and spirit.

Dickens' art was emotionally inclusive: he had a go at everything (often in a single novel), from the frivolous to the tragic, from the tender and sentimental to the terrific and macabre. Bagehot's comparison between the novels and a newspaper and London reminds us how hamstrung Dickens would have been had his art been confined to the characteristic locales of those other novelists whom I have mentioned, Jane Austen, George Eliot, and Hardy. Moreover, a novelist of conviviality, whether in crowds or round the domestic hearth, he also had a strong sense of its opposite, that loneliness which is most poignant and paradoxical when it is suffered in the midst of a huge community. In an early essay he announces this theme:

It is strange with how little notice, good, bad or indifferent, a man may live and die in London. . . . He awakens no sympathy in the breast of any single person; . . . he cannot be said to be forgotten when he dies, for no one remembered him when he was alive.[21]

For the refugee, or the fugitive from justice, this urban *anomie* can be comforting; Oliver Twist, running away from the Sowerberrys, makes for London, "that large place—nobody—not even Mr. Bumble—could ever find him there!" (ch. 8). Others are, and feel, condemned to "live solitarily in great cities, as in the bucket of a human well" (*Old Curiosity Shop,* ch. 15). Often, in such contexts, Dickens invokes the phrase (not peculiar to him), "the wilderness of London." When Nicholas Nickleby uses the phrase, Mr. Charles Cheeryble picks it up, in animated agreement:

> "Wilderness! Yes, it is, it is. Good! It *is* a wilderness. It was a wilderness to me once. I came here barefoot. I have never forgotten it. Thank God!" and he raised his hat from his head, and looked very grave. (*Nicholas Nickleby*, ch. 35)

Nicholas, like many of Dickens' other heroes, is a young man up from the country (a classic situation recurrent in nineteenth-century European fiction, as Lionel Trilling remarks in *The Liberal Imagination*). Another first impression of London is Pip's in *Great Expectations:*

> We Britons at that time particularly settled that it was treasonable to doubt our having and being the best of everything: otherwise, while I was scared by the immensity of London, I think I might have had some faint doubts whether it was not rather ugly, crooked, narrow and dirty. (ch. 20)

Pip speaks here for his creator, who in sundry essays and letters, and in authorial interjections in the novels, often makes the point without this thin veil of irony. In "The Boiled Beef of New England," for instance (in *The Uncommercial Traveller*, a collection of later essays, many of them germane to this theme; this one belongs to 1863):

> The shabbiness of our English capital, as compared with Paris, Bordeaux, Frankfort, Milan, Geneva—almost any important town on the continent of Europe—I find very striking after an absence of any duration in foreign parts. London is shabby in contrast with Edinburgh, with Aberdeen, with Exeter, with Liverpool, with a bright little town like Bury St. Edmunds. London is shabby in contrast with New York, with Boston, with Philadelphia. In detail, one would say it can rarely fail to be a disappointing piece of shabbiness, to a stranger from any of those places. There is nothing shabbier than Drury-lane, in Rome itself. The meanness of Regent-street, set against the great line of Boulevards in Paris, is as striking as the abortive ugliness of Trafalgar-square, set against the gallant beauty of the Place de la Concorde. London is shabby by daylight, and shabbier by gaslight. No Englishman knows what gaslight is,

until he sees the rue de Rivoli and the Palais Royal after dark.
    The mass of London people are shabby. . . . Probably there
are not more second-hand clothes sold in London than in Paris,
and yet the mass of the London population have a second-
hand look which is not to be detected on the mass of the Parisian
population.

Dickens often used Paris, polemically, in essays about English
social arrangements, acknowledging that more despotic
methods had been used in France to secure such handsome
and useful effects than would be tolerated by free Britons
(who never, never, would be slaves), but urging that some
means be quickly found to tidy up and clean up London, and
make living there more healthy and comfortable. "London
is a vile place, I sincerely believe," he wrote in the year of the
Great Exhibition, 1851. "I have never taken kindly to it, since
I lived abroad. Whenever I come back from the country now,
and see that heavy canopy [of smoke] lowering over the house
tops, I wonder what on earth I do there except on obligation."[22]
    A few years after this, he bought that country house: but
he continued to live much of the time in London, in his
bachelor *pied-à-terre* or in a house rented for the season, and
that "attraction of repulsion" kept his imagination faithful to
the city. He may be imagined echoing the other great poet
of the nineteenth-century city, Baudelaire—"Je t'aime, ô cap-
itâle infame!"—or as feeling for London as Catherine Earn-
shaw does about Heathcliff: ". . . a source of little visible
delight, but necessary. Nelly, I *am* Heathcliff! He's always,
always in my mind: not as a pleasure, any more than I am
always a pleasure to myself, but as my own being . . ." (*Wuth-
ering Heights*, ch. 9). He knew this environment, in far greater
depth than any other. "An author's best performance must
be achieved on his own ground," he told an American in-
terviewer in 1867 (so *Martin Chuzzlewit*, using his American
experiences, could not be among his best work): and he is
reported as saying, immodestly, "I suppose, sir, that I know
London better than any other man of all its millions." Forty
years earlier, he had impressed a fellow-clerk with his en-
cyclopedic knowledge—"I thought I knew something of the

town, but after a little talk with Dickens I found that I knew nothing. He knew it all from Bow to Brentford."[23] All his London pictures, he told the American, were "drawn from personal inspection," and some of his forays into the shadier and more dangerous purlieus were undertaken in disguise or with police protection. He was an energetic pedestrian, an urban explorer, highly observant and knowledgeable as well as imaginative and visually idiosyncratic. ("I have said to myself," a friend recalled, "when I have been with him, that he sees and observes nine facts for any two that I see and observe," and David Copperfield speaks for Dickens when he remarks, "I looked at nothing, that I know of, but I saw everything."[24]) Living through a period when London was rapidly changing and expanding, he registers better than any novelist of his time (Trollope is his only rival here) this remaking of the city—the classic passages about the railway's transforming the urban landscape (*Dombey and Son*, chs. 6, 15), or this from the same novel (ch. 33) about a suburban area which now is

> ... neither of the town nor country. The former, like a giant in his travelling boots, has made a stride and passed it, and has set his brick-and-mortar heel a long way in advance; but the intermediate space between the giant's feet, as yet, is only blighted country, and not town.[25]

Or, again in the same chapter, there is an excellent observation of urban immigration, the one-way traffic of travellers "always . . . in one direction—always towards the town. Swallowed up in one phase or other of its immensity, towards which they seemed impelled by a desperate fascination, they never returned . . . "

It was a commonplace of the day that some parts of the great cities were a *terra incognita*, like the blank parts on the map of the Dark Continent, and that novelists—eminently Dickens—were among the "explorers." As a reviewer in the *Quarterly Review*, June 1839, put it:

> Life in London, as revealed in the pages of Boz, opens a new world to thousands bred and born in the same city, . . . for the one half of mankind lives without knowing how the other half dies: in fact, the regions about Saffron Hill [Fagin's criminal

area] are less known to our great world than the Oxford Tracts, the inhabitants are still less . . .[26]

By the late 1830s, people were "doing" Oliver Twist's London, and readers who did not go that far could feel nevertheless that they had seen a new and previously hidden world. In *Oliver Twist* Dickens had, more explicitly than elsewhere, invited such a consciousness, such actual tours of the area indeed. A nice instance occurs when Bill Sikes is on the run after murdering Nancy. Chapter 50, which ends with his accidental but highly appropriate death by hanging, begins with a very long description of the Fagin gang's old hideout, where he takes refuge; at this exciting stage of the story, Dickens holds up the action, largely to make a social point:

> Near to that part of the Thames on which the church at Rotherhithe abuts, where the buildings on the banks are dirtiest and the vessels on the river blackest with the dust of colliers and the smoke of close-built, low-roofed houses, there exists the filthiest, the strangest, the most extraordinary of the many localities that are hidden in London, wholly unknown, even by name, to the great mass of its inhabitants.

"To reach this place," the narrative continues, "a visitor has to penetrate through a maze of close, narrow and muddy streets" (described at some length), and then:

> In such a neighbourhood, beyond Dockhead in the borough of Southwark, stands Jacob's Island, surrounded by a muddy ditch, six or eight feet deep and fifteen or twenty wide when the tide is in, once called Mill Pond, but known in the days of this story as Folly Ditch. It is a creek or inlet from the Thames, and can always be filled at high water by opening the sluices at the lead mills from which it took its old name. At such times, a stranger, looking from one of the wooden bridges thrown across it at Mill Lane, will see the inhabitants of the houses on either side lowering from their back doors and windows, buckets, pails and domestic utensils of all kinds, in which to haul the water up; and when his eye is turned from these operations to the houses themselves, his utmost astonishment will be excited by the scene before him.

Transparently, the reader is this "visitor," this "stranger," astonished by one of these parts of London "wholly unknown, even by name, to the great mass of its inhabitants" but now decisively put on the map: Folly Ditch was henceforth famous. It is worth noting, however, that Dickens, here as elsewhere, is delicately selective in what he tells the reader, often using such phrases as "every imaginable sign of desolation and disorder," "every repulsive lineament of poverty, every loathsome indication of filth, rot, and garbage." The enormities are left to the imagination of the ignorant and innocent. Thus, the teenage Queen Victoria, who read and admired *Oliver Twist* and felt instructed by it, probably did not altogether realize that the water being hauled up, for drinking and domestic use, was contaminated by the urine and faeces deposited into it from these very houses—but, had Dickens made such things plain, she would probably not have read the novel. There were prudent limitations to Dickens's realism.

Most of his fictional London, of course, is more familiar, less exotic than this: the City with its legal and commercial areas and Newgate and Smithfield, the centers of Government in Whitehall and elsewhere, that Covent Garden area to which he so often reverts, the great residential squares where the commercial aristocracy lived and the landed gentry had their town houses, the slum areas, the suburbs inner and outer, ranging from shabby-genteel to affluent, the river and dockside. Even Dickens could not know or depict the whole of London, but he conveys a rich sense of its vastness and multiplicity, and a marvellously detailed sense of the look and feel and smell and atmosphere of many particular aspects of its life—its dwellings, high and low, its places of work, its institutions, its places of entertainment, its streets and shops. How he conveys his sense of all this may, to recapitulate, be suggested by conflating those phrases quoted earlier—the "special correspondent to posterity," "the London Dante," the "fanciful photographer."

NOTES

1. "Travelling Abroad," in *The Uncommercial Traveller;* first published in *All the Year Round,* April 7, 1860.

2. I develop this and other comparisons between Dickens and Tennyson in "Tennyson in and out of time," in *Studies in Tennyson,* ed. Hallam Tennyson (London, 1981), and in *Tennyson, Poet of Lincolnshire* (Lincoln, forthcoming).

3. Charles Dickens, Jr., "Reminiscences of My Father," *Windsor Magazine* (Christmas 1934); rpt. in *Dickens: Interviews and Recollections,* ed. Philip Collins (London, 1981), I, 139.

4. John Forster, *Life of Dickens* (London, 1928), p. 11.

5. I have further discussed this phrase in my essay "Dickens and London," in *The Victorian City: Images and Realities,* ed. H. J. Dyos and Michael Wolff (London, 1973)—an essay obviously germane to my present topic but which I have striven to avoid echoing here.

6. Forster, p. 39. My "or almost became," and Forster's qualifying "in some sort," because the ten- to twelve-year-old Dickens could never have identified with the *lumpen-proletariat.* As his fragmentary autobiography (published in Forster's *Life*), and its fictional reflection in *David Copperfield,* ch. 11, make abundantly plain, he suffered at this time not as one of the "very poor" but as a middle-class boy thrown uncongenially among "common" (working-class) boys and men, who were in tolerably paid employment.

7. "The Short-Timers," in *The Uncommercial Traveller;* first published in *All the Year Round,* June 20, 1863.

8. "Charles Dickens," *National Review,* October 1858; rpt. in *Dickens: The Critical Heritage,* ed. Philip Collins (London, 1971), p. 394.

9. Donald Olsen, "Introduction: Victorian London," Pref., *The Government of Victorian London, 1855-1889,* by David Owen (Cambridge, Mass., 1982), pp. 10-12.

10. *Household Words,* January 1, 1853, VI, 362; rpt. in *Miscellaneous Papers,* ed. B. W. Matz (London, 1908), p. 361.

11. *Eclectic Magazine,* October 1861, N.S. I, 460.

12. Steven Marcus, *Engels, Manchester and the Working Class* (New York, 1974), pp. 142n, 198.

13. Asa Briggs, *Victorian Cities* (London, 1963), pp. 92-93. Lord Briggs remarks upon Dickens as an urban observer, in "Trollope the Trav-

eller," in *Trollope Centenary Essays,* ed. John Halperin (London; 1982), pp. 44-45.

14. Briggs, p. 113.

15. *Mugby Junction,* ch. 2; rpt. in *Christmas Stories.* See my "Dickens and Industrialism," *SEL,* 20 (1980), 657-60.

16. John Ruskin, "The Nature of Gothic," in *The Stones of Venice* (1851-53), II, 6, 16.

17. John Hollingshead, *According to My Lights* (London, 1900), p. 12.

18. *Eclectic Magazine, loc. cit.*

19. Moncure Conway, *Autobiography, Memories and Experiences* (London, 1904), II, 6.

20. Letter to W. H. Wills, September 24, 1858, *Letters of Charles Dickens,* ed. Walter Dexter (Bloomsbury, 1938), III, 58.

21. "Thoughts about People," *Sketches by Boz,* opening words.

22. *Letters,* II, 272.

23. Quoted from *Dickens: Interviews and Recollections,* II, 326; I, 12.

24. Sir Arthur Helps, quoted from *Dickens: The Critical Heritage,* p. 529; *David Copperfield,* ch. 27.

25. The same notion appears in George Cruikshank's famous engraving, *London Going Out of Town—or—The March of Bricks and Mortar* (1830), reproduced in *The Victorian City: Images and Realities,* opposite II, 464.

26. Quoted from *Dickens: Interviews and Recollections,* II, 326-27; I, 12.

The Social Explorer as Anthropologist: Victorian Travellers among the Urban Poor

Deborah Epstein Nord

Western peoples have often looked to images of non-Western cultures to describe themselves or to evoke aspects of their own culture.[1] In this tradition urban explorers of the nineteenth century developed the habit of comparing the English inhabitants of Victorian slums to Aborigines, South Sea Islanders and, most frequently, to African tribes. It seems that those English writers who reported back to the middle class on their travels into the unknown and uncharted areas of Manchester, Birmingham, and London could not resist making use of the almost obligatory analogy between the urban poor and the "uncivilized" peoples of truly foreign lands. Once the reader of that vast nineteenth-century literature of urban exploration notices the use of such analogies, she or he begins to see them everywhere, to realize that they constitute a virtual literary convention of that genre of writing. It also becomes apparent that the analogy takes on different meanings in different parts of the century and, indeed, as various writers exploited it.

I intend here to offer some speculations about why such a literary convention was used and needed by those social observers who wrote about the "denizens" of the slums. Was this anthropological analogy merely a rhetorical flourish to rouse the interest of readers, to get beyond their normally apathetic or antagonistic responses to the subject of urban poverty? Was the use of this literary convention a simple expression of Victorian racialism, of the earnest conviction that just as black Africans were a race apart from middle-class Englishmen, so too were slum-dwellers, street-laborers, and the unemployed? Or did this way of referring to the underclass help reformers, journalists, and social investigators to communicate something of significance to their readers that they otherwise might have found difficult to convey? I will begin to try to answer these questions by looking at the literature of urban exploration produced at the end of the century and work my way back to mid-century, ending with Henry Mayhew, in many ways the most important urban explorer of his time.

The England/Africa analogy appeared most prevalently in writings of the 1880s and 1890s, those late-Victorian decades in which poverty was "rediscovered" as a national issue and in which numerous middle-class explorers traveled into the *terra incognita* of urban slums, particularly those of the East End of London. A serious economic depression had hit England—and the rest of Western Europe—at the end of the 1870s; and throughout the 1880s unemployment, labor unrest, sporadic working-class violence, and the birth of the "new unionism" (the organization of unskilled workers) fed middle-class fears of social upheaval and prompted what was called the "socialist revival." Socialist groups like the Social Democratic Federation and the Fabians sought to analyze the causes of poverty; reform-minded professionals like Charles Booth mounted inquiries into the actual extent of poverty in English society; and journalists like W. T. Stead of the *Pall Mall Gazette* published exposés of slum housing, sweat shops, and the white slave trade.

Just as Manchester had been the focus for national interest in the ugly urban results of industrialization in the 1840s and 1850s, so the East End became the chief symbolic example of urban decay in the 1880s and 1890s. In 1845 Disraeli warned that England had become divided into two nations, "rich and poor," and in 1891 Margaret Harkness, chronicler of working-class life in London slums, echoed and amended Disraeli by identifying "two nations, *East* and *West*."[2] What had long been an actual physical contrast between the prosperous West End and the more solidly working-class East End was, in these last decades of the century, turned into what Raymond Williams calls an "interpretive image": the West represented all that was bright, open, dazzling, and enlightened; the East all that was dark, labyrinthine, threatening, and benighted.[3]

The dichotomy of West and East doubled, of course, for England and its Empire.[4] The era of the "rediscovery" of poverty was also the heyday of British Imperialism. The Great Depression at home and competition from Germany and the United States abroad gave Britain the impetus to expand trade and investment in its colonies; and the search for new markets in Africa and Asia brought in its wake missionaries, explorers, anthropologists, and travelers. They penetrated the "dark" continents in an effort to learn, conquer, and convert; and they captured the imaginations of an audience at home, eager for tales of exotic and torturous journeys, wild tribes, and miraculous conversions.

The literature of *urban* exploration depended in fact on this heightened interest in the Empire for much of its language, its form, its legitimacy, and its moral authority. In *How the Poor Live* George Sims, one of the better known popular social investigators of the 1880s, began a section on slum dwellings in this way:

> In these pages I propose to record the result of a journey into a region which lies at our own doors—into a dark continent that is within easy walking distance of the General Post Office. This continent will, I hope, be found as interesting as any of those newly-explored lands which engage the attention of the Royal Geographical Society—the wild races who inhabit it will, I trust, gain public sympathy as easily as those savage tribes for whose benefit Missionary Societies never cease to appeal for funds.[5]

If you can summon interest in and sympathy for "wild races" far away, Sims seems to be saying, then you can at least read what I have to say about those neglected people in your very midst. Sims is clearly using a rhetorical device to capture the attention of his readers, to enhance the exotic and even sensational quality of his squalid researches, but he is also admonishing the English public for its wilful ignorance of Whitechapel and Bethnal Green and for its facile enthusiasm for alien cultures.

A decade or so later Jack London expressed a similar sentiment with a somewhat sharper ironic edge in his *People of the Abyss*. "O Cook, O Thomas Cook & Son," he apostrophized,

Deborah Epstein Nord

path-finders and trail-clearers, living sign-posts to all the world, and bestowers of first aid to bewildered travellers—unhesitatingly and instantly, with ease and celerity, could you send me to Darkest Africa or Innermost Tibet, but to the East End of London, barely a stone's throw distant from Ludgate Circus, you know not the way![6]

While England gloried in its expanding Empire and spread "civilization" throughout the world, it forgot or never knew the hungry, unemployed, and poorly-housed denizens of its own cities. Jack London reminded his readers what and where the East End was: if the Empire never saw the setting of the sun, he quipped, the East End was that place over which the sun seldom rose.

The domestic social reformer who made his dependence on the African example most explicit was General William Booth, founder of the Salvation Army. In the summer of 1890 an explorer named Stanley—of Stanley and Livingstone fame—had published *In Darkest Africa,* an account of his journey across the "Lost Continent." Later that same year General Booth came out with a book outlining his plan for the alleviation of poverty in Great Britain: he called it *In Darkest England and the Way Out.* Booth begins this work with an account of Stanley's heroic entry into the "almost impenetrable" tropical forests of the Congo and his discovery of its predatory and godless population, and then interrupts his narrative to ask the inevitable question: "As there is a darkest Africa is there not also a darkest England? . . . May we not find a parallel at our own doors, and discover within a stone's throw of our cathedrals and palaces similar horrors to those which Stanley has found existing in the great Equatorial forest?"[7]

He introduces the already familiar analogy much as George Sims and Jack London did, but he takes it a step further by equating the Arab ivory raiders who exploit African forest dwellers with those Englishmen (he singles out pub-owners) who prey on the vulnerabilities of slum dwellers and unwittingly reduce them to criminals, drunkards, and layabouts. Booth suggests that the Englishman's guilt goes beyond mere *ignorance* of his poorer neighbors: he causes eternal misery, "brooding sullenness" and "dull despair"; he is a slave-driver and an agent of godlessness.

It is clear from these examples of the 1880s and 1890s that the language of domestic social investigation cannot be fully understood without an appreciation of England's place in the constellation of world politics, that England's national concerns—and the way they were discussed—were inseparable from its international ones. London had become the center of an empire, the docks of East London the conduit through which the Empire entered Britain; and the capital took on an aura of new and literal—not just metaphorical—internationalism in these decades. Waves of immigrants gravitated to London's central districts while native Londoners tended to spread out into the new suburbs and outlying areas. The "distant tribes" had more than an analogous relationship to Londoners: they had become Londoners, as London came to reproduce in miniature the world of the Empire. When Margaret Harkness wrote a novel about the Salvation Army, she quite appropriately followed the lead of General Booth by calling her book *In Darkest London,* further narrowing the focus of Booth's own title from benighted nation to benighted city. She opened the novel with a description of Whitechapel Road on a Saturday night:

> There one sees all nationalities. A grinning Hottentot elbows his way through a crowd of long-legged Jewesses. An Algerian merchant walks arm-in-arm with a native of Calcutta. A little Italian plays pitch-and-toss with a small Russian. A Polish Jew enjoys sauer-kraut with a German Gentile. And among the foreigners lounges the East End loafer, monarch of all he surveys, lord of the premises.[8]

The East End thoroughfare has become a Babel, a world in microcosm. The Jew, the Eastern European, or the Mediterranean is as alien to the Englishman as the Hottentot or the Pygmy; and each nationality is perceived as a cluster of stereotypical traits, each individual foreigner a caricature. The Empire brought with it into England the ironic coupling of great riches and great poverty; in this way it reproduced the dichotomy of West End luxury and East End squalor.

The literary convention of comparing the urban poor of England with Africans or other non-Western peoples was not,

Deborah Epstein Nord

however, a new one in the 1880s. To be sure, it was widely exploited in the last decades of the century because of the particular political and social circumstances of the period, but it was by then an already available and well-established convention. We have to look to earlier examples of this practice, therefore, for a fuller understanding of its various meanings. We remember, of course, the "Telescopic Philanthropy" chapter in Dickens' *Bleak House:* Mrs. Jellyby devotes herself to the natives of Borioboola-Gha on the left bank of the Niger, as well as to the cultivation of the coffee berry and the settlement of 200 "superfluous" British families there, while her own children fall down stairs, get their heads stuck between iron railings, and generally suffer neglect and misery at their mother's hands. Mrs. Jellyby, now often seen as Dickens' belittling parody of the socially engaged female, functions primarily as Dickens' indictment of the insensitive, myopic philanthropist. Her children represent not only the proper sphere of womanhood but the proper sphere of the reforming middle class: the poor of England.[9] Some eight years before Dickens began *Bleak House,* Friedrich Engels cited the remarks of an East End clergyman in his *Condition of the Working Class:* " 'I believe,' " recorded the Reverend G. Alston in the *Weekly Dispatch,* " 'that till the Bishop of London called the attention of the public to the state of Bethnal-green, about as little was known at the West-end of this most destitute parish as the wilds of Australia or the islands of the South Seas.' "[10] As early as 1844, then, the division of East and West and the veil of ignorance that presumably separated one part of London from the other were acknowledged by writers on urban poverty as social realities.

Both Dickens and Engels anticipated the later writers I have mentioned by admonishing their readers for ignoring what existed under their noses, for shutting out the misery around the corner while sentimentalizing the plight of those oceans away. But the real master of the particular analogy I have been discussing in the mid-Victorian decades was Henry Mayhew, the author of *London Labour and the London Poor.* It is his work that contains the most sustained and, I believe, the most purposeful use of the analogy. He not only employed the rhetorical strategies I have already discussed, but he chose to adopt the persona of the anthropologist.

Mayhew, a satirist, journalist, amateur actor, and member of the literary bohemia of the 1830s and 1840s (of which Dickens and George Cruikshank were also a part), was asked to undertake a series of articles on the conditions of the London working poor for the *Morning Chronicle* in 1849. The *Chronicle* appointed a number of journalists to cover various industrial cities throughout England, and Mayhew was made "Special Correspondent from the Metropolis."[11] The paper, which had liberal, reformist leanings, responded to the growing middle-class interest in problems of poverty and urban life in general. The cholera epidemic of 1849, which claimed the lives of the urban poor in far greater numbers than the rest of the population, served to focus even greater attention on the social issues already brought to public consciousness by the Depression of the early 1840s, by the Chartist Movement, and by the publication in 1842 of Edwin Chadwick's Poor Law Commission report on the sanitary conditions affecting the urban poor. The middle class reacted to these phenomenon of the decade with fear of social unrest, with some measure of repugnance, and with an often hesitant desire for reform.

Mayhew continued to publish his "letters" from the Metropolis in the *Chronicle* for just over a year until, in December of 1850, he broke with the paper and began to issue articles from an office of his own in twopenny weekly parts. In 1851-52 the pieces were bound together for publication as *London Labour and the London Poor,* and a four-volume edition was re-issued in 1861-62. In the Preface to the bound volumes Mayhew identified himself as a "traveller in the undiscovered country of the poor," who will supply information "concerning a large body of persons of whom the public had less knowledge than of the most distant tribes of the earth."[12] These remarks, as should by now be obvious, are not unusual and do not distinguish Mayhew from the other "travellers" who wished to capture the imaginations and sympathies of their readers. But, as we shall see, Mayhew was after more than sympathy: he wanted to alter the conventional judg-

Deborah Epstein Nord

ments of his audience by forcing it to see the working poor through the lens of moral science.

On the first page of this first volume, devoted to detailed accounts of London "street-folk"—sellers, buyers, finders, performers, artizans, pedlars, and laborers—Mayhew places himself among the "ethnologists."[13] He introduces the work of Dr. James Prichard on "wandering tribes," those groups of people who are neither pure nomads nor settlers but a "race" in between that attaches itself to various "civilized" tribes all over the globe. Such wanderers, according to Dr. Prichard in his *Natural History of Man*, have languages, physical characteristics, customs, and moral systems *distinct* from those of the settled tribes with whom they intermingle.

James Cowles Prichard, the ethnologist Mayhew mentions, was a leading member of the London Ethnological Society, founded in 1843, and the most influential British theorist of "monogenesis." Prichard and fellow-members of the Society believed, that is, in the " 'cherished unity of mankind' ": all of humanity was the product of a *single seed*, although various groups—or tribes—were to be found at different stages of development in the same evolutionary process.[14] There is essentially one race, and all variations among humankind can be attributed to *differences in external conditions* and to the different influences that derive from these conditions:

> That so great differences in external conditions, by the double influence of their physical and moral agency, should have effected during a long series of ages remarkable changes in the tribes of human beings subject to their operation,—changes which have rendered these several tribes fitted in a peculiar manner for their respective abodes,—is by no means an improbable conjecture. . . .[15]

Wandering tribes, then, would share the same characteristics—physical as well as "moral"—because they exist as nomads, under the same general conditions. Mankind is one but different, all of it moving toward a single point but at a varying pace.[16]

"It is curious," Mayhew concludes after establishing Prichard's theories, "that no one has yet applied the above facts to *the explanation of certain anomalies in the present state of society among ourselves.* That we, like the Kaffirs, Fellahs and Finns, are surrounded by wandering hordes—the 'sonquas' and the 'fingoes' of this country—paupers, beggars and out-casts. . . ."[17] Mayhew will, of course, go on to be the one to do just that, to treat the street-folk of London as an ethnologist observing foreign tribes. Using categories determined by the perception of street-folk as a separate culture, he catalogues their histories, dress, food, religion, language, politics, earnings, amusements, and education. The culture of the streets is not, however, monolithic in Mayhew's view: costermongers, prostitutes, pickpockets, watermen, and street-ballad sellers all have different ways of thinking and behaving, as well as working. In a section devoted to the "backwards slang" of costermongers Mayhew maintains the ethnologist's pose when he remarks that "in my present chapter the language has, I believe, been reduced to *orthography* for the first time."[18] The costers' slang, Mayhew explains, is the result of their desire to "shield their bargainings at market, or their conversation . . . from the knowledge of any Irish or uninitiated fellow-traders."[19] What appears a humorous or frivolous habit of speech to the "traveller" among the poor actually has its origins in the structure and customs of labor.

Mayhew takes an anthropologist's interest in the rules and mores that govern conjugal behavior among the street-folk. Costermen resemble North American Indians, he asserts, in their conduct toward their wives: they regard their women as "inexperienced servants" and punish female "disobedience" with physical abuse.[20] Among certain street-sellers matrimony is regarded as a waste of time and money: only one-tenth of all coster couples are legally married, and fidelity is as common among the unwed as among the wed.[21] But Mayhew wishes to emphasize that financial prohibitions make wedlock an undesirable choice. In Clerkenwell, he adds by way of evidence, as many as one-fifth of all coster couples do marry, quite simply because the incumbent of the parish marries them free of charge at Advent and Easter. If notions of morality among these people "agree strongly . . . with those of many savage tribes," if these "Nomades of England neither

Deborah Epstein Nord

know nor care for the enjoyments of home," Mayhew argues, it is because "*we* are the culpable parties."[22] If the "wandering tribes" of the London streets are improvident, ignorant in matters of religion, and careless of the rules of private property, it is because of the circumstances in which they live and because of our neglect of those circumstances. We deny them both a moral education and the means to make our own morality an expedient alternative to theirs.

What, finally, is the meaning of Mayhew's "ethnological" stance, and what does it add to our understanding of the oft-repeated analogy between the urban poor and the "uncivilized" tribes of foreign lands? Other critics of Mayhew's work have tended to dismiss or regret what Anne Humpherys has called his "weak anthropological analogy."[23] Humpherys herself treats the "wandering tribes" passages of *London Labour and the London Poor* as a lapse in Mayhew's writing and interprets quite literally his statements that the street-folk of London constituted a separate—and inferior—race of people. Further, she sees this lapse as evidence of the belief in "innate qualities" to which Mayhew was drawn periodically during the course of his study.[24]

Gertrude Himmelfarb contends that Mayhew succeeded only in "making 'foreigners,' aliens, out of the 'labouring population.' "[25] Mayhew represented the poor "less as a class in the Marxist sense," she remarks, "than a species in the Darwinian sense."[26] According to Himmelfarb, it is Mayhew and other reformers of his ilk that were responsible for creating the destructive notion of a "culture" of poverty. Both of these critics read Mayhew too literally, and yet neither takes what is quite obviously a conscious literary pose seriously enough.

There is no question that at the beginning of his first volume Mayhew sought to dramatize, even to sensationalize, his subject or that his rhetoric contained elements of crude, racialist thinking; but, more importantly, he sought a new vocabulary and a new perspective for the unimpassioned discussion of urban poverty. In his opening pages Mayhew was groping toward a new way of seeing and of writing about human behavior and of accounting for the disquieting variations in that behavior. He did not abandon this perspective after the first few dramatic pages, but continued to employ it throughout his analysis of the culture of the street-folk.

The language of early, even primitive, anthropology provided writers like Mayhew with the metaphor they needed to describe a new class, the inhabitants of a new kind of neighborhood in a new kind of city. Where would the language come from to discuss with some degree of seriousness the *lumpenproletariat* that dwelled in the slums of the industrial cities of the nineteenth century? If a writer wished to evoke the social scene neither as a pure entertainer nor as a rigidly censorious moralizer, if he or she wished to make an attempt at "scientific" objectivity, what tone and what attitude were available and acceptable?

In the 1830s and 1840s the British nation first attempted to come to terms with the facts of urban-industrial life, and a number of different methods of writing about the urban poor were or became available during these decades. Men like Peter Gaskell and Edwin Chadwick used statistical studies to examine infant mortality, birth rates, sanitation, and the spread of disease in slums; early socialists and revolutionaries developed a critique of industrial capitalism; hidebound moralists preached that slum-dwellers were an inherently inferior lot and deserved their squalid fates; popular writers described the high jinks of upper-class "slummers" in low-life settings; and novelists like Dickens, Disraeli, and Elizabeth Gaskell used fiction to evoke sympathy for the poor and bring about reconciliation between classes.

Social investigators like Mayhew represented yet another tradition; Mayhew was a *reformer* who wished to report in nonfictional form on the human conditions that statisticians represented numerically. He wished to impress upon his audience that the circumstances of slum life produced certain kinds of individuals and, by implication, to suggest that conditions would have to be transformed before individuals could be redeemed or "civilized." He had to convince his public that the people of whom he wrote were *of* English society though separate from it, *related* to the middle class but a "race" apart from it, fellow inhabitants of the same city but members

Deborah Epstein Nord

of a different "tribe." Ethnologists seemed to have solved the problem of considering "uncivilized" races abroad: they could embrace non-Western peoples on the grounds of the essential unity of mankind and yet they could explain apparently disturbing differences in customs and beliefs by theories of social evolution and of adaptive behavior. If this feat could be accomplished in regard to South Sea Islanders and African tribes, then surely there was a way to approach the urban slum-dweller as an object of study and not merely as an object of disapprobation, revulsion, or amusement.

NOTES

1. This paper was first presented as part of a multi-disciplinary panel on Western views of non-Western cultures at the Society of Fellows in the Humanities, Columbia University, April 1981.

2. Margaret Harkness ("John Law"), *In Darkest London: A Story of the Salvation Army* (London, 1891), pp. 67-68.

3. Raymond Williams, *The Country and the City* (London, 1973), p. 220.

4. See Peter Keating's introductory essay in *Into Unknown England: Selections from the Social Explorers* (Manchester, 1976). I am indebted to Keating's collection of the writings of social explorers and to his *The Working Classes in Victorian Fiction* (New York, 1971).

5. George Sims, *How the Poor Live* (1883), excerpted in Keating's *Into Unknown England*, pp. 5-6.

6. Jack London, *The People of the Abyss* (1903), excerpted in Keating, p. 224.

7. William Booth, *In Darkest England and the Way Out* (1890), excerpted in Keating, p. 145.

8. Harkness, p. 3.

9. See Charles Dickens' *Bleak House* (1852-3), Ch. IV.

10. Friedrich Engels, *The Condition of the Working Class in England*, trans. W.O. Henderson and W.H. Chaloner (Stanford, 1958), pp. 35-36.

11. See E.P. Thompson's introductory essay, "Mayhew and the *Morning Chronicle*," in *The Unknown Mayhew*, ed. E.P. Thompson and Eileen Yeo (Harmondsworth, Middlesex, 1971).

12. Henry Mayhew, *London Labour and the London Poor* (London, 1851), I, iii.

13. Mayhew, I, 1.

14. See J.W. Burrow, *Evolution and Society* (Cambridge, England, 1970), pp. 98-99, 120-24.

15. James Cowles Prichard, *The Natural History of Man* (London, 1843), p. 4.

16. Burrow argues that this and other Victorian evolutionary theories *avoided* "the unpleasantly relativist implications of a world in which many of the old certainties were disappearing" (p. 99). Mankind was *not* "everywhere the same," at least not at any given moment.

17. Mayhew, I, 2.

18. Mayhew, I, 23.

19. Mayhew, I, 24.

20. Mayhew, I, 43.

21. Mayhew, I, 20.

22. Mayhew, I, 43.

23. Anne Humpherys, *Travels into the Poor Man's Country: The Work of Henry Mayhew* (Athens, Georgia, 1977), p. 71.

24. Humpherys, pp. 71-72.

25. Gertrude Himmelfarb, "The Culture of Poverty," in *The Victorian City*, ed. H.J. Dyos and Michael Wolff (Boston, 1973), II, 719. Anne Humpherys concedes that Mayhew's assertions about the "wandering tribes" do indeed "support Gertrude Himmelfarb's charge that Mayhew contributed to the idea that the poor were a class apart." She defends Mayhew, however, by saying that the general introductory section on street-life was "less important than the rest of his work; it occupied only two pages out of all his volumes . . ." (Humpherys, p. 72). Rather than offering another interpretation of the passages in question, Humpherys simply minimizes their importance.

26. Himmelfarb, p. 711.

Manet and the Paris of Haussmann and Baudelaire

Theodore Reff

Manet's paintings, drawings, and prints of Parisian subjects, shown in a recent exhibition alongside those of his contemporaries,* have become so familiar through frequent reproduction that we tend to forget what a remarkable innovation they were in their time. Inseparable from two of the most popular aspects of our culture, impressionist art and modern Paris, they seem as "familiar, foreign, and near" as the Tuileries Gardens, the Folies-Bergère, and the Pantheon, each of which Manet painted. But like all authentic works of art, they are the product of a unique personality working in a unique milieu; they cannot be understood fully without first understanding certain aspects of Manet himself and the Paris of his time. For he was in background, manners, and taste the most thoroughly Parisian of the impressionist artists, at home only there, and even there only in an elite society centered on the fashionable cafés of the boulevards and the artists' cafés of Montmartre.

At the same time, he was influenced by two developments that began in the 1850s and continued in the following decade, when he produced his first images of Paris. One was the transformation of the city both physically and socially into the first truly modern metropolis, with a monumental grandeur and scale and a richness of cultural life that made it a model for capital cities throughout the world. The other was the devel-

---

*Manet and Modern Paris, National Gallery of Art, Washington, December 5, 1982–March 6, 1983. The catalogue essay is reprinted here with minor changes; © copyright National Gallery of Art, reprinted with permission. References within the text to Manet's paintings are to vol. I of Rouart and Wildenstein (see note 14).

opment of modernism itself as the highest value of avant-garde and eventually of popular culture and of the urban milieu as the source of that modernism for over a century. The one achievement was largely due to Baron Haussmann, Napoleon III's master planner in the rebuilding and expansion of Paris in the Second Empire; the other to Baudelaire, Manet's guide in the discovery of modern urban life as a source of subject matter and stylistic innovation. To understand what made Manet's images of Paris specifically modern, rather than merely contemporary like those of his predecessors, we must understand how they were shaped by his own vision and values, as well as by the modernization effected by Haussmann and the modernism advocated by Baudelaire.

*

All those who knew him agreed that Manet was more than a resident of Paris; he "personified the sentiments and customs of Parisians, raised to their highest power."[1] Unlike many of his fellow citizens, moreover, he was "comfortable only in Paris," and despite his fascination with Spain and Spanish art, he found the cuisine of Madrid so inferior to that at home that he cut short his trip in 1865 and hurried back.[2] He did stay longer at Boulogne, where the food was presumably better, on a summer vacation in 1868, but toward the end he admitted, "I think only of returning to Paris, for I do nothing here."[3]

Born and bred a Parisian, he came from a prominent, well-to-do family in which the traditions and social graces of the old bourgeoisie of the July Monarchy were still valued. On his father's side, his ancestors had been wealthy landowners and local officials at Gennevilliers and respected magistrates in Paris for several generations; on his mother's, they had been equally distinguished diplomats and army officers. From them Manet acquired a taste for fashionable society and, equally important, the means to satisfy it. "He confessed to me," wrote Zola in 1867 in his first essay on the artist, "that he adored society and discovered secret pleasures in the perfumed and brilliant delights of evening parties."[4] Fantin-Latour's well-known portrait, painted in the same year, shows

Manet wearing elegantly cut clothing and a tall silk hat, with a gold chain in his vest and a walking stick in his gloved hands, a costume we are told he always wore, in the country as well as the city. Even at the end of his life, when he was very ill, he "dressed like a clubman" and, preserving "a smiling demeanor, welcomed many friends in his studio . . . now that he was unable to walk along the boulevards."[5]

The boulevards, from the Porte Saint-Denis to the Madeleine, and especially the few hundred yards between the rue de Richelieu and the Chaussée d'Antin comprising the boulevard des Italiens, had been the center of Manet's social life since the late 1850s, as indeed they had been for several generations of worldly and talented Parisians for twenty years before that. Here were concentrated the most fashionable theaters, restaurants, and cafés—above all the Café Tortoni on the corner of the rue Taitbout, the very heart of boulevard society and of Manet's as well. "The Café Tortoni was the restaurant where he had lunch before going to the Tuileries Gardens," his friend Antonin Proust recalled, "and when he returned to the same café from five to six o'clock, people vied with each other in complimenting him on his studies."[6] Here, on the boulevard, were edited and published the ephemeral newspapers, with names like *Le Nain jaune, La Vie parisienne,* and *Le Boulevard* itself, devoted to chronicling the activities and gossip of that elite society, and in a witty, sophisticated style that summed up its urbane spirit perfectly. Among the topics treated in their columns and abundant illustrations were the theater, the racetrack, the beaches and spas, the public concerts and festivals, and the lives of the fashionable courtesans—all subjects Manet too treated in the 1860s. Among the contributors were Banville, Champfleury, Baudelaire, and Gautier, all friends of his; indeed Baudelaire's only essay on him appeared in *Le Boulevard,* edited by the socially prominent photographer and satirist Carjat, and Manet in turn contributed a satirical print to one of Carjat's previous publications, *Le Diogène.*[7]

It was also on the boulevard des Italiens, in the enterprising Galerie Martinet, a forerunner of those which later supported impressionism, that Manet had his first one-man exhibition in March 1863. Among the pictures he showed was the one in which, for the first time, he portrayed himself amid this boulevard society and made its elegant, allusive style his own— the *Concert in the Tuileries* (fig. 1). Some of those who have been identified in it were indeed among the leaders of that society: Gautier, the bohemian turned court writer and entertainer; Offenbach, the composer of lighthearted operettas; Aurélien Scholl, the journalist admired for his wit; Baudelaire, the poet and self-styled dandy; and Manet himself, the unofficial painter of this elite circle.[8] Unofficial but not unacknowledged, for in depicting himself and a fellow artist at the left edge of his composition, he imitated the poses and positions of figures then thought to represent Velázquez and Murillo, in a picture in the Louvre then attributed to Velázquez, thus implying that he was to this new aristocracy what his idol had been to the old aristocracy of Madrid.[9] For the fulfillment of this fantasy, at once serious and playful, the public gardens adjacent to the Palais des Tuileries provided a suitably courtlike setting, just as the band concerts given there biweekly provided a suitably fashionable and animated atmosphere.

Contemporary observers were by no means agreed, however, on the value of such an atmosphere or setting. If in the politically neutral *La Vie parisienne* a society draftsman like Crafty could describe a concert in the Tuileries with coy amusement,[10] in the republican paper *L'Evénement* an opposition writer like Jules Vallès could only find it ridiculous: "It is the worn-out and the idle who sit there under the tall chestnut trees, proper gentlemen and charming ladies," he remarked, bitterly regretting that in creating a new street Haussmann had not "mutilated" the Tuileries Gardens, rather than the Luxembourg Gardens dear to the Latin Quarter.[11] It was indeed in defiance of publications like Carjat's *Le Boulevard* that Vallès chose as the running title of his columns "La Rue," a term with a lower-class connotation: "I am of the people and my column too," he announced.[12] Manet, for all his well-known republican views, was of course a friend of Carjat and not of Vallès, an habitué of the boulevard and not of the street. Yet he was more complex than such a simple opposition implies: for if, as a later admirer of Vallès noted,

Theodore Reff

Fig. 1. Edouard Manet, *Concert in the Tuileries,* oil on canvas, 1862. The National Gallery, London.

the street suggests "the pavement or, better yet, the barricade,"[13] Manet too could represent the barricade with power and compassion, as he did three times during the Commune.[14] He could also represent the street itself and the streetwise inhabitants of its slums, as he did in the *Old Musician* (RW 52), painted in the same year as the *Concert in the Tuileries* and shown with it in the same exhibition at the Galerie Martinet— an extraordinary confrontation between *le boulevard* and *la rue,* to which we shall return.

Nor was it the only such confrontation his work of the early 1860s provided: in contrast to *Fishing* (RW 36), based on a print after Rubens' *Landscape with the Castle Steen* and depicting himself and his future wife, stands the *Gypsies* (RW 42-44), based on a print after Louis Le Nain's *Harvesters* and perhaps on his *Forge* in the Louvre, models of lower-class rural life appropriate for this image of dispossessed, wandering gypsies. In contrast to the *Women at the Races* (RW 95), a group of elegant spectators at the Longchamp racetrack, stands the *Street Singer* (RW 50), an itinerant performer emerging from a low tavern. These too were aspects of contemporary Parisian society to which Manet, an artist keenly aware of his society, could not help responding.

In the kind of company he himself chose, however, he remained to the end the *boulevardier* he had been from the beginning, "one of those for whom the frequentation of the boulevard was a habit all his life" and even, as its character became increasingly cosmopolitan and commercial, "one of the last representatives of that form of existence."[15] In the 1870s, after having established the Café Guerbois and then the Café de la Nouvelle-Athènes in Montmartre as the meeting place of his circle of artists and writers, he continued to return to the Café Tortoni and the Café de Bade—the only one in that circle who did so, indeed the only one, except perhaps for Degas, who *could* do so. Manet's work was received at Tortoni's, once his closest friends were gone, with indifference and even with hostility, yet "he came back every day simply as a Parisian, driven by the need to tread the select ground of the true Parisian."[16] When his failing health prevented him from going there, he recreated the boulevard milieu in his studio, filling it every afternoon with friends and acquaintances, even setting out beer and apéritifs for them; it became, as his wife remarked, "an annex of the Café de Bade."[17] He also invited society ladies and well-known cocottes to sit for their portraits, executed in the lighter medium of pastel; among them were Méry Laurent and Valtesse de la Bigne, demimondaines who brought with them "a circle of fashionable artists, financiers, and wealthy foreigners."[18]

Valtesse was one of the many links between Manet's present society and that of the Second Empire: she had begun her career singing in Offenbach's operettas and had been a model for Zola's and perhaps Manet's treatment of Nana, the very type of the wealthy courtesan of the Empire.[19] Henriette Hauser, the actress who actually posed for Manet's painting, was another link; she too had performed in boulevard comedies and achieved her greatest notoriety toward the end of the Empire. And Léontine Massin, who starred in the stage version of *Nana* in 1881, was another of those whom Manet portrayed at this time (RW 2:54).

Several of his recent pastel portraits, including that of Valtessse de la Bigne, figured in the exhibition Manet held in April 1880 in the galleries of *La Vie moderne*, an illustrated weekly founded the year before, which now played much the same role in his life as *Le Boulevard* had in the previous decade. Its offices and galleries were in fact on the boulevard, and its pages were filled with articles of topical interest for polite society, avoiding politics and stressing social and cultural activities of the kind that the previous publication had featured; although it appealed to a broader middle-class audience, its articles were written in a similarly sophisticated and witty style. The editor of *La Vie moderne*, Emile Bergerat, was a friend of Manet's and persuaded him to contribute several drawings—Renoir and Forain were more regular contributors—and to participate in a few benefit shows. About his own exhibition the journal carried a long and predictably favorable review, assuring its readers that Manet was a man of "perfect education, excellent manners, cultivated spirit, and amiable character, a Parisian by race."[20] He was, in short, both the painter of modern Paris and the embodiment of its spirit, at least that side of its spirit valued by *La Vie moderne* and *Le Boulevard*.

What they valued was precisely what characterizes Manet's own style: allusive, elegant, subtle, effortless, it is the style of the boulevard society to which he remained loyal throughout his life. In his youth it had still been the self-contained society of whose domain Musset noted with satisfaction, "It is only a few steps from one end to the other; nevertheless they contain the whole world."[21] In such a closed milieu, subtle allusions could be made with the assurance that they would be appreciated: allusions to well-known figures in one's circle, like those in the *Concert in the Tuileries,* or even to oneself in an historical guise, like that in *Fishing;* but also quotations from famous works of art, like that of Titian's *Venus of Urbino* in *Olympia* (RW 69), though it was scarcely noted by contemporary reviewers. If the design of *Olympia* is patterned on Titian's *Venus,* its style is altogether modern, closer to that of the boulevard writers in its elegance and concision. As Zola astutely observed, "that elegant austerity" marks "the personal savor" of works like *Olympia,* while "certain exquisite lines, certain slender and lovely attitudes," reveal Manet's "fondness for high society."[22]

Much the same concision, a form of visual wit, characterizes the svelte drawing and simplified modeling in the *Balcony* (RW 134) and the *Gare Saint-Lazare* (RW 207). In their color harmonies, dominated by relatively neutral tones with accents of brighter hue, these pictures reveal a refined feeling for nuance, for subtlety and understatement, that was also a familiar feature of the boulevard style. Even in an intrinsically colorful subject like the *Ball of the Opera* (RW 216), Mallarmé could "only marvel at the exquisite nuances in the blacks: in the dress coats and dominoes, in the hats and masks . . ."[23] The same could be said of the subtly varied shades of black, olive green, and white in the *Dead Toreador* (RW 72). For all their apparent simplicity and ease, both pictures were, as we know, the result of a long struggle; and in this effort to make them seem effortless, Manet reveals still another feature of his boulevard style. It was the natural expression of a society that disdained hard work as bourgeois or plebeian and admired the virtuoso performance. All those who watched him paint have remarked that "he labored greatly on the pictures he sent to the Salon, yet they looked like sketches," and that he reworked a portrait "again and again, [yet] every time it came out brighter and fresher."[24]

To match the style of a social group with that of a single artist is always somewhat arbitrary; and in this case to isolate four qualities, while ignoring others which may characterize the group better than the artist—the amusing banter, witty repartée, and ephemeral journalism said to express the spirit of the boulevard[25]—or the artist better than the group—the "harmony, clarity, economy, and concentration on essentials" said to distinguish Manet's finest pictures[26]—may seem particularly arbitrary. But in its allusiveness, elegance, subtlety, and virtuosity, Manet's style does reflect that of the milieu whose values had formed his own and continued to inform them throughout his life. Zola, the first to hint at such a connection, noted that Manet's art is "intelligent, witty, spirited" and "could only have developed in Paris; it has the slender grace of our women, made pale by gaslight; it is truly the child of an artist who loved high society and exhausted himself determining to conquer it."[27] In the twenty years it took him to do so, however, that society changed and the city itself changed dramatically, thanks largely to the ambitious program of renovation and expansion undertaken in the Second Empire and completed early in the Third Republic.

*

Napoleon III's grandiose plans for the modernization of Paris, formulated before he became emperor in 1851 and amplified by Haussmann, his Prefect of the Seine, were a response to many urgent problems. The most obvious was demographic: in the two decades preceding 1851, the city's population had doubled, rising from 576,000 to 1,053,000; in the three decades following, the population doubled again, reaching 2,270,000; thus within Manet's lifetime it increased fourfold. The new railroads that led directly to the capital, the annexation by the city of its suburbs in 1860, and the influx of workers from rural areas, partly drawn by Haussmann's construction projects, all contributed to the demographic explosion. In addition to overcrowding, there were other serious problems: the housing in many of the oldest and poorest quarters was dangerously decrepit; the narrow streets made circulation difficult within neighborhoods and impossible between them; the outmoded sewage system was a threat to public health and was polluting the Seine; and both the central markets and the public parks were inadequate for the increased population.

To these problems the emperor and his prefect, for all the ruthlessness of their methods and the political bias of their motives, which favored above all "the new class of daring financiers, large scale building contractors, big department store owners, hotel operators, and the rest of the *nouveau riche* commercial breed,"[28] brought energetic and farsighted solutions. They demolished many slums in the central and eastern parts of the city and promoted construction of new housing there and in the recently developed areas to the north and west; they cut through wide boulevards to provide access to railroad stations and commercial centers and to link the separate neighborhoods; they so greatly improved the sewage and drainage systems that Napoleon could be complimented on having "found Paris stinking and [having] left it sweet";[29] and they built modern markets at Les Halles and large parks at Boulogne, Vincennes, and elsewhere in the city.

The results were impressive, but so were the costs, not only the 2.5 billion francs that Haussmann estimated having spent, much of it borrowed through the irregular schemes that eventually brought him down, but also the less easily quantified costs that critics such as Victor Fournel added up: the destruction of old buildings and streets of great historic value and charm; the ruthless insistence on broad, straight boulevards of monotonously uniform design; and the imposition everywhere, on private as well as public buildings, of a pompous, banal, official style.[30] And those other costs, more social than aesthetic, that Zola listed in a scathing attack on the brutal demolition of entire neighborhoods, the cynical indifference to those who were evicted—those urban vagabonds for whom Haussmann expressed hatred even as he increased their numbers—and the masking of new slums by new facades; in short, it was "an immense hypocrisy, a colossal Jesuitical lie."[31] And though these critics did not mention it, others pointed out that the broad boulevards were also a "strategic embellishment" that would faciliate the movement of troops and the razing of barricades in any future insurrection, which indeed they did in 1871.[32]

Manet's reaction to the drastic changes taking place around him is hard to assess. The only direct evidence is Proust's memoir of their stroll one day—it must have been in 1860–1861—through a ghetto being demolished to make way for the new boulevard Malesherbes, one of Haussmann's major projects and the subject of many prints like the one by Martial illustrated here (fig. 2). The memoir focuses exclusively on Manet's delight in the novel visual effects provided by a tree left standing in a destroyed garden and by the whiteness of a workman's clothing against a white plaster wall: " 'There it is,' he exclaimed, 'the symphony in white that Gautier speaks of.' "[33] But this purely aesthetic response could not have been his only one; for he could hardly ignore the moral and social implications of the demolitions, any more than Daumier did in depicting the bewilderment of suddenly dispossessed tenants and the glee of suddenly enriched landlords in prints of the 1850s, or than Baudelaire did in revealing "how the modernization of the city at once inspires and enforces the modernization of its citizens' souls" in prose poems of the 1860s.[34]

Fig. 2. Martial (Adolphe Potémont), *Petite Pologne*, etching, 1861. Bibliothèque Nationale, Paris.

If Manet was fascinated by the visual aspects of the rebuilding, the way draftsmen like Martial and photographers like Marville were, he did not record them in his art; whereas he did represent, in a picture of haunting, melancholy power, the displaced inhabitants of Petite Pologne, the once notorious area of decrepit slums whose destruction he had witnessed that day. This picture, his first of modern Paris on a monumental scale, is of course the *Old Musician* (fig. 3), painted in his new studio on the rue Guyot, a street recently opened in a still undeveloped area west of the boulevard Malesherbes, not far from Petite Pologne. In it he describes sympathetically not only those undesirable types Haussmann wished would go away—an itinerant musician, a quack peddler, a chronic alcoholic, an orphan girl—but also a street urchin whose incongruous, Pierrot-like costume alludes to the Parisian home

Fig. 3. Edouard Manet, *The Old Musician*, oil on canvas, 1862. National Gallery of Art, Washington (Chester Dale Collection).

of the commedia dell'arte, the Théâtre des Funambules, itself a victim of urban renewal; along with other popular theaters on the boulevard du Temple, it was about to be destroyed.[35] Thus the *Old Musician*, far from being "Manet's last portrayal of peasant life in a more romantic manner" before he turned to modern urban subjects later in 1862,[36] is actually his first portrayal of lower-class street life in a realist manner—or rather, a manner half romantic and half realist.

He had, it is true, already painted the alcoholic whom he repeats in the *Old Musician* three or four years earlier; but this *Absinthe Drinker* (RW 19), although posed by a rag-picker and iron-monger Manet had met in the Louvre—the slums in its neighborhood, among the worst in Paris, had only recently been cleared—remained a wholly romantic image of pathos and shadowy mystery, without the roots in a particular time and place of the later work. Much closer to the *Old Musician* in that respect is the *Street Singer* (fig. 4), painted at about the same time. It was in fact inspired by the same exploration of the area occupied by Petite Pologne; for Proust's memoir of their stroll through the area concludes with an account of their chance meeting with just such an itinerant singer: "A woman was leaving a suspicious-looking cabaret,

Theodore Reff

Fig. 4. Edouard Manet, *The Street Singer*, oil on canvas, 1862. Museum of Fine Arts, Boston.

lifting her skirts, holding her guitar. Manet went straight up to her and asked her to come and pose for him."[37] She refused, laughing, and he used a model instead; but his immediate interest in the street singer—not as a picturesque genre figure, but as a performer of a certain class, encountered in a certain part of Paris—remains significant. Nor is it the last expression of such an interest in his work: the so-called *Philosophers* (RW 99, 100), painted in 1865, were not only traditional types based on Velázquez' *Aesop* and *Menippus*, but also thoroughly contemporary Parisians; although Haussmann had succeeded in driving them from the new commercial and residential districts, they still flourished in the old ones around the Hôtel de Ville and along the rue Mouf-fetard.[38] And the *Rag-Picker* (RW 137), painted in 1869, al-though by then a familiar type in popular art and literature, was likewise associated with particular parts of the city, above all the bizarre colony called the "Villa des Chiffoniers" near the place d'Italie which, according to a contemporary guide to the Paris underground, contained hundreds of their tiny, tin-roofed hovels, "a city within a city, . . . the capital of pov-erty lost in the midst of the country of luxury."[39]

However revealing of Manet's social sympathies these pic-tures of the "capital of poverty" may be, most of those he painted of Parisian subjects represent the "country of luxury," and not only in the last decade of the Empire but also in the first decades of the Republic. In this respect the Republic did not differ from its predecessor, completing all the projects Haussmann had left unfinished and adding a few of its own. The pictures of "luxury," moreover, are often more topical than the others, more deeply rooted in aspects of the city's social life currently in vogue and even in certain places and streets only recently built, as in these examples:

The *Concert in the Tuileries* (RW 51), painted in the spring of 1862, depicts a milieu which, to judge from the attention given it in the illustrated weeklies, of which the drawing in *La Vie parisienne* already cited and an article in *Le Boulevard* exactly contemporary with Manet's painting are examples, was then at the height of its popularity among the men about town and demimondaines who pursued each other there.[40]

The *Spanish Ballet* and the portraits of Lola de Valence and Mariano Camprubi (RW 53-55), which date from the fall of the same year, describe performers who appealed not only to the Hispanophile in Manet but also to the connoisseur of urban entertainment; in the company of Baudelaire, he at-tended their performances nightly at the Hippodrome, an arena on the place Victor-Hugo that had opened five years earlier.

The *Races at Longchamp* (RW 98), painted in 1864 and repeated several times thereafter, treats a subject which had become one of the major events of the social season and, after the founding of the Grand Prix de Paris the year before, an international sporting event as well; moreover, its setting was the new racetrack in the Bois de Boulogne, completed in 1857 as part of the grandiose development of that park.

The *World's Fair of 1867* (RW 123), one of Manet's few panoramic views of Paris, was inspired by a truly topical event, an exhibition open for only seven months, but one of great significance for the Second Empire, which built immense galleries on the Champ de Mars to house it, and for the artist himself, who had a smaller structure built opposite it on the place de l'Alma to house a retrospective exhibition of his own work.

The *Balcony* (RW 134), shown at the Salon two years later, represents an architectural motif which, although not invented by Haussmann's builders, was a standard feature of their new apartment houses, including the one on the rue Saint-Pétersbourg where Manet recently moved; a feature that afforded the kind of extension of private into public space that he describes here and that the younger impressionists were soon to exploit.[41]

The *Gare Saint-Lazare* (RW 207) and the *Ball of the Opéra* (RW 216), both dating from 1873, show recently built or currently fashionable aspects of Paris—the one the Saint-Lazare railroad station and yard, enlarged six or seven years earlier, and the Pont de l'Europe, constructed in the same years; the other the traditional carnival ball which, to judge again from the frequency of coverage in the illustrated papers, was especially popular at the time.[42]

Nana (RW 259), exhibited amid much notoriety in 1877, portrays the type of wealthy courtesan of the Second Empire who dominates Zola's novel, published two years later, but who also appears in his *L'Assommoir,* issued serially while the picture was in progress; and just as Zola had interviewed a *grande cocotte* of that era, so Manet used as his model an actress and cocotte of his own era.[43]

The *Rue Mosnier Decorated with Flags* (RW 270), painted on June 30, 1878, depicts not only a specific occasion, the celebration of the success of the latest world's fair, but a specific location as well, the street Manet saw from his studio windows; opened by Haussmann nine years earlier in the development of the Quartier de l'Europe, it was still so new it was named three years after the picture was completed.

The *Bar at the Folies-Bergère* (RW 388) of 1882, the last of Manet's large Parisian subjects, is also one of the most topical; although this gaudy music hall on the rue Richer had been noted for its glittering decor and varied spectacles for almost a decade, its greatest vogue came later; witness Forain's picture of 1878, cartoons in the illustrated press of that year, and Huysmans' description in a prose poem of 1879.[44]

The most ambitious of all Manet's pictures of Haussmann's Paris would have been the murals he proposed to paint in the new Hôtel de Ville but never received permission to execute. The building, almost entirely destroyed during the Commune, was reconstructed between 1873 and 1882 and inaugurated in July of that year; but its decoration dragged on for almost two decades, so that most of the murals were commissioned in the late 1890s, long after Manet's death. Hence his proposal, in a letter to the president of the Municipal Council in April 1879,[45] seems rather premature—until we learn that one month earlier the authority to determine subjects and choose artists, at least for the sculptural decoration, had been shifted from the central administration to the council itself[46] and that its membership included Manet's brother Gustave and the friendly critic Castagnary. Manet's hopes "to paint the life of Paris in the house of Paris"[47] were however soon dashed: his letter received no reply. And when the council eventually awarded commissions, it was to artists such as Bonnat, Gervex, and Roll, who could cleverly combine contemporary urban subjects with traditional allegorical motifs; Gervex's ceiling on the theme of music, for example, shows a group of performers and putti floating on clouds and below them a concert in a modern theater strongly reminiscent of scenes by Manet and Degas.[48] What is interesting in the series of subjects Manet proposed on "the public and commercial life" of his day is that every one of them referred to structures, infrastructures, or public amenities created by Haussmann and Napoleon III: "I would have," he explained, "Paris-Markets, Paris-Railroads, Paris-Bridges, Paris-Underground, Paris-Racetracks and Gardens." And

Theodore Reff

three of them were subjects he had already treated in images of the Gare Saint-Lazare (fig. 5), the Pont de l'Europe (RW 2: 321), and the races at Longchamp (RW 98).

Fig. 5. Edouard Manet, *The Gare Saint-Lazare*, oil on canvas, 1872-73. National Gallery of Art, Washington.

The recently built Pont de l'Europe and rebuilt Gare Saint-Lazare were appropriate symbols of the new city that had emerged, were indeed at the heart of the recently developed Quartier de l'Europe, an upper-middle-class residential area west of the administrative and commercial centers. Although laid out in the 1820s, it had remained largely undeveloped until the nearby slums of Petite Pologne were demolished over thirty years later.[49] It was the former inhabitants of Petite Pologne, symbols of the old city that had disappeared, whom Manet painted in the *Old Musician* a decade before painting the *Gare Saint-Lazare* in the same neighborhood. Thus the differences between the two pictures are not only stylistic— a realism tinged with romanticism that leaves the setting vague and evocative versus a full-blown naturalism that defines it explicitly—but are also rooted in the urban development of Paris. They parallel the differences in style and urban content between the *Absinthe Drinker* (RW 19), posed for by a rag-picker who frequented the Louvre in the oldest part of the city, and *At the Cafe* (RW 2: 502), set in a tavern near the place de Clichy on the edge of the new quarter; or those between the portrait of Rouvière (RW 106), a neglected tragedian who played Hamlet on the old boulevard du Temple, and the portrait of Faure (RW 256), a world-famous baritone who performed *his* Hamlet in the splendid new Opera.

In the earlier period, Manet himself had preferred marginal, somewhat destitute neighborhoods, living in apartments on the rue de l'Hôtel de Ville (Batignolles) and the boulevard des Batignolles, in an outlying area only recently annexed by the city, and working in studios on the rue Lavoisier, a street or two away from Petite Pologne, and on the rue Guyot, a remote street behind the still undeveloped Parc Monceau. But in those years he had also frequented the fashionable Café Tortoni, identifying himself with its boulevard clientele, and in that isolated studio, "surrounded by workshops, all sorts of warehouses, courtyards, and huge vacant lots,"[50] he had painted the Tuileries Gardens, the races of Longchamp, and the elegant courtesan Olympia.

In the later period, such a dichotomy was much less apparent: he lived and worked and often chose his subjects in a relatively restricted area between the place de l'Europe and the place Pigalle, in the western part of the Ninth Arrondissement and the extreme eastern part of the Eighth. For many years his apartment was on the rue Saint-Pétersbourg and his studio was on the same street or on the rue d'Amsterdam, both of them in the Quartier de l'Europe; his favorite haunts were the Café Guerbois, near the place de Clichy, and the Café de la Nouvelle-Athènes, on the place Pigalle, though he continued to frequent Tortoni's on the boulevard; and his Parisian subjects included, in addition to the Gare Saint-Lazare and the Pont de l'Europe, others in the same *quartier:* the balcony of a building on the rue Saint-Pétersbourg (RW 134), the celebration of a holiday on the rue Mosnier (RW 270), and the garden of a friend on the rue de Rome (RW 237). Several of the other sites he painted were clustered around the place de Clichy a few blocks away: the Brasserie de Reichshoffen (RW 312), the restaurant of Père Lathuille (RW 291), and the bustling traffic of the *place* itself

(RW 273); or they were not much further away: the ice skating rink on the rue Blanche (RW 260), the old opera house on the rue Lepelletier (RW 216), and the Folies-Bergère on the rue Richer (RW 388). Of Manet's other Right Bank subjects, only the world's fair viewed from the Trocadéro (RW 123) and a *café-concert* on the Champs-Elysées (RW 310) were further afield, and both clearly had a universal Parisian appeal. As for the Left Bank, he painted only one view—a very impressive one, it is true—of the area around the Pantheon (RW 162) and a small sketch of the southern suburb of Montrouge (RW 159).

To a large extent, then, Manet's Paris from the late 1860s on was that of the Ninth Arrondissement and contiguous parts of the Eighth and Seventeenth. It was an area of the city in which were crowded together a remarkable number of artists, writers, theater people, newspaper offices, music halls, opera houses, and cafés of every variety, an area of which it could still be said many years later, "Of all the Parisian *arrondissements*, this one is without doubt the most Parisian."[51] It was thus an appropriate setting for the most Parisian of the impressionist painters. But it is doubtful that he would have assimilated its spirit so thoroughly if he had not been convinced that a truly modern art had to be rooted in the experience of modern urban life; and this conviction he owed above all to Baudelaire.

*

The early 1860s, when Manet began painting Parisian subjects, after a decade of painting copies and pastiches of Velázquez, Titian, and other old masters, were just the years when he was most closely acquainted with Baudelaire, who had long been an eloquent advocate of such subjects, and also the years when Baudelaire himself was most deeply involved in treating them in both poetry and prose. This double coincidence is something to savor but also something to distrust, for by mid-century Baudelaire was hardly alone in urging that artists and writers "be of their own time." The importance of depicting contemporary scenes and figures rather than historical ones, and in a contemporary language or style rather than a classical one, had already been stressed more than thirty years earlier, when one of the leading romantics had insisted that writers be of their time "before everything and in everything."[52] Manet himself, while still a *lycée* student in the mid-1840s, had rejected Diderot's dictum "When a people's clothes are mean, art should disregard costume" by asserting bluntly, "That is really stupid; we must be of our time and paint what we see."[53]

Yet Baudelaire's brilliant elaboration of the idea does mark a turning point in its history: he was the first to recognize that "the heroism of modern life" was to be found above all in modern urban life, the first to declare that "the life of our city is rich in poetic and marvellous subjects."[54] For the romantics, "being of one's time" had largely been a theoretical demand in their battle against the established rules and canons of correctness and their search for freshness and novelty in contact with nature and everyday life. For the realists, it had a more concrete meaning—that of recording the manners and customs of their own society, especially of its neglected lower classes, in a sincere and serious style—and it had a greater application in practice. But if realist critics like Champfleury called for the imaging of "present-day personalities, the derbies, the black dress-coats, the polished shoes or the peasants' *sabots*,"[55] and artists like Courbet painted them on the monumental scale formerly reserved for the heroic figures of history and myth, these "present-day personalities" were largely drawn from rural and small-town society and thus remained images of its familiar and timeless types. What Baudelaire had discovered, however, and urged Manet to discover, was "the transitory, fleeting beauty of our present life," by which he meant urban life, whose energy and complexity constituted a new source of inspiration.[56]

It was not the urban-industrial milieu as such that he first claimed for modern art. Gautier had already argued in 1848 that "a modern kind of beauty," different from that of classical art, could be achieved if "we accept civilization as it is, with its railroads, steamboats, English scientific research, central heating, factory chimneys,"[57] almost all of which Manet

Theodore Reff

went on to paint. He may indeed have heard his teacher Couture extoll the power of the locomotive, "that grandiose and modern chariot," and the heroism of the engineer, whose "mission has made him grow taller,"[58] and this too he eventually planned to paint. What he would have learned from Baudelaire, and only from him, was the value of immersing himself in the dynamism of urban life, of "setting up house in the heart of the multitude, amid the ebb and flow of movement."[59] This was the writer's prescription for "the perfect *flâneur*" in his essay "Le Peintre de la vie moderne," published in 1863, when he was in almost daily contact with Manet and had recently been "his habitual companion when Manet went to the Tuileries, making studies outdoors," that is, acting like the perfect *flâneur* himself.[60]

In the painting that emerged from those studies, the *Concert in the Tuileries* (RW 51), Baudelaire occupies as we have seen a prominent position. That Manet does not hold a corresponding position in Baudelaire's essay, that the painter of modern life is identified instead as Constantin Guys, a relatively minor draftsman, has often been taken as a sign of the writer's failure to appreciate Manet's work sufficiently. And just as often it has been explained as an unavoidable failure, given the date of the essay (1859-1860) and his unadventurous production up to that time. When Manet showed his more recent work in 1862, Baudelaire was quick to acclaim in it evidence of "a vigorous taste for reality, modern reality," as well as of "a lively and abundant imagination."[61] He could hardly have spoken of that taste in the earlier essay if indeed he was the one who later stimulated it and had even, as is sometimes stated without proof, suggested the Tuileries concert as a suitably modern subject.

For such a subject, however, Manet had other sources as well, which were equally familiar to Baudelaire. One of them, a wash drawing by Guys of fashionable people gathered in the gardens of the Champs-Elysées, was in fact in the writer's collection; and if it is not quite as "analogous in conception" as has been maintained,[62] it is nevertheless the kind of authentic record of contemporary life that Manet too would have found congenial. The many wood engravings of the

Tuileries Gardens and of the concerts given there, which appeared in illustrated newspapers around 1860, would have been equally helpful; this was precisely the kind of imagery, unpretentious yet filled with the flavor of its time, that Baudelaire had been one of the first to appreciate. In "Le Peintre de la vie moderne," while implicitly acknowledging the limitations of Guys's drawings, many of them made for newspapers, he affirms their importance as "precious archives of civilized life," alongside those of Debucourt, Gavarni, and others,[63] which were likewise precedents or sources for Manet.

But if the *Concert in the Tuileries* is Manet's first important picture of modern life, it is because it transcends those precedents and captures what Baudelaire called the "heroism" of that life, in a medium and on a scale associated with ambitious Salon paintings. Pictures of equally familiar Parisian sites with figures in contemporary dress had, it is true, been shown by Bouhot, Dagnan, and others at the Salon earlier in the century;[64] but the figures had been small and the sites rendered in a static, topographic manner. With Manet, not only is the scale larger and the ambition greater, but the merely contemporary becomes truly modern; he conveys the immediacy of the urban *flâneur's* experience, the force and freshness of his sensations, however mediated by memories of Velázquez. And in this he is indebted to Baudelaire, who affirms in the same essay: "The pleasure which we derive from the representation of the present is due not only to the beauty with which it can be invested, but also to its essential quality of present-ness."[65]

The years around 1860, when Baudelaire wrote and sought to publish this essay, were also those when he was most deeply involved in conveying his experience of modern Paris in both his critical and his imaginative writings. The one kind of writing reinforced and may well have influenced the other; for in the art that he discussed, he discovered those aspects of the city's social life and physical fabric that most fascinated him as a poet. In Daumier's lithographs, he saw "parading before [his] eyes all that a great city contains of living monstrosities, in all their fantastic and thrilling reality";[66] in Guys's drawings, "all the various types of fallen womanhood" to be seen in "that vast picture-gallery which is life in London or Paris";[67] and both are familiar themes in *Les Fleurs du mal.* Also familiar, at least in the poems of these years, which for the first time bore titles like "Rêve parisien" (dedicated to Guys) and "Paysage parisien," are evocations of what he called, in a memorable passage on Meryon's etchings of old streets and monuments, "the natural solemnity of a great capital."[68] This passage first appeared in the "Salon de 1859," where he also discussed for the first time "the landscape of great cities, . . . that collection of grandeurs and beauties which results from a powerful agglomeration of men and monuments."[69]

In these years too Baudelaire wrote most of the prose poems—some published during his lifetime, the rest only posthumously—that constitute the *Spleen de Paris,* his most profoundly original meditations on the modern city, and he grouped his recent poems on Parisian subjects with several older ones to create, in the second edition of the *Fleurs du mal* (1861), the section entitled "Tableaux parisiens." One of the new poems, "Le Cygne," is about Haussmann's transformation of Paris: set in the place du Carrousel, the great public space created six years earlier when the old streets and tenements adjacent to the Louvre were demolished, it evokes the bohemian life that once flourished there and laments its disappearance: "The old Paris no longer exists (the form of a city changes more quickly, alas, than the heart of a mortal)."[70]

How much of this writing had an impact on Manet, it is hard to say. The poet's somber vision of Paris, summed up in the famous verse in which he calls it "hospital, brothel, purgatory, hell, prison," seems at first to bear little resemblance to the painter's essentially luminous vision. In fact they shared a more complex, ambivalent attitude toward the city, one that revealed itself explicitly in Baudelaire's oscillation between "lyrical celebrations" and "vehement denunciations" of modern life[71] and only implicitly in Manet's alternation between themes of middle-class pleasure and lower-class alienation. Two examples of convergence in their treatment of *la vie élégante* have been noted: the *Concert in the Tuileries*

(RW 51) and the picture in "Les Veuves" of a military concert in a public garden, where "shimmering gowns trail on the ground; glances cross each other; idlers, tired of having done nothing, loll about"; and *Olympia* (RW 69), the very type of the elegant Parisian courtesan, and the image in "Les Bijoux" of the poet's beloved lying naked before him, wearing "only her sonorous jewels," with "her eyes fixed on [him] like a tamed tigress."[72] An example in their treatment of *la vie de bohème* has also been cited: the *Absinthe Drinker* (RW 19) and the portrait in "Le Vin des chiffoniers" of a solitary rag-picker in an old, decrepit neighborhood, absorbed in his reverie, "intoxicating himself with the splendors of his own virtue,"[73] and to it can be added a second example: the *Philosopher* (RW 100) and the vivid sketch in "La Fausse Monnaie" of a beggar encountered outside a tobacco shop, "holding out his cap with a trembling hand," with "a look of mute eloquence in his pleading eyes."[74]

Contrasts of this sort, inspired by a deep awareness of the contradictions in urban society, are familiar in the work of Baudelaire; much less so in that of Manet. Yet it is sufficient to compare his two major paintings of modern life of 1862, the *Concert in the Tuileries* (fig. 1) and the *Old Musician* (fig. 3), one set in a formal garden near an imperial palace, the other in a wasteland near a recently demolished ghetto, one summing up "the pageant of fashionable life," the other "the thousands of floating existences,"[75] to realize how keen his own awareness was. It was indeed, for all his so-called detachment, that of the "perfect *flâneur*" who becomes "one flesh with the crowd," for Manet is present in both pictures— in the one quite literally, as a Baudelairean dandy and *boulevardier;* in the other symbolically, as a Baudelairean beggar and alter ego for the artist. But the two worlds do not come together; whereas in the *Painter's Studio* (fig. 6), exhibited seven years earlier, and long recognized as a source for both of Manet's pictures, Courbet had shown them sharing the same space and himself poised between them. At the right are the writers, musicians, intellectuals, patrons, and other members of his circle, among them the ubiquitous Baudelaire; at the left, the beggar, the poacher, the mountebank,

Theodore Reff

Fig. 6. Gustave Courbet, *The Painter's Studio,* oil on canvas, 1855. Musée du Louvre, Paris.

the Wandering Jew, and other disinherited types whom Courbet had also met. But the latter remain anonymous types, while the former are individuals, just as the people in Manet's *Concert* are all individuals, while the old musician and his friends are types.[76]

Ultimately, what links Manet's images of modern Paris with Baudelaire's, beyond the social contradictions implicit in their subject matter, is the depth of their understanding of the distinctly modern forms and content of urban life. This is most evident, in the writer's work, in the prose poems of the late 1850s and 1860s, initially entitled *Spleen de Paris,* more than half of which have a Parisian setting; and in the artist's work, in paintings and pastels of the late 1860s and 1870s, when he had largely abandoned his dialogue with older art and confronted modern life directly. That he recognized the value of Baudelaire's book and its roots in urban experience is clear from his offer to provide an etched portrait of the author, based on that in the Tuileries picture, "wearing a hat, in fact out for a walk," as a frontispiece for the posthumous edition.[77] To convey the very look and feel of that experience, each of them sought to stretch the limits of his art. For the poet, this meant inventing a new language, "a poetic prose, musical without rhythm and rhyme, supple enough and rugged enough to adapt itself to the soul's lyrical impulses, the undulations of revery, the leaps and jolts of consciousness," a prose derived "above all from the exploration of enormous cities and from the convergence of their innumerable connections.[78] For the painter, it meant breaking with conventional rules of composition, perspective, and finish to create images of the city in which key figures are placed off-center or cut by the frame, as in the *Ball of the Opera* (RW 216); space becomes disjunctive and objects within it incommensurable, as in the *World's Fair* (RW 123); and sensations are recorded in a swift shorthand that gives the appearance of a sketch, as in the *Funeral* (RW 162). And for both it meant employing a previously spurned vernacular style, whether it was the racy language of the streets or illustrations in the popular press.

It is above all their treatment of certain themes, which "carry a mythic resonance and depth that . . . transform them into archetypes of modern life,"[79] that reveals the profound affinities in their vision. Three such "primal modern" themes in particular stand out: estrangement in the midst of conviviality, indifference in the presence of death, and suicide, that uniquely modern form of revolt. Baudelaire treats the last of these in "La Corde," which is dedicated to Manet and inspired by an event he had related, the suicide by hanging of a poor, deranged boy whom he had befriended and used as a studio assistant and occasional model.[80] Always said to have taken place some years earlier, it must actually have occurred in 1861-1862 in Manet's studio on the rue Guyot; this is what his widow recalled[81] and what the poem itself suggests in locating the studio, like Manet's, in an "out of the way neighborhood . . . where great grassy spaces still separate the houses."[82] It was there that he painted the *Old Musician* (fig. 3) early in 1862, in which a poor boy is shown standing beside the gypsy violinist: does the narrator of "La Corde" have this in mind when he says, "I would disguise him, sometimes as a little gypsy . . . with the vagrant musician's violin"?[83] And did Manet himself have the poet's conception of suicide as "*the* achievement of modernism in the realm of passions,

Theodore Reff

... the only heroic act that remained"[84] in mind when he painted the victim of a self-inflicted death lying alone in a sparsely furnished room, a pistol still held in his hand (RW 258)?

Death is also the theme of "Le Tir et le cimetière," published shortly after Baudelaire was buried in the Montparnasse Cemetery and at about the same time Manet painted the *Funeral* (fig. 7), which is set there and may commemorate

Fig. 7. Edouard Manet, *The Funeral,* oil on canvas, c. 1867. The Metropolitan Museum of Art, New York.

that event.[85] Both works deal with the burial of the dead by stripping it of its earlier meaning—the pathos of a personal tragedy, as in romantic art; the dignity of a communal ceremony, as in realist art—and investing it instead with the familiar modern feelings of indifference, cynicism, and irony. Baudelaire's *flâneur* has come upon a tavern opposite a cemetery, a self-styled "Cemetery View Tavern," and after he has "drunk a glass of beer facing the graves and slowly smoked a cigar," has decided to walk among them; but his thoughts are "interrupted at regular intervals by shots from a nearby shooting gallery."[86] In short the modern city, in all its vulgarity and violence, has encroached on the once-sacred "sanctuary of Death." In Manet's picture indifference takes a different form: the funeral cortège seems lost amid tall trees and public buildings, its figures small and blurred; the day is gloomy and the weather threatening, as if nature shared the pervasive malaise. But this detachment too has an ironic twist: the Pantheon, resting place of some of France's most illustrious writers, is not quite aligned with the much maligned poet's hearse.

Not death as such but alienation, a kind of living death, is the theme of "Les Yeux des pauvres," which is set "in front of a new café forming the corner of a new boulevard,"[87] one of those created by Haussmann. It is also the theme of Manet's café pictures, especially the one showing a café on the place du Théâtre-Français (fig. 8), another new establishment in a

Fig. 8. Edouard Manet, *A Café in the Place du Théâtre-Français,* oil and pastel, 1881. The Burrell Collection, Glasgow Museums & Art Galleries.

public space created by Haussmann. Both are depicted as opulent and dazzling, the gas lamps "lighting with all their might the blinding whiteness of the walls, the expanse of mirrors, the gold cornices and moldings," but in both works this luxury only heightens the poverty of human relationships. Baudelaire's couple are doubly estranged—unable to cross the class barrier separating them from the poor family in the street who observe them enviously, and equally unable

Theodore Reff

to reconcile their own differences in facing such a challenge. Manet's café-dwellers may all belong to the same world socially, but it is a world of strangers adrift in a seemingly limitless space, who are cut off severely at its edges, reflected ambiguously in its mirrors, remote from each other even when seated together, and like the man at the left no more substantial than smoke. In images such as these we rediscover the city of today, the truly modern city in all its contradiction and complexity, of which the Paris of Manet and Baudelaire was the first example and for almost a century the last type.

It was, however, much more than a city of alienated classes and individuals, of dreary funerals and disrespect for the dead, of suicides in remote studios and furnished rooms, however "primal" these themes may be for later modernist experience. For it was also a city of theaters, restaurants, and *cafés-concerts,* of international fairs and patriotic celebrations, of masked balls at the Opera and concerts in the Tuileries Gardens, of beggars, rag-pickers, and gypsy musicians, of common streetwalkers and fashionable courtesans, and at times of barricades in the streets and warfare between the classes. These too were Parisian subjects, and as such were also treated by Manet and his contemporaries in paintings, drawings, and prints.

NOTES

1. Théodore Duret, *Manet* (1902; 4th ed., Paris, 1926), p. 158.

2. Duret, p. 47.

3. Etienne Moreau-Nélaton, *Manet raconté par lui-même,* 2 vols. (Paris, 1926), I, 103.

4. Emile Zola, "Une nouvelle manière en peinture: Edouard Manet" (1867); rpt. in *Salons,* ed. F. W. J. Hemmings and Robert Niess (Geneva and Paris, 1959), p. 86.

5. Jacques-Emile Blanche, *Manet,* trans. F. C. de Sumichrast (London, 1925), pp. 9-10.

6. Antonin Proust, *Edouard Manet. Souvenirs* (Paris, 1913), p. 42.

7. Beatrice Farwell, "Manet and the Nude: A Study in Iconography in the Second Empire," diss. University of California, Los Angeles, 1973, pp. 82-83, 120-24.

8. Martin Davies, *National Gallery Catalogues, French School,* revised by Cecil Gould (London, 1970), pp. 91-92.

9. Nils Gosta Sandblad, *Manet: Three Studies in Artistic Conception* (Lund, 1954), pp. 37-39.

10. *Concert in the Tuileries Gardens,* wood engraving in *La Vie parisienne* (May 28, 1864).

11. Jules Vallès, *La Rue* (1866), ed. Pierre Pillu (Paris, 1969), p. 36.

12. Vallès, pp. 8-9.

13. Henri Guillemin, cited in Vallès, pp. 8-9.

14. In the lithographs *The Barricade* and *Civil War* (Jean C. Harris, *Edouard Manet: Graphic Works* [New York, 1970], nos. 71, 72) and in the watercolor *The Barricade* (Denis Rouart and Daniel Wildenstein, *Manet. Catalogue raisonné,* 2 vols. [Paris, 1975], 2, no. 319).

15. Duret, p. 159.

16. Duret, p. 160.

17. Pierre Schneider, *The World of Manet* (New York, 1968), p. 135.

18. Blanche, p. 52.

19. Werner Hoffman, *Nana: Mythos und Wirklichkeit* (Cologne, 1973), p. 90.

20. Anne Coffin Hanson, *Manet and the Modern Tradition* (New Haven, 1977), p. 132.

21. Siegfried Kracauer, *Orpheus and Paris: Offenbach and the Paris of His Time,* trans. Gwenda David and Eric Mosbacher (New York, 1938), p. 75.

22. Zola, pp. 91, 97.

23. George H. Hamilton, *Manet and His Critics* (New Haven, 1954), p. 183.

24. Hanson, p. 160.

25. Firmin Roz, *La Lumière de Paris* (Paris, 1933), pp. 206-11.

26. John Richardson, *Edouard Manet* (New York, 1958), p. 29.

27. Emile Zola, "Edouard Manet" (1884), in *Salons,* ed. Hemmings and Niess, p. 261.

28. Howard Saalman, *Haussmann: Paris Transformed* (New York, 1971), p. 113.

29. David Pinkney, *Napoleon III and the Rebuilding of Paris* (Princeton, 1958), p. 127.

30. Victor Fournel, *Paris nouveau et Paris futur* (Paris, 1865), pp. 218-29.

31. Emile Zola, "Lettre parisienne," *La Cloche* (June 8, 1872).

32. Walter Benjamin, "Paris—Capital of the Nineteenth Century," *New Left Review,* no. 48 (March-April 1968), p. 87.

33. Proust, pp. 39-40.

34. Marshall Berman, *All That Is Solid Melts into Air: The Experience of Modernity* (New York, 1982), p. 147.

35. George Mauner, *Manet, Peintre-Philosophe: A Study of the Painter's Themes* (University Park, 1975), p. 55.

36. Sandblad, p. 28.

37. Proust, p. 40.

38. Alexandre Privat d'Anglemont, *Paris anecdote,* 2nd ed. (Paris, 1864), pp. 305-06.

39. Privat d'Anglemont, p. 218.

40. Joel Isaacson, "Impressionism and Journalistic Illustration," *Arts Magazine* 56, no. 10 (June 1982), 115, n. 85; Farwell, pp. 80-82.

41. See Kirk Varnedoe, in *Gustave Caillebotte: A Retrospective Exhibition,* Museum of Fine Arts, Houston, October 22, 1976—January 2, 1977, pp. 147-48.

42. Isaacson, p. 105.

43. Hoffman, pp. 22-23, 90-91.

44. Lillian Browse, *Forain the Painter* (London, 1978), pl. 2; Isaacson, p. 110; Joris-Karl Huysmans, "Les Folies-Bergère en 1879" in *Croquis parisiens* (1880), ed. Lucien Descaves (Paris, 1928), pp. 14-18.

45. Edmond Bazire, *Manet* (Paris, 1884), p. 142.

46. Marius Vachon, *L'Hôtel de Ville de Paris* (Paris, 1905), p. 120.

47. Proust, p. 95.

48. Louis d'Hancour, *L'Hôtel de Ville de Paris à travers les siècles* (Paris, 1900), pp. 742-47.

49. Jacques Hillairet, *Dictionnaire historique des rues de Paris*, 2 vols. (Paris, 1963), I, 79, 489.

50. Duret, p. 86.

51. Albert Dauzat and Fernand Bournon, *Paris et ses environs* (Paris, 1925), p. 91.

52. Linda Nochlin, *Realism* (Baltimore, 1971), p. 104.

53. Proust, p. 7.

54. Charles Baudelaire, "Le Peintre de la vie moderne" (1863), in *The Painter of Modern Life and Other Essays*, trans. Jonathan Mayne (London, 1964), p. 40.

55. Nochlin, p. 28.

56. Baudelaire, "Le Peintre de la vie moderne," p. 40.

57. Matei Calinescu, *Faces of Modernity: Avant-garde, Decadence, Kitsch* (Bloomington, 1977), pp. 45-46.

58. Thomas Couture, *Méthode et entretiens d'atelier* (Paris, 1867), p. 254.

59. Baudelaire, "Le Peintre de la vie moderne," p. 9.

60. Proust, p. 39.

61. Charles Baudelaire, "Peintres et aqua-fortistes" (1862), in *Art in Paris, 1845-1862*, p. 218.

62. Lois Boe Hyslop and Francis E. Hyslop, "Baudelaire and Manet: A Re-Appraisal," in *Baudelaire as a Love Poet and Other Essays*, ed. Lois Boe Hyslop (University Park, 1969), p. 102.

63. Baudelaire, "Le Peintre de la vie moderne," p. 40.

64. See *Paris vu par les peintres de Corot à Foujita, Bulletin du Musée Carnavalet*, XXXI, 1978, nos. 6-9, 29, etc.

65. Baudelaire, "Le Peintre de la vie moderne," p. 1.

66. Charles Baudelaire, "Quelques caricaturistes français" (1857), in *The Painter of Modern Life and Other Essays*, p. 177.

67. Baudelaire, "Le Peintre de la vie moderne," p. 37.

68. Baudelaire, "Peintres et aqua-fortistes," p. 221.

69. Charles Baudelaire, "Salon de 1859," in *Art in Paris, 1845-1862*, p. 200.

70. Charles Baudelaire, *Les Fleurs du mal* (2nd ed., 1861), ed. Jacques Crépet and Georges Blin (Paris, 1942), p. 96.

71. Berman, p. 134.

72. Hyslop and Hyslop, pp. 99-100, 111-12.

73. Hanson, p. 55.

74. Charles Baudelaire, *Petits poëmes en prose* (1869), trans. Louise Varese (New York, 1970), p. 58.

75. Baudelaire, "Salon de 1846," p. 118.

76. Farwell, p. 91.

77. William Hauptman, "Manet's Portrait of Baudelaire: An Emblem of Melancholy," *The Art Quarterly*, new series, I (1978), p. 215.

78. Baudelaire, *Petits poëmes en prose*, pp. ix-x.

79. Berman, p. 148.

80. Baudelaire, *Petits poëmes en prose*, pp. 64-67.

81. Etienne Moreau-Nélaton, *Manet, graveur et lithographe* (Paris, 1906), no. 10, and *Manet raconté par lui-même*, I, 38.

82. Duret, p. 86.

83. Mauner, p. 18.

84. Walter Benjamin, *Charles Baudelaire: A Lyric Poet in the Era of High Capitalism*, trans. Harry Zohn (London, 1973), p. 75.

Painters of Modern Life:
Baudelaire and the Impressionists

Michele Hannoosh

La vie parisienne est féconde en sujets poétiques et merveilleux.
—Baudelaire, *Salon de 1846*[1]

French painting of the latter half of the nineteenth century had a special relationship to the theme of the modern city, for it treated city life as a distinctive feature of the modern experience that it sought to express. For Baudelaire, Manet, and the Impressionists, modernity became a catchword and, more seriously, an aesthetic criterion, in which the city itself played a large part. The reason why this was so is not easily determined; calls for modern subjects in art and literature had been issued since the early part of the century, and yet by 1850 they had not inspired any significant movements dedicated to representing modern life. Paris was changing, and certainly Haussmann's grand boulevards provided remarkable views, but the city had been no less a source of intriguing subjects before that. And although urban subjects figured prominently in modern painting, they alone do not suffice to account for "modernity in art." One needs to question the specific concept of modernity that the late-nineteenth century held, and the role played by the city in its development.

Baudelaire constitutes an appropriate point of departure for this inquiry, for several reasons. First, he was a gifted and sensitive art critic and, in that capacity, the most eloquent spokesman for the modern in art that the nineteenth century produced. His interest in the modern is present in his early *Salons* of 1845 and 1846, appears in various essays of his middle period, and culminates in the great art critical piece of 1859, *Le Peintre de la vie moderne*. Second, Baudelaire is acknowledged to be not only the first great modern poet but, more pertinently for us, the first great poet of the modern city. Paris constitutes one of the principal themes of the *Fleurs du mal*, not only in the "Tableux parisiens" section of poems specifically about the city, but also in the longest section, "Spleen et idéal." The theme of the city also informs the *Petits poèmes en prose*, subtitled *Le Spleen de Paris*, in which he gives his modern subject the added distinction of an appropriately novel form, the prose poem. This "Parisian" aspect of Baudelaire's vision and of his poetry was perceived even during his own time as one of his unique qualities and one of his poetic strengths. In his own words, he discerned and conveyed "le charme profond et compliqué d'une capitale âgée et vieillie dans les gloires et les tribulations de la vie" (1083).[2] Third, Baudelaire had identifiable historical connections with the future Impressionist painters, a term I use cautiously and for convenience to designate Manet and those whom we now consider to be the representatives of this group, e.g., Monet, Renoir, Pissarro, Raffaëlli, Morisot, and Cassatt. He was a friend and supporter of Manet after 1859, and although he wrote little on him, he nevertheless described him approvingly as one who combined "un goût décidé pour la réalité, la réalité moderne—ce qui est déjà un bon symptôme—et cette imagination vive et ample, sensible, audacieuse" (1146).[3] The statement is significant for, as we shall see shortly, Baudelaire associated these same two qualities with true art. Various proposals have been advanced to measure the influence of Baudelaire on Manet at this time, as he moved from his Spanish manner to the more modern vision of the *Concert in the Tuileries* (1862) in which, of course, he depicted Baudelaire himself. Although the precise nature of his impact on Manet can only be surmised, it is generally agreed that Baudelaire greatly influenced Manet's evolution toward Parisian subjects and the aesthetic of modern city life.[4]

Baudelaire's views, in particular his call for a painter of modern life, touched others besides Manet, however. In fact, they influenced most of the innovative painters of the generation immediately following. But how does Baudelaire conceive of the modern in painting, how does the city figure in this conception, and in what ways do his ideas relate to the theory and practice of Impressionism? I shall address these questions from three points of view: style and technique, subject matter, and aesthetic, that is, a particular notion of beauty and of truth. I hope to show that Baudelaire's urban vision is inseparable not only from modern subject matter but also from his aesthetic as a whole.

I. Qui dit romantisme dit art moderne
—Salon de 1846

Baudelaire's reflections on a modern style were inspired principally by Romantic painting and thus would seem to have little bearing upon the innovations of Impressionism. But his particular interpretation of Romanticism in fact anticipates constantly specific Impressionist techniques and theories of composition. Baudelaire consistently associated the modern with Delacroix, that is to say, with the *coloristes*—those who employed color rather than line as the chief means of expression and the primary way of establishing form and composition. In a section of the 1846 *Salon* devoted to the theory of color, he describes the colorist as one concerned with rendering movement, the atmospheric effects of light and air, and by his choice of tones, feeling—three qualities that he attributes to modern art and that will certainly become predominant in Impressionism.

Line drawing, for Baudelaire, is an abstraction: the colorist's line is really a fusion of colors; his contours are indefinite and his forms floating for, as in nature, his figures are delimited by "la lutte harmonieuse des masses colorées" (885)[5]; his modeling comes from the harmony formed by the juxtaposition of colors and its contrast with shadow. He is aware of the importance of the air in the perception of color, and he accounts for it with his palette, thus rendering by a gradation of tones the kind of aerial perspective that the Impressionists would later use consistently. For the colorist, "forme et couleur sont un" (882)[6]; color replaces line as the major formal and compositional factor.

Baudelaire especially admired Delacroix' *Dante and Virgil*

Michele Hannoosh

in Hell (1822, fig. 1) for these effects of movement, color, and atmosphere. He felt that the painting achieved its greatest effect at a distance, a quality that he associated with aesthetic

Fig. 1. Eugène Delacroix, *Dante and Virgil in Hell*, oil on canvas, 1822. Musée du Louvre, Paris.

Fig. 2. Edouard Manet, *Copy after Delacroix' Dante and Virgil*, oil on canvas, 1854. Metropolitan Museum of Art, New York.

unity. "*Dante et Virgile*, par exemple, laisse toujours une impression profonde dont l'intensité s'accroît par la distance" (891-892).[7] Manet seems to have perceived these radical aspects of the painting, since he did a copy of it that features amorphous forms, masses of color, and a sense of movement (1854, fig. 2). Baudelaire also associates the modern style of the colorist with the "vibration perpétuelle" of nature (880) and the poetic, interpretative rendering of a subject. The choice and combination of tones convey an emotional effect. As he puts it, "Les purs dessinateurs sont des philosophes et des abstracteurs de quintessence. Les coloristes sont des poètes épiques" (885).[8] Impressionism, too, emphasizes the vibrations of light and color that the eye perceives and assimilates into a unified image, and also the subjectivity of the impression so rendered.

Although Baudelaire's ideas on style were distinctly modern, they were nevertheless made in connection with an established school of painting and in a relatively conventional critical language. His most obvious contribution to modern painting was in the area of subject matter. Although he admitted all types of subject matter, and although his favorite painter, Delacroix, avoided modern subjects, he makes a call from the early *Salons* onward for a painter of modern life.[9] He first expresses this in a memorable conclusion to the *Salon de 1845*. Deploring the lack of invention, ideas, or personal vision ("tempérament") in the Salon paintings that year, he observes:

> Au vent qui soufflera demain nul ne tend l'oreille; et pourtant l'héroisme *de la vie moderne* nous entoure et nous presse. . . . Celui-là sera le *peintre*, le vrai peintre, qui saura arracher à la vie actuelle son côté épique, et nous faire voir et comprendre, avec de la couleur ou du dessin, combien nous sommes grands et poétiques dans nos cravates et nos bottes vernies. (866)[10]

At this point, Baudelaire raises specifically only the question of fashionable dress, but in his *Salon* of the following year he extends his notion of modern life to include not only modern dress but more generally the life of the big city. First, he describes the suit as "la pelure du héros moderne,"[11] then notes "sa beauté et son charme indigène" (950),[12] and finally relates

Michele Hannoosh

this attire to what he considers the distinctive spirit of the age:

> N'est-il pas l'habit nécessaire de notre époque, souffrante et portant jusque sur ses épaules noires et maigres le symbole d'un deuil perpétuel? Remarquez bien que l'habit noir et la redingote ont non seulement leur beauté politique, qui est l'expression de l'égalité universelle, mais encore leur beauté poétique, qui est l'expression de l'âme publique;—une immense défilade de croque-morts, croque-morts amoureux, croque-morts bourgeois. Nous célébrons tous quelque enterrement. (950)[13]

Despite its humor, the remark brings out a significant point of Baudelaire's aesthetic, namely his association of modern life with suffering, a sentiment that he expressed variously as melancholy, spleen, even ennui. As we shall see later, this emotion was a crucial aspect of the "modernism" of the late-nineteenth century, unlike the more energetic and aggressive spirit of the early twentieth with which we usually associate the term.

Moreover, Baudelaire implies that by modern life he means specifically city life. "La vie parisienne est féconde en sujets poétiques et merveilleux. Le merveilleux nous enveloppe et nous abreuve comme l'atmosphère; mais nous ne le voyons pas" (952).[14] By the heroism of modern life, Baudelaire does not mean simply contemporary subjects. Painters have frequently depicted modern scenes of public, official subjects, but the subject alone does not suffice to make a painting modern, especially, Baudelaire adds, since the government commissions them to produce such pictures. By modern, Baudelaire understands the particular beauty that derives from the distinctive spirit of the age, "la beauté particulière, inhérente à des passions nouvelles" (951).[15] This includes "le spectacle de la vie élégante," that is to say, fashionable women and dandies. He describes the latter, in fact, as "la suprême incarnation de l'idée du beau transportée dans la vie matérielle"[16] and "le dernier éclat d'héroisme dans les décadences" (1179).[17] In a later essay, he specifically names the places that such elegant people frequent as being appropriate subjects for the modern painter: the public gardens, the racetrack, the theatre, the opera. These, of course, became favorite Impressionist subjects, beginning with Manet's *Concert in the Tuileries* (1862), and that movement was linked with the representation of fashionable Parisian life. Baudelaire saw ladies' fashions as an especially suitable subject. He evokes "la haute spiritualité de la toilette" (1183)[18] and describes fashion as "un effort . . . vers le beau, une approximation quelconque d'un idéal dont le désir titille l'esprit humain non satisfait" (951).[19]

But he also called for the representation of more "low life" subjects ("des milliers d'existences flottantes qui circulent dans les souterrains d'une grande ville—criminels et filles entretenues")[20] and more industrial features of the city. In the 1859 *Salon*, he devotes a section to landscape painting and regrets the absence of a special type of landscape,

> un genre que j'appellerais volontiers le paysage des grandes villes, c'est-à-dire la collection des grandeurs et des beautés qui résultent d'une puissante agglomération d'hommes et de monuments, le charme profond et compliqué d'une capitale âgée et vieillie dans les gloires et les tribulations de la vie. (1083)[21]

He cites Meryon as a painter who does produce such cityscapes, but as usual Baudelaire's examples permit him to elaborate further his own views. Here, he speaks of the beauty of industry and construction:

> Les majestés de la pierre accumulée, les clochers *montrant du doigt le ciel,* les obélisques de l'industrie vomissant contre le firmament leurs coalitions de fumée, les prodigieux échafaudages des monuments en réparation, appliquant sur le corps solide de l'architecture leur architecture à jour d'une beauté si paradoxale, le ciel tumultueux, chargé de colère et de rancune, la profondeur des perspectives augmentée par la pensée de tous les drames qui y sont contenus, aucun des éléments dont se compose le douloureux et glorieux décor de la civilisation n'était oublié. (1083)[22]

Such a beauty is evoked, for example, in Monet's *Gare Saint-Lazare* (1877), with the open work of the canopy, the iron and glass, the puffs of smoke, and the deep perspective that permits a view out onto the city (fig. 3).

This hybrid term—"paysage des grandes villes"—is significant, for it applies a term customarily reserved for nature to the city, and Baudelaire began increasingly to connect these

Michele Hannoosh

Fig. 3. Claude Monet, *The Gare Saint-Lazare*, oil on canvas, 1877. The Art Institute of Chicago.

two normally opposed domains.[23] For example, in *Le Peintre de la vie moderne* he calls modern life an "immense dictionary," thus replacing nature in his earlier formulation of 1846: "Pour Eugène Delacroix, la nature est un vaste dictionnaire" (891).[24] The idea of nature as a dictionary had been expressed previously by Delacroix himself, as Baudelaire tells us in the *Salon de 1859;* by his substitution, Baudelaire transfers all the aesthetic implications of the term "nature" to modern city life.

The significance of the dictionary metaphor becomes clear when we read his explanation of Delacroix' use of it:

"La nature n'est qu'un dictionnaire", répétait-il fréquemment. Pour bien comprendre l'étendue du sens impliqué dans cette phrase, il faut se figurer les usages nombreux et ordinaires du dictionnaire. On y cherche les sens de mots, les générations des mots, l'étymologie des mots; enfin on en extrait tous les éléments qui composent une phrase et un récit; mais personne n'a jamais considéré le dictionnaire comme une composition dans le sens poétique du mot. Les peintres qui obéissent a l'imagination cherchent dans leur dictionnaire les éléments qui s'accordent à leur comception; encore, en les ajustant avec un certain art, leur donnent-ils une physionomie toute nouvelle. Ceux qui n'ont pas d'imagination copient le dictionnaire. (1041)[25]

Painters of Modern Life   175

As Baudelaire understood the phrase, nature was a vast dictionary from which the artist selected his materials, which he then combined, by virtue of his creative imagination, into a meaningful utterance.[26] When he makes modern life the dictionary, he marks it not only as subject matter but as the very material of art, that which the artist's imagination interprets and arranges. In a note for "L'Art philosophique" (1857-1860), Baudelaire also suggests that the experience of modern life, and specifically that of urban life, provides the aesthetic sensation that the Romantics felt in the midst of nature. He likens the "vertige" experienced in a big city to that had in nature, for both provide the same "délices du chaos et de l'immensité" (1107).[27] The city thus provided not only matter for art, but in the "ivresse religieuse des grandes villes" (1248)[28] supplied an aesthetic sublimity formerly reserved for the communion with nature.

After style and subject matter, a third aspect of Baudelaire's concept of the modern remains, what I have called an "aesthetic of modernity." It embraces three main areas: the notion of beauty as transitory, an emphasis on the artist's subjective rendering of his subject, and a pervasive mood of melancholy. These three points provide yet another link with the modern vision of the Impressionist painters and in many ways articulate what would become the dominant themes of late nineteenth century aesthetics.

Baudelaire relates the modern aesthetic, first, to a particular conception of beauty, as it is found in the circumstantial and the transitory. He sees ideal, absolute beauty as merely an abstraction:

> Toutes les beautés contiennent, comme tous les phénomènes possibles, quelque chose d'éternel et quelque chose de transitoire,—d'absolu et de particulier. La beauté absolue et éternelle n'existe pas, ou plutôt elle n'est qu'une abstraction écrémée à la surface générale des beautés diverses. L'elément particulier de chaque beauté vient des passions, et comme nous avons nos passions particulières, nous avons notre beauté. (950)[29]

Although here, in 1846, he admits that beauty contains "quelque chose d'éternel," he very nearly ignores the idea in his subsequent writings, and when it does appear he has qualified it by suggesting that it depends on the transitory: "Il s'agit

Michele Hannoosh

. . . de dégager de la mode ce qu'elle peut contenir de poétique dans l'historique, de tirer l'éternel du transitoire" (1163).[30] Baudelaire thus identifies the task of the modern artist, to find the special beauty of his own era, for only this will ensure the authenticity and the durability of his art. Only by finding the universal and the eternal in the transitory, the ephemeral, the contingent, the historical, in short the *modern*, can we assure that the art of our time will become timeless, worthy of being to future generations what the great art of the past is to us. Baudelaire presents this not only as desirable, but more sternly as a necessity, a moral obligation on the part of the artist:

> Cet élément transitoire, fugitif, dont les métamorphoses sont si fréquentes, vous n'avez pas le droit de le mépriser ou de vous en passer. En le supprimant, vous tombez forcément dans le vide d'une beauté abstraite et indéfinissable, comme celle de l'unique femme avant le premier péché. (1163-1164)[31]

It is acceptable to imitate art of the past to develop technique, but not for inspiration:

> Malheur à celui qui étudie dans l'antique autre chose que l'art pur, la logique, la méthode générale! Pour s'y trop plonger, il perd la mémoire du présent; il abdique la valeur et les privilèges fournis par la circonstance; car presque toute notre originalité vient de l'estampille que le *temps* imprime à nos sensations. (1165)[32]

In so far as "le temps" includes both "time" and "the times," Baudelaire's comment relates the aesthetic of the transitory directly to the aesthetic of modern life. Modern life, especially Parisian life, inspires distinct emotions, and these produce the special beauty of an age, that "beauté particulière" (951) which was, for him, Beauty itself.

The passage on Guys just cited reflects a second characteristic of Baudelaire's aesthetic, namely the importance of what he variously calls personality, temperament, and finally imagination. Art is not the representation of nature, but the artist's interpretation of it, the image of nature in his mind. Baudelaire had expressed this notion from the very beginning of his critical career, in connection with Romanticism. In the 1846 *Salon*, he had defined a beautiful painting as "la nature réfléchie par un artiste" (877)[33] and had said of Delacroix:

> Delacroix part donc de ce principe, qu'un tableau doit avant tout reproduire la pensée intime de l'artiste, qui domine le modèle comme le créateur la création. (891)[34]

Of Guys, he wrote in 1859:

> M. G. traduit fidèlement ses propres impressions . . . et l'imagination du spectateur . . . voit avec netteté l'impression produite par les choses sur [son] esprit. Le spectateur est ici le traducteur d'une traduction toujours claire et enivrante. (1166)[35]

In light of late-nineteenth-century art, Baudelaire's use of the word "impression" is striking. He used the term frequently in his art criticism as an indication of the artist's imaginative rendering of his subject. But even more important, it seems to me, is his notion of artistic creation as a kind of translation. He states this clearly in the 1846 *Salon* where, while stressing the need for rendering one's personal impression, he insists on the importance of technique in this activity: "l'effet produit sur l'âme du spectateur est analogue aux moyens de l'artiste" (891).[36]

Baudelaire attributes to modern art an emphasis on the subjective, that is, the artist's own vision of the exterior world, according to his moral, psychological, even physiological constitution (i.e., his temperament), which is translated, rendered into an intelligible utterance, by the conventional language of technique. As we shall see, this same argument will be made by the theorists of Impressionism to establish its objectivity, to reconcile the obvious subjectivity of the impression with the communicability and intelligibility associated with great art.

Perceiving and rendering the heroism and poetry of modern life involves a third aesthetic characteristic, the communication of its pervasive and distinctive emotion, which Baudelaire identifies consistently as melancholy. In the early *Salons,* he associates this mood with Delacroix and feels that it makes him a distinctly modern painter:

> Il me reste . . . à noter une dernière qualité chez Delacroix, la plus remarquable de toutes, et qui fait de lui le vrai peintre

Michele Hannoosh

du dix-neuvième siècle: c'est cette mélancolie singulière et opiniâtre qui s'exhale de toutes ses oeuvres. . . . (898)[37]

Since, as we have seen, Baudelaire links beauty with passing time, it follows that it must also include sorrow for what has been lost, and most of what Baudelaire finds supremely beautiful possesses this melancholy quality: autumn, setting suns, twilight, and that living image of beauty, the dandy: "comme l'astre qui décline, il est superbe, sans châleur et plein de mélancolie" (1180).[38] More than merely an aspect of beauty, melancholy is inseparable from it. As he wrote in his journal:

> Je ne prétends pas que la joie ne puisse s'associer avec la beauté, mais je dis qu'elle est un des ornements les plus vulgaires; tandis que la mélancolie en est pour ainsi dire l'illustre compagne. (1255)[39]

Significantly, in the 1859 *Salon* Baudelaire locates this emotional quality in the city itself, "le douloureux et glorieux décor de la civilisation" (1083).[40] Transitory, subjective, melancholic, Baudelaire's sense of modernity can be summed up in the qualities that he attributes, a little too generously perhaps, to the city drawings of Constantin Guys:

> La beauté passagère, fugace, de la vie présente. . . . Souvent bizarre, violent, excessif, mais toujours poétique, il a su concentrer dans ses dessins la saveur amère ou capiteuse du vin de la Vie. (1192)[41]

In its style, subject matter, and conception of beauty, modern art indeed renders the "bitter savour" of modern life, but for Baudelaire the vision is softened and always poetic. The melancholic mood that he attributes to modernity is lyrical and elegiac, as are so many of his city poems, and this tone will also inform much Impressionist painting.

II. L'imagination du spectateur . . . voit avec netteté l'impression produite par les choses sur l'esprit de M.G.
—Le Peintre de la vie moderne

Impressionist paintings of modern life do not all convey such melancholy. However, they do generally treat even the most sordid or miserable of urban subjects with a poetic brush, thus softening the mood in the way Baudelaire had described. Raffaëlli's *Absinthe Drinkers* (1879), for example, has none of the excessively depressing quality that we might expect of the subject. Rather, the two figures look almost thoughtful as they lean forward with their shoulders sloping gently, the muted tones of their black suits set against a luminous wall, the soft play of light on the stools and the ground. The picture conveys not misery but gentle warmth, with a touch of sadness. Even Raffaëlli's bleaker pictures, such as the illustration

Fig. 4. Edouard Manet, *The Bar at the Folies-Bergère,* oil on canvas, 1882. Courtauld Institute Galleries, London.

to Huysmans' *Croquis parisiens* (1880), were seen not as social commentary on the misery of city life, but rather as the expression of a new, specifically urban beauty.

Manet's *Bar at the Folies-Bergère* (1882, fig. 4) provides another, more complex example of a potentially vulgar setting that creates nevertheless a poetic image. The excitement and activity of a café-concert surround the central immobile figure of the barmaid, to whom the attention is irresistibly drawn by virtue of her incomparably sad gaze. Her contours are firmer and more well-defined than those of the blurred forms that surround her and that suggest the bustle of activity in the crowded room. Her image in the mirror, however, is fuzzy, as at the waist and sleeve of the dress, and this softening relates her mirror image to the activity around her, thus identifying her social self. This makes the contrast with the full-face figure, her private side, all the more striking. By placing her melancholy gaze within a scene that is distinctly modern in both subject and style, Manet suggests the profound sadness to be found in the contrast between her "poetic," private reflections and her implied relation to the gentleman reflected in the mirror whom, with her conspicuous décolleté, she serves.

As the *Bar at the Folies-Bergère* suggests, Baudelaire's ideas for appropriate modern topics became favorite Impressionist motifs, for all the painters associated with this group depicted modern Parisian subjects. These include two main groups: first, views of Paris—the railroad, cafes, the opera, the theatres, the boulevards, industrial buildings, low life, and social outcasts; and second, scenes of elegant life, featuring in particular modern dress—dandies, courtesans, racetrack scenes, luncheon parties, and so on.

A more complicated issue, however, is that of style. Baudelaire meant his remarks on style to apply to Romantic painting, or more precisely to Delacroix, and thus I do not wish to suggest that they announced Impressionism in any historical sense. However, certain aspects of Baudelaire's theory became dominant elements of the Impressionist manner. As we have seen, he insisted above all on the importance of color over line for form and composition, and on the importance of a sense of movement. This included such techniques as establishing perspective through gradation of color, taking atmospheric conditions into account in the rendering of color, juxtaposing bright, contrasting tones, and rendering the effects of light to suggest movement. All these techniques were well-suited to the portrayal of modern life. Impressionism carried out Baudelaire's suggestions: making color responsible for composition, using a sketch-like brush stroke, contrasting bright tones, using dabs of paint, blurring forms and contours, and creating a sense of the instantaneous by cutoff and off-center figures, an oblique viewpoint, and crowd-

Fig. 5. Edouard Manet, *The Races at Longchamp*, oil on wood, 1872-75. National Gallery of Art, Washington.

ing of objects within the pictorial space. Manet's *Races at Longchamp* (1872–1875, fig. 5) features some of these techniques, for example. The image itself vibrates with the sketchlike brush stroke, the touches of blue and pink against the more dominant green, blue, and brown tones, and the effect of movement and light. There is no bold linear definition, the horses being the most striking example of this. The spectators are merely dabs of paint in a general blur, sending our attention more properly to the central action of the picture, the race. A sense of immediacy is rendered by the head-on viewpoint and the conspicuously short foreground.

The *Bar at the Folies-Bergère* employs similar devices for a subject less obviously concerned with movement: the confusion of forms in the crowd, the unfocused reflections in the mirror, the fleeting feet of the trapeze artist, all create a sense of movement, activity, and instantaneity. As I have remarked previously, however, the central figure is in focus, as are some of the objects on the bar—the oranges, the flowers, the bottles. In addition to the main figure, certain things do stand out amid the confusion, and our eye is drawn to them, as they in this way formally anchor the picture: for example, the two gaslights that punctuate the background,

Michele Hannoosh

a couple of figures in the crowd, and even the looming, overly-large head of the customer.

Finally, Impressionist aesthetics involve two principal issues, and both of these relate closely to Baudelaire's views on the modern. In fact, his theory even suggests a way out of what many believed to be the Impressionist dead end, that is, the question of subjectivity. The aesthetic of Impressionism held that beauty was located in the momentary, the transitory, the ephemeral, and the whole concept of the impression derives from this idea. It is the controlling theme of the movement, and all its stylistic innovation and thematic concerns reflect it. As we have seen, this was also a keystone of Baudelairean aesthetics as he elaborated them in his art criticism and related them to modern life. The second distinctive feature of Impressionism is its emphasis on subjectivity and temperament, also included in the concept of the impression. As the critic Castagnary stated explicitly after the first Impressionist exhibit in 1874, "they are impressionists in the sense that they render not the landscape but the sensation produced by it," reminding us of Baudelaire's similarly formulated remarks on the modern painter.[42] This posed, however, a basic problem: if the Impressionist calls attention to the originality of his sensation, to his personal vision of the exterior world, how can his painting embody objective truth, that is to say, how could it be understood by others? Furthermore, by what standards could such an image be judged, if only fidelity to one's own subjective impression counted?

Baudelaire's views suggest a solution to these questions and provide a basis upon which to justify the subjectivity of Impressionism, indeed to affirm its objectivity and its universality. He maintained that a painting is the artist's impression of nature translated by a language of technique, a language that is a convention and thus intelligible to everyone. The Impressionists, too, conceived of the image as a subjective impression rendered intelligible by technique, but they were unwilling to accept the state of the received language, which they felt to have lost its expressive power. In fact, they could not accept such a convention, because to do so would be to compromise or sacrifice their commitment to a personal vision by associating them immediately with an established manner or school. Instead, they reformed the language and revised the conventional procedures of technique, to suit the exigencies of the impression.

This new language, however unusual it may have seemed to some, was nevertheless considered to be easily accessible to all for two reasons: first, it was thought to be faithful to the laws of vision—the eye perceives light vibrations, not theoretical perspective and line drawing; secondly, it was thought to be sufficiently faithful to the appearance of nature, which everyone would understand if freed from the falsifying constraints of painterly convention and the prejudice of centuries of art. This qualification assured the status of the painting as the representation of an objective truth, intelligible and able to be evaluated, that nonetheless embodied the subjective, individual truth of the artist's vision.[43]

Although Baudelaire died long before the Impressionist controversy arose, an examination of his views of the modern in art is instructive for the history and theory of that movement. His notion of the modern is, in some ways, a period one and contradicts some of the things that we associate with modernism. But his concept of the modern, in terms of the three areas that we have investigated—a subject matter drawn from modern, especially urban life; a technique founded primarily on the use of color; and an aesthetic defined in terms of the fleeting and poetic qualities of a distinctly modern experience—bears directly upon the creations of Impressionism and upon the late-nineteenth century as a whole. Today we tend to view that period by way of the early developments of the twentieth century; the line from Delacroix to Baudelaire, and from Baudelaire to the Impressionists, may serve to qualify our views and to suggest to what degree the modern vision of the late nineteenth century extended, and of course revised, the traditions of its Romantic heritage.

NOTES

1. "Parisian life is rich in poetic and wondrous subjects." Charles Baudelaire, *Oeuvres Complètes,* ed. Y.G. Le Dantec and Claude Pichois

Michele Hannoosh

(Paris, 1961), p. 952. Subsequent references noted parenthetically. Translations from the French are my own.

2. "The profound and complicated charm of an aged capital grown old in the glories and tribulations of life."

3. "A vigorous taste for modern reality—which is already a good sign— and a lively, sensitive, bold and abundant imagination."

4. Theodore Reff has called Baudelaire one of the two formative influences on Manet's "Parisian sensibility," the other being the transformation of the city itself. See *Manet and Modern Paris* (Washington, 1982), pp. 13 and 23.

5. "The harmonious struggle of masses of color."

6. "Form and color are one thing."

7. "*Dante and Virgil,* for example, always leaves a deep impression whose intensity increases with distance." On this subject Baudelaire also remarks: "La bonne manière de savoir si un tableau est mélodieux est de le regarder d'assez loin pour n'en comprendre ni le sujet ni les lignes. S'il est mélodieux, il a déjà un sens . . ." (883). ["The right way to tell if a painting is melodious is to look at it from far enough away that you cannot understand either the subject or the lines. If it is melodious, it already has a meaning . . ."] Baudelaire had just defined melody as "l'unité dans la couleur, ou la couleur générale . . . c'est un ensemble où tous les effets concourent à un effet général" (883). ["unity in color, or the general color . . . it is a whole where all effects contribute to a general effect."]

8. "Pure draughtsmen are philosophers and given to abstract reasoning. Colorists are epic poets."

9. The question of why Baudelaire chose Constantin Guys, a minor illustrator, for his painter of modern life has caused some perplexity. Attention to dates explains why he did not name Manet instead of Guys: although the essay did not appear until 1863, it was written late in 1859, and Baudelaire had only just encountered Manet and his work around that time. And at the time, Manet was still painting in his Spanish manner; he had not yet begun to represent scenes of modern life. The painter whom Baudelaire considered the true modern painter was Delacroix; but because Delacroix avoided specifically modern subjects, he did not fit the theme of Baudelaire's essay.

10. "To the wind that will blow tomorrow, no one is lending an ear; and yet the heroism *of modern life* surrounds us and presses upon us. . . . The painter, the true painter, will be he who knows how to tear from contemporary life its epic side and make us see and understand, with

color or line, how great and poetic we are in our neckties and our polished boots."

11. "The outer husk of the modern hero."

12. "Its beauty and its native charm."

13. "Is it not the necessary dress of our suffering epoch, which bears even on its thin black shoulders the symbol of perpetual mourning? Note that the black suit and the frock coat have not only their political beauty, which is the expression of universal equality, but also their poetic beauty, which is the expression of the public soul;—an immense parade of undertakers, undertakers in love, bourgeois undertakers. We all celebrate some funeral."

14. "Parisian life is rich in poetic and wondrous subjects. The marvelous surrounds and overwhelms us like the atmosphere; but we do not see it."

15. "Particular beauty, inherent to new emotions."

16. "The supreme incarnation of the idea of the beautiful transported into material life." "Notes nouvelles sur Edgar Poe," in Poe, *Histoires,* trans. Baudelaire, ed. Y.G. Le Dantec (Paris, 1932), p. 704.

17. "The last burst of heroism in a declining age."

18. "The high spirituality of dress."

19. "An effort toward beauty, some kind of approximation of an ideal, the desire for which titillates the dissatisfied human mind."

20. "Thousands of floating existences that move in the underworld of a big city—criminals and kept women."

21. "A genre that I would call the landscape of big cities, that is, that collection of grandeurs and beauties that result from a powerful agglomeration of men and monuments, the profound and complicated charm of an aged capital grown old in the glories and tribulations of life."

22. "The majesty of piled-up stone, the spires pointing to heaven, the obelisks of industry spewing forth against the firmament their packets of smoke, the prodigious scaffolding of monuments under repair, applying against the solid body of the architecture their open-work architecture of such paradoxical beauty, the tumultuous sky, charged with anger and rancor, the depth of perspective increased by the thought of all the dramas that are contained therein, none of the complex elements of which the mournful and glorious decor of civilization is composed was forgotten."

Michele Hannoosh

23. F. Leakey traces such a conception to Balzac, who entitles one of the chapters of *Splendeurs et misères des courtisanes* as "Un Paysage parisien." See F. Leakey, *Baudelaire and Nature* (Manchester, England, 1969), p. 163. Cf. also Baudelaire's poem of 1857, "Paysage parisien," later re-entitled simply "Paysage" (1861). He uses the phrase in two other essays of the period, *Le Peintre de la vie moderne* and *Peintres et aquafortistes*.

24. "For Eugene Delacroix, nature is a vast dictionary."

25. " 'Nature is only a dictionary', he used to say frequently. In order to understand completely the extent of the meaning implied in this sentence, it is necessary to consider the numerous ordinary uses of the dictionary. We look in it for the meaning of words, the origin of words, the etymology of words; finally we take from it all the elements that make up a sentence and a narrative; but no one ever considered the dictionary as a composition in the poetic sense of the word. Painters who obey the imagination look in their dictionary for the elements that agree with their conception; then, by adjusting them with a certain art, they give them an entirely new physiognomy. Those who do not have any imagination copy the dictionary."

26. In his *Salon* of 1844, Théophile Gautier had also used this phrase: "la nature n'est que le dictionnaire ou il cherche les mots dont il n'est pas sûr." Baudelaire had read Gautier's *Salon*, as he alludes to it in his own *Salon* of the following year (817). On the relation of Gautier's ideas to Baudelaire's on this question, see D. Kelley, *Baudelaire: Salon de 1846* (Oxford, 1975), p. 93. Delacroix seems to have used the phrase in print only once, in a note on realism. See M. Gilman, *Baudelaire the Critic* (New York, 1943), p. 38.

27. "Pleasures of chaos and immensity."

28. "Spiritual intoxication of big cities."

29. "All types of beauty contain, like all possible phenomena, an element of the eternal and an element of the transitory,—of the absolute and of the particular. Absolute, eternal beauty does not exist, or rather it is only an abstraction skimmed from the general surface of diverse beauties. The particular element of each type of beauty comes from the emotions, and as we have our particular emotions, we have our own beauty."

30. "It is a question . . . of extricating from fashion what it can contain of the poetic in the historical, of drawing the eternal from the transitory."

31. "This transitory, fugitive element, whose metamorphoses are so frequent, you do not have the right to scorn it, you fall necessarily into

the void of an abstract, undefinable beauty, like that of the only woman before the first sin."

32. "Woe to him who studies the ancients for anything other than pure art, logic, the general method! For plunging too deeply into it, he loses his memory of the present; he abdicates the value and the privileges furnished by circumstance; for nearly all our originality comes from the mark that the times imprint on our sensations."

33. "Nature reflected through an artist."

34. "Delacroix starts from this principle, that a painting must above all reproduce the private thought of the artist, which dominates the model, as the creator dominates his creation."

35. "M. G. translates faithfully his own impressions . . . and the imagination of the viewer . . . sees clearly the impression produced by things on his mind. The viewer is here the translator of a translation always clear and intoxicating."

36. "The effect produced on the soul of the viewer is analogous to the means of the artist."

37. "It remains for me to note one last quality in Delacroix, the most remarkable of all and the one that makes him the true painter of the nineteenth century: it is this singular, obstinate melancholy that is given out by all his works. . . ."

38. "Like the sun which sinks lower on the horizon, [dandysm] is superb, without warmth, and full of melancholy."

39. "I do not maintain that joy cannot go along with beauty, but I say that it is one of beauty's most vulgar ornaments; whereas melancholy is, so to speak, beauty's illustrious companion."

40. "The mournful and glorious decor of civilization."

41. "The passing, fleeting beauty of contemporary life. . . . Often bizarre, violent, excessive, but always poetic, he has been able to concentrate in his drawings the bitter or heady savour of the wine of Life."

42. Quoted in R. Shiff, "The End of Impressionism. A Study in Theories of Artistic Expression," *Art Quarterly*, Autumn 1978, New Series I, 4, p. 338.

43. Jules Laforgue, one of the early theorists of Impressionism, explained it in these terms. R. Shiff has discussed various other theories of the movement and related them to positivist psychology. See n. 42.

Michele Hannoosh

Culture and Architecture: Some Aesthetic Tensions in the Shaping of Modern New York City

Thomas Bender and William R. Taylor

> It's possible a little dose of history
> May help us in unravelling this mystery.
> —W. H. Auden

In May 1981, the New York State Urban Development Corporation invited proposals for the Forty-second Street Development Project. This request for proposals was accompanied by an impressive two-volume compendium of detailed design guidelines, prepared by the architecture and planning firm of Cooper, Eckstut Associates. The publication of the guidelines for Forty-second Street, moreover, followed by only a few months the selection of Cesar Pelli's proposal for the development of Battery Park City, a proposal based upon another equally ambitious set of design guidelines by the same firm.

What is most striking about these guidelines, at least to an historian, is their evocation of the city's past. There is an assumption that there is an older New York that belongs to common memory, like panels in some imaginary mural. Perhaps even more striking are the tacit assumptions contained

This is a shortened version of an essay that was written for *Controspazio*. It appears here as revised by Thomas Bender.

in these guidelines about how the city "worked" at particular moments in the past and the attendant desire, at this late date, to recapture some of the operational magic of its shapes, vistas, and some of the dramaturgy of its principal thoroughfares and the public places where these thoroughfares converged.

The past inferred in these guidelines might be styled 'Early Modern' New York, a city that was in the throes of dramatic changes, absorbing thousands of immigrants, becoming the administrative center for American corporate capitalism and the center of American intellectual and cultural life. Perhaps most important of all, it was the city of progressive urban reform, which involved as one of its principal aims the definition, in the political and architectural realms, of modern public life and culture.

Between the 1890s and 1930, New York acquired its famous skyline, as well as the monumental classical structures that continue to define its public spaces. It is a period when an indigenous New York urban aesthetic took form.

The authors of the guidelines sense this past but they are unable to articulate it. In part the cause for this is simple to understand; they are operating at the level of fundamental cultural premises that are, by definition, assumed and not stated. But one of the tasks of history, of intellectual history in particular, as Arthur O. Lovejoy pointed out many years ago, is to penetrate and elucidate the unstated premises of a culture in a way that makes reflection on them possible.[2]

The task assumed by Cooper, Eckstut Associates in the case of Forty-second Street is to give architectural expression to the street's importance; they want to monumentalize a street as a public space. They almost instinctively draw upon a suppressed history of New York when they propose that a horizontal rather than vertical emphasis can monumentalize and give civic significance to urban space. They seem to recognize that in the history of urban form in New York horizontal monumentalism implies civic or public purposes, while the tower represents the power of corporate capitalism. In their guidelines they propose to emphasize the civic or public character of Forty-second Street by keeping the "5-story building wall" uniform in order to produce a "low-rise corridor." Tow-

Thomas Bender and William R. Taylor

ers are to be kept well back from the street wall. In doing this they make a strong statement for public values, and they appeal to the city's history as authority. Yet this history has never been written or raised to a level of critical discussion. This paper represents a first attempt at such a written history, and it seeks to locate in particular the cultural sources of this distinctive aesthetic history.

Probably no modern city—and certainly none with its acknowledged importance—has been dealt with as harshly and as sparingly by architectural historians as New York. Ironically, New York, the first modern city in the world, has received only scant and damning mention in the historical works that have canonized modern architecture and planning. Only the city's parks and parkways receive ritual praise. It has otherwise been regarded as a city dominated by its monotonous, mindless grid, its neoclassical or renaissance facades, and its devotion to mercantile values and Beaux-Arts aesthetics. Nowhere does one find discussion of the interesting tug-of-war that took place between private and civic values, between vertical and horizontal structure, and, in planning, between laissez-faire values and deliberate and detailed efforts to give shape and unity to the city's heterogenous and often conflicting functions.

With an important exception—LeCorbusier—the giants among the moderns have been uniformly abusive of New York's architecture and planning achievements. Louis Sullivan, for example, characterized Lower Manhattan as "a plague spot of American architecture."[3] In no one modernist work is the combined condemnation and neglect of New York's place in the history of urban design more clearly registered than in Sigfried Giedion's now classic *Space, Time and Architecture: The Growth of a New Tradition* (1941 et seq.). Giedion unfolded what has now become the authoritative cultural history of modern architecture and planning in its relation to the realities of its time and to modernism in the other arts.

In Giedion's story, late-nineteenth-century Chicago fared very well, since it was there that architectural expression most closely matched structural changes. That city, accordingly, produced more than its share of modernist forerunners. New

York, for Giedion, represented neoclassical architectural and planning schemes, sometimes referred to broadly as Beaux Arts or eclectic, which he scorned as being in the "troubadour spirit, pitting song against the din of modern industry." New York developments were perceived as detours, even perversions, of the logic of modernist architectural progress. He made the dual charge that the Beaux Arts eclectic neoclassicism was not responsive either to technology or to function. In a similar way he dismissed those who engaged in city planning from a neoclassical perspective: "the urbanist like the popular painter, lost himself in the composition of idylls."[4]

These charges must now be examined skeptically and critically. More than that, it seems appropriate to make a counterclaim. Such a claim would go something like this: Buried within the Beaux Arts education and locked into the work of Americans trained in Paris was a preoccupation with "ensemble," with the pattern of construction perceived collectively. This particular concern with ensemble in turn resonated with certain civic attitudes toward the city that have now all but disappeared. In New York, where in the 1890s one finds the greatest concentration of Beaux Arts trained architects in America and where one finds them developing an evident self-consciousness, this orientation was incubated awaiting the opportunity of the ebullient building spirit at the turn of the century.[5]

A certain preoccupation with what we would call planning was implicit in the way Beaux Arts architectural students were trained to conceive of the buildings they designed. The full implications of this aspect of architectural education have never been adequately appreciated. The Beaux Arts training may not have insisted upon specific sites for buildings, but it did stress siting in general just as it stressed street level perspectives. To some students, the next step was easy to take. And several of the best students at the Ecole assumed an urbanistic perspective: Henri Proust, Ernest Hebrard, and, most widely known and the only one acknowledged by Giedion, Tony Garnier.[6] This "radical" side of the Beaux Arts tradition was available as well to "provincials" who traveled to Paris, and it is clear that Americans trained in Paris were very receptive to it. The American version appears to have had its most pronounced expression in the architecture and urban design of New York, although Daniel Burnham may well have given it its most concise expression.[7]

The Chicago World's Fair of 1893, identified so often with Burnham and the New York architects, is the crucial event in the historiography of modernism in America. How one interprets that event, located in the American midwest, largely determines, ironically, one's capacity for understanding the urbanistic heritage of New York. The modernist interpretation, much simplified to be sure, is something like the following. In Chicago, the orthodox story goes, a commercial ethic and new technology had produced in the decades after the fire a steel-frame architecture of tall commercial buildings that exemplified what later became the dictum of modernism: form follows function. When Daniel H. Burnham, who with his partner John Wellborn Root had helped pioneer this new architecture, invited a group of eastern, particularly New York architects, to Chicago to design the most important buildings for the World's Fair, the logic of architectural history was perverted. In contrast to the modern architecture being born downtown in Chicago, the neoclassical White City they built in Jackson Park was simply *retardaire*. Louis Sullivan's lament echoes through the history books: The Fair unleashed a "virus" that produced "an outbreak of the Classic and Renaissance in the East . . . The damage wrought to this country by the World's Fair will last a half century . . ."[8] According to Giedion:

> At the very moment when the Chicago school gained a mastery of the new means which it had created, its further development and influence was abruptly choked off. The event which directly effected this change was the Chicago World's Fair of 1893 (the World's Columbian Exposition), but influences working in this direction had set in long before in another section of the country. American architecture came under many different influences during the nineteenth century, but none was so strong or came at such a critical moment as the rise of power of the mercantile classicism developed in the East.

Giedion also provided a truncated historical motivation for

this anomalous turn of events.

> Public, artists, and literary people believed themselves to be witnessing a splendid rebirth of the great traditions of past ages. The immense appeal of this re-created past in "the White City" can only be laid to a quite unnecessary national inferiority complex . . . Only Louis Sullivan had sufficient inner strength to hold fast in the midst of a general surrender.

New York, as the home of "mercantile classicism," had a sinister role to play.

> Mercantile classicism had been developing and gaining strength in New York since the eighties, but it won its country-wide ascendancy at the World's Columbian Exhibition of 1893. The spirit behind it had now come to possess authority for American architecture as a whole. The Fair should, indeed, have stood in New York; it so thoroughly represented the influence of that city.[9]

Yes, there is a sense in which the Fair belonged to New York. But it is important to understand what Burnham and his New York associates were up to and how their achievement was received and interpreted. The Beaux Arts architects of New York brought to Chicago their preoccupations with a unified neoclassical city, and at the Fair, under the leadership of Daniel Burnham, the Superintendent of Construction, accomplished something that was broadly urbanistic, rather than narrowly architectural. Writing at the time, Montgomery Schuyler, the best architectural critic in America, observed that "the success is first of all a success of unity, a triumph of ensemble. The whole is better than all its parts." This could not be said of any American city at the time, though some hoped it might be. Schuyler went on to point out that this unity derived from two decisions: first, the choice of a neoclassical architectural motif, and second, the regulation of cornice heights, which produced a "visually continuous skyline all around the Court of Honor." It was this horizontal visual unity that gave the Fair its public impact, not the character or architectural expression of individual buildings. Among classicists, at least, this lesson was remembered. In a major article published in *Architectural Record* (1916) under

Thomas Bender and William R. Taylor

the title "Twenty-five Years of American Architecture," A.D.F. Hamlin acknowledged the "revolutionary" impact of steel framing developed in central Chicago, but he also insisted on the importance of the Fair. It represented, he argued, the first example of American design since Thomas Jefferson's plan for the University of Virginia in which a "monumental group of buildings [was] planned as an ensemble." It was, he continued, "an object lesson in the possibilities of group-planning, of monumental scale, of public decorative splendor and harmony. . . ."[10]

In retrospect, it seems clear that the modernist preoccupation with individual buildings, with overturning the architectural style of surrounding structures, and with historically singling out the new and experimental architectural expression of any age, overlooks the aesthetic lesson that can be learned from the progressivist side of the Beaux Arts tradition. This side of Beaux Arts classicism found its fullest realization not in Paris, but in America, in projects deeply influenced by New York architects. The most important of these projects were the Fair and the plans for Washington (1901) and Chicago (1909). It is probably accurate, moreover, to say that it was Charles McKim, upon whom Burnham most relied at Chicago and who took the lead in the collaboration with Frederick Law Olmsted, Jr., and Burnham on the Plan for Washington (1901) who brought this Beaux Arts ideal, via New York, to Burnham and Chicago where it was clarified and purified before returning to New York.[11]

This progressive neoclassicism sought to monumentalize and unify the late-nineteenth-century city. It moved from the architecture of the buildings to the urbanism of comprehensive planning. It stressed the street perspective, the uniform cornice, the nineteenth-century tradition of the five story street wall, and it was a functionalist expression of new technologies of urban transportation. Giedion and other modernist historians were able to dismiss the whole enterprise because—despite their ideology of organicism and functionalism—they focused their attention, ironically, on stylistic detail, on surface. The neoclassicists "decorated" buildings; form did not express function, nor did it reveal the building technology. That was enough, apparently, to justify dismissing Burnham and the New York architects. What Giedion, preoccupied with style, did not see was the important urbanistic achievement of the Fair's neoclassicism. Such devaluation of the urbanistic dimension is hard to justify in terms of urban history, for surely the crisis of the industrial city was one of ensemble, not one of style. Most revealing of all, perhaps, is the way in which differences in style made Giedion overlook the remarkable similarities between the *Cité industrielle* of Tony Garnier, the rebel *within* the Ecole and a hero in Giedion's story, and Burnham's *Chicago Plan*.

Garnier's plan for an "industrial" city, first developed between 1901 and 1904, though published a decade or so later, is architecturally modern in a way that Burnham's contemporaneous Chicago Plan is not. (Garnier, for example, uses reinforced concrete and emphasizes functional expression and the cleanness of materials.) Yet as understandings of urban form—and reform—the two are remarkably similar, even though one is the work of a European "socialist" and the other one of corporate capitalism's most favored architects.

The impulse behind all these plans was a desire to rationalize the perceived chaos in existing cities and to link these sprawling, amorphous conglomerations of population to the countryside and surrounding communities. It is difficult for us to realize how high a priority such an object could have had, nor the price those making such plans were willing to pay for their fulfillment—or even something approaching fulfillment. Transportation and movement was for such planners the fundamental reality of the city. They sought to have these lines of movement converge upon a city "center" at once functional and symbolic, a central axis in a wheel and spoke arrangement.

In no city were the issues faced by architects and planners as vexed, the aesthetic tensions as visible, as in New York where record population growth, commercial and industrial expansion, and novel metropolitan status were heaped upon a restricted island and an old premodern city within the compass of half a century. It is this battleground quality, and the unique character of the aesthetic treaties that resulted from it, that gives New York its architectural interest.

Thomas Bender and William R. Taylor

New York has the reputation of being a vertical city, and indeed the tall buildings crowding the battery have long been a spectacular symbol of its modernism. Yet, if we grant modernist legitimacy to certain horizontal impulses and locate New York's verticality in a dialectical relationship to that horizontalism, one finds a far richer heritage of architectural invention than a preoccupation with unrestrained thrust for height suggests.

When Henry James returned to the United States in 1904, he was displeased by the sight of the skyscrapers that had risen over the five-story city he had left twenty-five years before. As was sometimes his wont, James suggested that the thinness of American culture rendered it incapable of resisting such expressions of unrestrained commerce. New York grew skyscrapers, he seemed to say, because it lacked the density of culture required to guide growth away from purely economic and technical considerations, because it lacked in his words "the ancient graces." There was no higher aspiration capable of keeping the buildings down, so they "over-topped" his beloved Trinity Church.

Another view is possible; one can read New York's development quite differently. One can see technology, economics, and a particular cultural disposition in favor of horizontal urban order interacting to form a distinctive urban form in New York City. One cannot but be struck by evidence of a sustained resistance to a vertical architecture, indeed even to the perception of verticality when it first appeared.

A case in point is the Haughwout Building, a cast-iron building put up in 1857 and still standing on the corner of Broome Street and Broadway, one of New York's most remarkable buildings. It is the first building to have an Otis elevator, and it is a building that Ada Louise Huxtable credited with anticipating all the essential elements of the skyscraper, except that it is only five stories high. But this exception is important because it points toward the essentially horizontal perception of urban form in the nineteenth century. Two illustrations of the Haughwout Building, one a wood engraving made when the building was new, the other a photograph taken when the building was nearly a century old, provide some fascinating evidence (figs. 1, 2). Today, we who have accepted the aesthetic of a vertical city, apparently view the buildings differently from the New Yorkers who first confronted it. The engraving makes the building look

Fig. 1. Haughwout Building (1859), Courtesy of Otis Elevator Building.

flatter, less high, wider than in the photograph. Note also that the engraver faces the building head-on at street level, while the photographer, used to vertical perspectives, chooses a location well above street level to snap his photo. Since New Yorkers were unused to tall buildings in the 1850s, one would have thought that contemporaries would have been struck by the height of a building like the Haughwout. Indeed, might not one expect the engraving to exaggerate its height, thus leaving the photograph with the task of cutting it down to its proper scale? Apparently, the engraver was prepared to perceive the city in terms of horizontal rather than vertical lines. That his perception of this building was part of a collective horizontal perception of the city is suggested by a contemporaneous series of drawings on New York architecture (by many hands) run in *Putnam's Magazine* in 1853. The anonymous author of this series, probably Clarence Cook, verbalized the mid-nineteenth-century urban bias toward horizontalism in discussing A. T. Stewart's famous depart-

Thomas Bender and William R. Taylor

Fig. 2. Haughwout Building (1952), Courtesy of Otis Elevator Building.

ment store (1846), the Italianate structure still standing at Broadway and Chambers Street. While he admired the building, he worried that it was too tall, or that it gave the impression of being too tall. "This might have been remedied," he reflected, "by making the horizontal lines of the building more prominent than the perpendicular."[12]

This perceptual or, if you will, cultural resistance to verticality or height provides a crucial context for some comments of Montgomery Schuyler concerning the slow development of the skyscraper. Writing in 1909, on "The Evolution of the Skyscraper," Schuyler insists that technology and economic incentive were there before tall buildings were materialized. This discussion reveals how the technology Huxtable finds in the Haughwout building was fitted into a frame of cultural or architectural perception that stressed not new possibilities of verticality but rather a continuation of the traditional five-story city. The elevator, Schuyler remarks, did not suggest an unlimited number of floors. Rather its "humble office" was simply "to equalize the desirableness of rooms on the fifth floor with that or rooms on the second." Such was the case for nearly a decade. "Such a creature of habit is man . . . that, throughout that decade, it did not occur to anybody that the new appliance might enable the construction of taller buildings." The first building to go beyond five stories with the assistance of the elevator was the Equitable Building (1870). It went to seven. "The addition of two stories now seems timid enough; then doubtless it seemed audaciously venturesome." By the mid-1870s, the Tribune and Western Union Buildings not only went higher, but they expressed their capacity to rise above the traditional city in the architectural treatment, particularly in Richard Morris Hunt's Tribune Building with its tower. Yet the evolution of the skyscraper in New York remained slow. Schuyler can find no technical reason for the delay in moving beyond the load-bearing wall to steel frame construction several years before it occurred. "Necessity," he remarks, "seems to have been singularly protracted."[13]

The resistance of New Yorkers to tall buildings is interesting in itself, one that has dimensions other than aesthetic; but certain architectural ideas, ones that stressed horizontal, massive, and monumental forms seem to have preoccupied New Yorkers, blunting their capacity to perceive monumentality in vertical terms. It was assumed that an appropriate civic presence, monumentalism, could be best achieved in the context of traditional horizontal lines.

This nineteenth-century configuration of urban monumentalism reached its fullest development with Pennsylvania Station (1906-1913). While retaining the ideal of the nineteenth-century street wall, this massive and magnificent railroad station by McKim, Mead, and White extended itself to cover two entire blocks. In fact, it faces another civic structure,

Thomas Bender and William R. Taylor

the new post office, that monumentalizes an adjoining grid. Instead of giving the station monumental status by placing it at the termination of a diagonal avenue, as was being done in late-nineteenth-century Paris, McKim, Mead, and White achieved their purpose by making the block itself a monument.

The nearly contemporaneous Grand Central Terminal (1903-1913) continues the monumentalization of New York civic space along horizontal lines, but it does not so much monumentalize a block in the grid as create a megablock that in certain (but not in other) ways anticipates Rockefeller Center. It moves beyond the block on a massive scale, but rather hesistantly. By placing the station astride Park Avenue, moreover, the planners created a dramatic vista on both sides of the station that acted to monumentalize the avenue and underscore the North-South movement of traffic through the city. The circumferential drive preserves the Park Avenue street flow, while at the same time allowing Grand Central Terminal to monumentalize a perspective. While Forty-third Street is blocked, the municipal authorities insisted that the fenestration on the east and west walls be aligned so that, if necessary, a bridge could carry Forty-third Street traffic through the main concourse. Quite a similar effect was obtained in McKim, Mead, and White's contemporary Municipal Building, which stood in 1911 astride an arch that permitted a clear east-west vista along Chambers Street, once again underscoring the grid, even at the cost of certain neoclassical oddity. The structure of Grand Central itself does not attempt to maintain the traditional five-story wall, but it saves the general principle, simply raising the height and maintaining a uniform cornice along Park Avenue. In this quarter of Manhattan, the New York Central and its landholding company created in microcosm fulfillment of the sort of urbanism one finds in the proposals of Garnier and Burnham. Both of them focus on the hubs of rail and street traffic as the site to monumentalize. Modern technology makes it possible for the city to accommodate the railroad underground while monumentalizing a unified horizontal perspective above ground.

The lineage just traced from the Haughwout Store to Grand Central outlines the expansion of the horizontal vision of New York before World War I in its most pristine form. Other examples of neoclassical civic architecture could be cited and discussed. Richard Morris Hunt's Lenox Library (1870-75), which Schuyler in 1895 rated as unrivaled when built for its achievement of "monumental dignity" and, of course, one must note Hunt's East Wing of the Metropolitan Museum of Art. While the massive New York Public Library (1911) is also an obvious example of horizontal monumentalism, realized with a sense of commodiousness and liberality, a much smaller building, one called by Schuyler "a modern classic," emphasizes that it is not a mere matter of size that is at issue. The Knickerbocker Bank (1904), on Fifth Avenue at Thirty-fourth Street, by McKim, Mead, and White was only three stories high, but according to Schuyler its very restraint in the matter of height gives it strength. With its tetrastyle front, the building was, in Schuyler's words, "ample in scale for purposes of impressiveness. Since it holds its own against the huge mass of the many storied Astoria, it is not likely to be put out of countenance by any succeeding erection."[14] Finally, as further examples of horizontal monumentalism, we should note the neoclassical uptown campuses McKim, Mead, and White designed for New York University and Columbia University in the 1890s.

At Madison Square, however, we can trace a complicated pattern of development and of perception that bring us closer to the tensions between horizontal and vertical lines in the development of New York's distinctive urban aesthetic. When the Fifth Avenue Hotel opened on Madison Square in 1859, it boasted the first hotel passenger elevator in the city. Yet it was architecturally and urbanistically of a piece with the old Astor House (1836) downtown, the hotel it replaced as New York's most fashionable place to stop and be seen. It remained within the five- to six-story street wall tradition, and it presented itself to the street. Both hotels are on Broadway frontage facing a triangular park, but such siting is clearly more comfortable for the Astor House, located as it was on Lower Broadway, before Broadway came into tension with the grid

Thomas Bender and William R. Taylor

imposed on New York in 1811. With the Fifth Avenue Hotel we begin to notice some of the complexity involved in imposing horizontal order on the New York grid (fig. 3). Not only is the facade broken, but the multiple lines of movement

Fig. 3. Broadway and Fifth Avenue, Courtesy of Brown Bros.

produced by Broadway, Fifth Avenue, the Park, and the street car rails produce not only an aesthetic tension in photographs and engravings, but also personal problems of movement and orientation in the city. This tension is multiplied further when one's gaze widens to include the curvilinear pattern of the paths in Madison Square.

Part of the success that was achieved at Penn Station and Grand Central Terminal was the result of responding to developments in transportation technology (electrification) that allowed rail transportation—both subways and trains—to be placed underground where it would not disrupt the grid. The triumph of the street level grid over the underground technology in defining horizontal movement in New York is embodied in the names given the subway stations. The subway lines do not follow a grid pattern, but the system surfaces only at streets on the grid. In contrast to the Paris Metro, for example, which is "place" oriented (very few stations are named for streets, almost all for places, such as L'Opera,

L'Odeon), almost all Manhattan subway stops refer to streets. What could easily have been called the Madison Square station is called the Twenty-third Street station. This tension between surface and sub-surface legibility in New York underlaid the wide discussions and controversy over the introduction of a new subway map four years ago.

When the Fifth Avenue Hotel was opened, Madison Square was a major transportation node. The depots of the New York & Harlem and the New York, New Haven & Hartford railroads were located just off the northeast corner of the Square. In 1873, after the first Grand Central Terminal was opened at Forty-second Street, Barnum transformed the property into a concert garden. In 1879, it was named Madison Square Garden and ten years later the famous Madison Square Garden designed by Stanford White was constructed on the site (fig. 4). White's building is fundamentally horizontal, but it points to New York's distinctive skyscraper aesthetic. Reminiscent of the tower in Italian city states and following the New York lead of Richard Morris Hunt's Tribune Building (1873-75), White placed an expressive tower on top of a blockish building. Twenty years later, McKim, Mead, and White would do much the same thing, though with the scale vastly increased, with the Municipal Building (1911) that went up across from Hunt's earlier Tribune Building. These developments, in effect vertical towers designed to enhance buildings of horizontal monumentality, contain the germinal aesthetic of the New York skyscraper some twenty years later. The aesthetic rationale for the modern skyscraper, ironically, was the campanille fully as much as the steel frame. But we are moving too fast. Actual events moved much slower. Madison Square Garden was not perceived as a precursor of the skyscraper. It was an entertainment center built along horizontal lines as was traditionally appropriate for monumental public architecture.

Ten years later, south of the square, another building went up. The Fuller or Flatiron Building (1901), designed by the Chicago firm of Daniel Burnham, is recognized for its height and for its steel frame construction as one of the links in the evolution of the modern skyscraper. Yet we must ask how,

Thomas Bender and William R. Taylor

Fig. 4. Madison Square Garden, blt., 1899, Courtesy of the Museum of the City of New York.

in the context of the tradition of horizontal urban perception that we have traced, this architectural innovation was perceived. We gain insight into this problem by examining one of the most famous and compelling photographs made of this building, which was taken by Alfred Stieglitz in 1903 (fig. 5). It is one of the few photographs that Stieglitz talked about, and it is worth quoting him.

> In the early months of 1903 I stood spellbound, during a great snowstorm, before the Flat Iron Building. It had just been erected on Twenty-third Street at the junction of Fifth Avenue and Broadway.
>
> Watching the structure go up, I felt no desire to photograph

Fig. 5. Flatiron Building (1903), Alfred Stieglitz, Courtesy of the Metropolitan Museum of Art.

the different stages of its development. But with the trees of Madison Square covered with fresh snow, the Flat Iron impressed me as never before. It appeared to be moving toward me like the bow of a monster ocean steamer—a picture of a new America still in the making . . .

Recalling those early days, I remember my father coming upon me as I was photographing in the middle of Fifth Avenue. "Alfred," he said, "how can you be interested in that hideous building?" "Why Pa," I replied, "it is not hideous, but the new America. The Flat Iron is to the United States what the Parthenon was to Greece." My father looked horrified . . .

Later the Flat Iron appeared rather unattractive to me, after years of having seen even taller and more extraordinary sky-

Thomas Bender and William R. Taylor

scrapers—the Woolworth shooting into the sky, and then still others . . . I no longer considered it handsome, nor representative of the coming age, nor was I tempted to photograph it.[15]

There are many things about this passage that are of interest: Stieglitz's father's abhorrence in 1903 of a vertical aesthetic, Stieglitz's almost mystical association of urban structure with destiny, but the evocation of the ocean steamer is of particular relevance here. The image of the ship's prow suggests not vertical but horizontal conceptions of the development of the city and of American culture generally. One thinks of railroads crossing the continent, or of the streetcar lines crossing in front of the Flatiron more easily than one thinks of, say, the Empire State Building. Ships' prows were high, especially since in 1900 passengers and friends walked or rode right up to the bow of the ship at nearly the water line, but they moved horizontally. The cornice line of the Flatiron building, from this perspective, suggests that there is more to come, hence the plausibility of his speaking of the building as the leading edge of a progressive American culture. In 1903 the dynamism of American culture and urban development, at least for Stieglitz, was horizontal. Later, after a perceptual shift which we will soon describe, verticality became central to progressivism. And with many taller buildings to be seen, the Flatiron building could no longer be impressive. It was caught in a shift in urban aesthetics from horizontal to vertical. When it was the world's tallest building, Stieglitz and, we assume, others viewed it in terms of the horizontal lines it suggested. When they began to view buildings with a sensitivity to or preference for verticality, the Flatiron was no longer tall enough.

A clearer idea of the evolution of the New York skyscraper and of the perceptual shift we are discussing can be obtained still within the square by turning our attention to the Metropolitan Life Building and Tower designed by Napoleon LeBrun & Sons (business block, 1893; tower, 1909, fig. 6). The Metropolitan Life building accommodates the tower by placing it on top of a horizontal business block. This strategy echoes the campanille characteristic of early Renaissance Ital-

Fig. 6. Metropolitan Life Building (1909), *King's Views of New York, 1896–1915* (New York: Arno Press, 1974).

ian civic architecture, and it was not new in New York in 1909; we have already mentioned Hunt's Tribune Building and White's Madison Square Garden tower. Such a treatment of bulk—often with Italian or French Renaissance architectural detailing, was a New York tradition extending back to the era of the Haughwout Building. And its pervasiveness explains Le Corbusier's remark upon first seeing New York's skyscrapers in the 1930s:

> It is an odd thing that the modern skyscrapers are the weak ones. The Italian Renaissance skyscrapers are of excellent quality, in contradiction with what I imagined before seeing them. For, prior to 1925, Brunelleschi and Palladio were in control. . . .

Thomas Bender and William R. Taylor

In New York, then, I learned to appreciate the Italian Renaissance. It is so well done that you could believe it to be genuine. It even has a strange, new firmness which is not Italian but American.[16]

The monumental scale of the Metropolitan Life Building is impressive; it fills a whole block in the grid. It goes beyond the traditional five stories, yet the power of traditional perceptual catagories is strong. The architectural treatment divides the facade into six units, thus modulating its break from nineteenth-century urban scale. It is worth noting, moreover, that it is oriented more to the grid than to the park, and its primary public face is the horizontal business block facade on Twenty-third Street rather than as we might have expected, given our later aesthetic assumptions, the tower side facing the park.

If one looks at the two pictures of the Metropolitan Life Building shown here, both taken from Moses King's *Views of New York,* one from the 1909 edition and the other from the 1915 edition (fig. 7), it is possible to see an important perceptual shift within the city that points toward the eventual acceptance of the tower itself rather than as a campanille. The 1909 view from south of Madison Square emphasizes the business block and shows the tower to be behind it. The 1915 view, by contrast, is taken from north of the square, and the tower is in the foreground and dominates the picture. In the period of six years, monumentalism had come to be more identified with verticality. By 1961, when the tower was renovated, it was visually separated from the business block, suggesting two structures rather than one. By then, the tower could stand alone. When those renovations were undertaken, the idea of a free standing tower caused few aesthetic tensions, but before about 1930 the dominant urban aesthetic in New York could not accommodate such unabashed verticality.

In 1909 the Metropolitan Life Building and the Singer Tower that Ernest Flagg placed on top of a French Baroque business block represented the basic *form* of the New York skyscraper. They differed from the strong expression of uncompromising verticality that Louis Sullivan prescribed for the tall office building and which he achieved to a remarkable

Fig. 7.   Metropolitan Life Building (1915), *King's Views of New York, 1896–1915* (New York: Arno Press, 1974).

degree in his only New York building—the Condit Building (1898)—perhaps appropriately, in terms of our argument, hidden away on Bleecker Street on the "wrong" side of Broadway. What Sullivan prescribed in his famous essay, "The Tall Office Building Artistically Considered" (1896), was alien to New York skyscraper architecture. Sullivan wrote:

> What is the chief characteristic of the tall office building? . . . [A]t once we must answer, it is lofty. This loftiness is to the artist nature its thrilling aspect . . . It must be in turn the dominant chord in his expression of it, the true excitant of his imagination. It must be tall, every inch of it tall. The force and power of altitude must be in it, the glory and the pride of

Thomas Bender and William R. Taylor

exaltation must be in it. It must be every inch a proud and soaring thing, rising in sheer exultation that from bottom to top it is a unit without a single dissenting line . . .[17]

Cass Gilbert's Woolworth Building (1913, fig. 8), the building that Stieglitz mentions in describing his devaluation of

Fig. 8. Woolworth Building, blt., 1913, *King's Views of New York, 1896–1915* (New York: Arno Press, 1974).

the Flatiron Building, achieved a sense of soaring exultation that no earlier New York building had achieved. But he achieved this effect in the context of the New York campanille tradition rather than in the manner prescribed in Sullivan's essay or exemplified in his Condit Building.

From Broadway today the Woolworth Building appears to

be a tower. We do not see, unless we approach it from the rear, the familiar New York business block base that is prominent in pictures of it at the time it was completed. It is a massive version of the New York campanille. With a difference. Gilbert, for his "Cathedral of Commerce," as it was called during the opening ceremonies, used the Gothic rather than Renaissance motif. If you want to soar, Gothic soars toward the heavens. The height of the horizontal cornice, as well as the tower, surpassed anything previously built in New York, but Gilbert's concessions to the nineteenth-century city are striking. Although the business block is higher than ever before, the architectural detailing continues to associate it with the traditional five or six-story cornice line. There is an expanded base and cornice, and there are four intermediate horizontal divisions marked by architectural treatment. This decoration of the building may be read as a failure to achieve functional expression or it may be seen as an intentional and comforting echo of the nineteenth-century urban building tradition. For a narrowly architectural history, the former explanation is appropriate. But for any urbanistic understanding of what Gilbert was doing the latter explanation is compelling.

Until the mid-1920s photographs and paintings reveal resistance to verticality. The most common and striking perspective on New York's tall buildings from the 1890s through 1930 was the view of the skyline across the water. Yet such views, it must be noted, do not really take advantage of the possibilities of verticality. Instead they array the city's tall buildings along a horizontal axis. The city, in such views, is a mountain range; the ensemble is perceptually more important than the individual peaks.

It was not until the few years between about 1925 and 1931, particularly with the publication of the New York Regional Plan volume on *The Building of the City* in the latter year, that the skyscraper as tower got its full aesthetic justification and its first examples, with the Radiator Building (1925), the Chrysler Building (1930), and the Empire State Building (1931). During these years two extraordinary and visionary architects, Raymond Hood and Hugh Ferriss, along

Thomas Bender and William R. Taylor

with Thomas Adams, director of the Regional Plan project, rejected the skyline as mountain range in favor of the portrayal of distinct towering peaks (fig. 9).

Fig. 9. "Two Views of the New York Skyline," Regional Plan Association, *Building the City,* 1931.

Hood seems to have been the one with the initial vision that was picked up by the other two, but whatever the precise pattern of influence among the three, they articulated a new vision of the city. And the two architects, by getting their vision incorporated into the proposals of the well-connected and powerful Regional Plan Association, insured for them a significant hearing. Hood and Ferriss offered visions of New York as a city of widely spaced towers. Hood proposed to place towers at express tops of subways, thus using the underground transportation system rather than the street grid to define the horizontal space of the city. Ferriss, in his book *The Metropolis of Tomorrow* (1929) contrasted the coming skyscraper city with the present skyscraper city that had been built up over the past fifty years (fig. 10). Acknowledging the visionary thinking of Hood, he writes of the city represented in his drawings:

Fig. 10. *Imaginary Metropolis*, Hugh Ferriss, in *Architectural Visions: The Drawings of Hugh Ferriss* by Jean Ferriss Leich (New York: Whitney Library of Design, 1980).

Thomas Bender and William R. Taylor

. . . we are struck by certain peculiarities in the disposition of the towers now before us. In the first place, no two of them rise in close juxtaposition to each other . . . Also, there is a certain degree of regularity apparent in their disposal throughout; while they are not all precisely equidistant, and their relation does not suggest an absolutely rectangular checkerboard scheme, yet it is obvious that they have been located according to some citywide plan.

The bases of these 1,000-foot (or more) towers cover from four to eight city blocks. In between the towers, in the "wide districts . . . which make up the greater area of the city—the buildings are comparatively low. The average six stories . . .[18]

With Harvey Wiley Corbett, designer of One Fifth Avenue, the dialectic evaporates and one finds a complete—and amusing—assimilation of verticality and beauty. Writing in the *Yale Review* in 1928, Corbett explained that the vertical is always more attractive than the horizontal; it provides an effect of slenderness that is more pleasing. "We have vertical stripes on our clothes because we think they add to our appearance. And, conversely, how are ugly clothes—clothes that we do not want copied, the uniforms of convicts—how are such clothes designed? They have broad horizontal stripes. No one would willingly wear anything so hideous. In his buildings, too, man has liked lines that accentuate heights and carry the eye upward."

Verticality had been accommodated into a new urban aesthetic. And photography could celebrate it in a way that Stieglitz did not and could not in 1903. The new fascination with verticality is apparent in New York photography of the 1930s, in the cropping done by Berenice Abbott in *Exchange Place* or in the exploration of the vertical lines of the Empire State Building in *The Maypole* by Edward Steichen, or in the choreography and cinematography in the 1930s movie *Forty Second Street*.

Yet we must not exaggerate, even in the 1930s, how far New Yorkers moved from the neoclassical civic vision of Burnham at the turn of the century. The New York Regional Plan, which incorporated the ideas of Ferriss and Hood, was a direct off-spring of the Chicago Plan. The two individuals most responsible for the establishment of the plan in New York under the auspices of the Russell Sage Foundation, Charles Dyer Norton and Frederic Delano, had been actively involved earlier in the Chicago Commercial Club's sponsorship of the Chicago Plan. There are, it is true, more towers (Burnham and Garnier proposed one each in their plans, while the Regional Plan—and Ferriss and Hood—proposed many), but it is, like Burnham's, an attempt to express civic unity by producing a neoclassical urban form for the modern American city.

There is more to be said about the persistence of the horizontal civic tradition. If the Empire State Building is the premier example of the skyscraper as a block-filling tower, it is important to remember that its street wall is only six stories, as the authors of the Forty-second Street guidelines remember in specifying the relation of tower to street they desire. And recall that the public or civic extension of Rockefeller Center's Promenade is flanked by the low-rise French and British Pavillions that terminate in a six-story street wall. It was undoubtedly this historical low-rise horizontal tradition for civic architecture that Lewis Mumford was drawing upon when he complained in the forties of the unabashed verticality of the United Nations Secretariat building, comparing it unfavorably with the New York Public Library.[20] Finally, to mention a more recent example of New York civic architecture, the neoclassical horizontalism of Lincoln Center further underscores the persistent interest in horizontal monumentality. Indeed, the relation of Lincoln Center to the street, the gridiron, and the transportation center at the convergence of Broadway and Ninth Avenue recall all of the tensions over the horizontal cityscape that marked Madison Square at the turn of the century.

The distinction we make between civic horizontalism and corporate verticality was recognized, in a strikingly paradigmatic way, in the Regional Plan in 1931. In the course of a discussion of New York's architectural distinctiveness, the authors of the plan present two pages of pictures. The first portrays public buildings, the second business structures. All of the former are horizontal, while all of the latter are vertical.[21]

Thomas Bender and William R. Taylor

Business has appropriated the tower as a means of expressing corporate power. The feeble but not yet extinguished expression of civic life continues to find limited expression at the street level. Indeed, the particular pattern of civic "contribution"—or retribution—exacted by the City Planning Commission (in return for allowing businesses to make their symbols—and profits—of "private" power higher) derives from the New York tradition associating civic purpose with the five-story street wall, horizontalism, and street access. When, for example, Citicorp sought permission to exceed the "as of right" height for its tower on Lexington Avenue, a variety of civic demands might have been placed before them. But tradition (and, consequently, the zoning laws) restricted those options to civic amenities at the street level. So we got the "Market" and a street level church for St. Peters. The struggle for civic authority and public space in the city will not, one hopes, be fought in the streets, but it will be fought at the street level.

NOTES

1. Cooper, Eckstut Associates, *Forty-Second Street Development Project: Design Guidelines* (New York, 1981).

2. Arthur O. Lovejoy, *The Great Chain of Being* (Cambridge, 1936), chap. 1; idem, *Essays in the History of Ideas* (Baltimore, 1948), chap. 1.

3. Sullivan quoted in Sigfried Giedion, *Space, Time and Architecture: The Growth of a New Tradition,* 5th edition (Cambridge, 1965), p. 854.

4. Giedion, p. 780.

5. Montgomery Schuyler noticed the increased presence—both because of numbers and because of their growing self-confidence and aggressiveness—of Beaux Arts-oriented architects in New York in the 1890s. Montgomery Schuyler, *American Architecture,* ed. William H. Jordy and Ralph Coe, 2 vols. (Cambridge, 1961), I, 575-78.

   This is not the place to identify all Beaux Arts influences in New York, but it may be useful to say a bit about the leading architects, mostly born in the 1850s, who came of age professionally in New York in the 1890s. These architects were either trained directly at the Ecole des Beaux Arts or they studied in New York offices of Ecole graduates. The first American trained at the Ecole was Richard Morris Hunt (b. 1827), and his New York office provided training on the Ecole model for many men who later became leaders in the profession in New York, most notably George B. Post (b. 1837) and William Ware (b. 1832), the latter having decisively shaped the training programs of the architecture schools at MIT and, later in the 1880s and 1890s, Columbia. Charles McKim (b. 1847), who was trained at the Ecole, in turn trained one of New York's most important architects, Cass Gilbert (b. 1859), who had very little other study beyond his experience in the McKim, Mead, and White firm. McKim's later partner Stanford White (b. 1853) studied in the New York office of Beaux Arts-trained Henry Hobson Richardson (b. 1838). John Carrère (b. 1858) and Thomas Hastings (b. 1860), architects of the New York Public Library, were both trained at the Ecole, as was Ernest Flagg (b. 1857). Whitney Warren (b. 1864) who was primarily responsible for the architectural design work of Grand Central Terminal studied at the Ecole des Beaux Arts, returning to New York City in 1896, after an extended residence in Paris. Finally, Henry Hardenberg (b. 1847), architect of the Plaza Hotel and the Dakota, studied in New York with Beaux Arts-trained Detlef Lienau.

6. On the Ecole des Beaux Arts and urban planning, see the forthcoming work by Gwendolyn Wright, *At Home and Abroad: Colonialism and French Urban Planning, 1870-1930*, chap. 1.

7. While I was working on this paper—and developing this notion of the progressivist side of the Beaux Arts tradition—Domenico Cecchini shared a brief and helpful paper developing the notion of conservative and progressive sides of classicism ("The Meanings of Classicism and the Image of the City," 1981).

8. Louis Sullivan, *The Autobiography of an Idea* (1924; rpt. New York, 1956), pp. 324-25.

9. Giedion, pp. 393-95.

10. Schuyler, II, 559-60; *Architectural Record* (July, 1916), 3-4. It should be noted that Schuyler in the essay cited above also saw (and quite rightly) certain dangers in misreading the urbanistic lesson of the Fair, pointing out that it was unreal, that it was not fitted into the dense fabric of the city.

11. On Charles McKim's special influence at the Fair and at Washington, see John Reps, *Planning Monumental Washington* (Princeton, 1967), p. 93 (on the Fair) and *passim* for Washington.

12. "New York Daguerrotyped," *Putnam's Magazine*, I, (1853), 13.

13. Schuyler, II, 424-28.

14. Ibid., II, 595-96. Schuyler is cited frequently in part for convenience

sake, but also because he is a contemporary observer of the evolution of modern architecture generally appreciated by modernists.

15. Dorothy Norman, *Alfred Stieglitz: An American Seer* (New York, 1973), p. 45.

16. Le Corbusier, *When Cathedrals Were White* (New York, 1947), pp. 59-60.

17. Louis Sullivan, *Kindergarten Charts and Other Essays,* ed. Isabella Athey (New York, 1947), p. 206.

18. Hugh Ferriss, *The Metropolis of Tomorrow* (New York, 1929), p. 109.

19. Harvey Wiley Corbett, "New Heights in American Architecture," *Yale Review,* 17 (July 1928), pp. 692-93.

20. Lewis Mumford, *From the Ground Up* (New York, 1956), pp. 20-60.

21. They may be seen in New York Regional Plan, *Building the City* (New York, 1931), pp. 69-70.

Tokyo and the Borders of Modern Japanese Fiction

Paul Anderer

Readers may recall the scene in Tanizaki's *The Makioka Sisters* in which Sachiko, the one sister on whom everyone relies, eats too much steak and is stricken with jaundice. At the advice of the family doctor, she takes to her bed, drinks only clam broth, and patiently suffers the muggy weather that precedes the June rains. Her daughter, Etsuko, enters the sick room and we encounter the following passage:

> "What is that flower, Mother?" She pointed at the flower in the alcove.
> "A poppy."
> "I think you should take it away."
> "Why?"
> "Look at it. It sucks you up inside it."
> "I see what you mean." The child had a point. Sachiko herself had been feeling strangely oppressed by something in this sick room, and, without being able to say what it was, she could not help thinking that the cause was right before her eyes. Etsuko had put her finger on it. In the fields, the poppy was a pretty enough flower, but the single poppy in the alcove was somehow repulsive. You felt as though you were being sucked up inside it.[1]

It is a trivial passage, given the scope and complexity of this book, which traces a proud merchant family's decline and gradual displacement from the country toward city life. But for Tanizaki, as we know, the trivial is like a fetish and has a special significance: a poppy misplaced, a phone call unanswered, and we are reminded of what the narrator has said elsewhere about how "the merest trivialities determine a person's future."[2] In Sachiko's case, it is true, the poppy is removed, and deciding against lilies, against anything natural at all, she has her husband write a poem, a "fresh, clean poem" we are told, and this she hangs in the alcove:

A far off evening shower, on the Peak of Atago
Soon it will be roiling over Clear Cascade.[3]

This substitution, this rearrangement of spatial detail, trivial in itself, makes a difference. On the following day the jaundice is gone and Sachiko has recovered.

It would be convenient but incorrect to say that throughout this novel Tanizaki takes disorderly details—facial blemishes and fevers, a flood in Kobe and a typhoon in Tokyo, an unmarried woman past her prime and a young, rebellious woman—and rearranges them for a pleasing or beautiful effect. Improbable as it seems, a well-placed poem may cure Sachiko's jaundice, but no manner of artfulness can conceal the spots of the aging sister, Yukiko. *The Makioka Sisters* begins in an effort to arrange Yukiko's marriage, and proceeds from there to reveal a self-conscious concern to arrange everything, including the spatial details of an interior and an exterior landscape, until we regard the darkly glowing wooden floors of the old Ashiya home as the very medium through which these figures are apprehended along their dim and mostly hesitant passage. In such a novel Yukiko's marriage remains problematic. The book ends, we notice, before her marriage is consummated. Symbol of the old, she does not seem destined for a new life. On the train en route to the ceremony, she has diarrhea. As a further ominous sign, she is traveling toward Tokyo, where in this and in so many other modern Japanese novels, as I will have occasion to point out, nothing ever seems happily arranged or consummated.

It is a measure of Tanizaki's integrity as a writer that he acknowledges and dramatically portrays situations in life that do not yield to arrangement. The fictional lives of the sisters often do not or cannot be made to conform to an aesthetic pattern. Yet Tanizaki, like many of the finest Japanese writers, subtly persuades us that any significant breach of artistic decorum is a mistake. Not freedom and possibility but loss and violation are signaled by it. Better the unremarkable but familiar garden behind the old provincial house, susceptible as it has always been in Japanese literature to aesthetic arrangement, than the grey sooty expansiveness of western Tokyo; better a life of domestic routine, adhering to traditional patterns of conduct, than one unregulated, as the youngest sister's is, subject to the vagaries of the market place, to romantic love, and to an unsanctioned pregnancy. Such violations are seen as being aesthetically as well as physically tragic, ending with telling metaphorical significance in the child's death at birth.

I will continue to draw Tanizaki and other writers into our discussion, and will have more to say about Tokyo, but for now I want to focus on the essential topic of this essay—The Borders of Japanese Fiction—an admittedly vague topic, which I hope to make clearer. The borders I have in mind are reasonably specific but not chronological—not a date, say, 1887, when Futabatei's *Ukigumo* was written. I mean, rather, the way Japanese fictional space is arranged, the lines by which a given scene is drawn and a sense of place emerges. In my own reading experience, these topographical borders and the space that they enclose are remarkably consistent, and since in so much Japanese fiction, the setting determines and often seems even to dominate character and plot, I feel compelled to come to terms with how this setting is shaped and formed. What has become clear to me in reading Japanese fiction and criticism is that there is nothing haphazard or nebulous about these borders. It is rarely a question of "the country" or "the city" or "Nature" writ large. The Japanese fictional landscapes, which recur in serious literature and which we have come to anticipate and value, have common features of stability, domesticity, and familiarity. They are particular rural villages or urban neighborhoods or temple grounds—Ashiya, Asakusa, Kiyomizu; particular mountains and rivers—Yoshino, Daisen, Sumidagawa, place names often previously celebrated in Japanese poetry and prose, and which we recognize as semi-metaphorical presences within a culturally domesticated homeland.

In the twentieth century, to be sure, the issue appears more complicated. We notice certain transgressions of the homeland's borders, explorations of new and alien territory: Arishima's forays into Hokkaido, America and a ship at sea;

Mishima's myth-haunted expedition to Southeast Asia; Endo's spiritual journey to Nueva Espana and Rome; Abe's allegorical urban wastelands. These fictions need to be acknowledged and accounted for, and yet they appear to be anomalous. It remains possible to say, even today, that Japanese fiction takes place within intelligible borders, and when it does not, it is, like the poppy in Sachiko's sick room, out of place.

The power of the literary tradition in this regard should not be overestimated. Contrary to a naive belief, the cosmopolitan, reform-minded literati of the late-nineteenth century did not jettison the old literature, indeed, it was hardly their intention to do so. Modern Japanese literary history does not conform to a deconstructionist model, literary history seen not as a continuum but as a series of ruptures and discontinuities. Some modern Japanese writers have ignored and some have honored their literary past; but few have really struggled against it, and even among those who have there seem to be no unambiguous victories. Instead, the record of fictional experiment in defiance of the tradition shows an initial daring, followed by disillusionment and defeat: Arishima's heroine in *A Certain Woman,* who left for the New World with such hope, returns to Tokyo, a tainted woman, and there loses her mind; Mishima's adventure in Thailand yields, by the end of the tetralogy, not a new vision but a very old one, of silence and forgetfulness in the quiet of an almost medieval retreat; Endo's recent globe-trotting leads of course to martyrdom, and the only figure fully conscious at the end is not Japanese at all but European; and Abe, the most consistent border transgressor of all, has turned from fiction to drama, as though even he found it difficult to sustain an earlier, imaginative vision. That most modern Japanese fiction does not end in such disillusion and defeat, preferring to represent the subtle, unrelenting, yet somehow tolerable pressures of everyday life, signals an awareness of literary limits that remains strong, even in the face of Western literary influence, and the desire, expressed by a few, to write a new literature. For now I want to insist that this sense of limits, these largely unspoken but widely practiced rules of conduct in one's choice of a fictional setting, are not modern at all but have deep roots in the past.

The touchstone on this issue, as on so many issues concerning Japanese literature, is the *Tale of Genji*. It is possible, I suppose, to go back even further, to the earliest chronicles and gazeteers: the eighth-century *Kojiki* and the *Fudoki*, with their litanies and etymologies of ancient place names, and their implication that spiritual and even practical value resides in the physical features of the land; the headnotes to the poetry in the *Manyoshu* and subsequent imperial poetic anthologies, which specify the context of an emotion, the lyric always associated with a particular occasion and setting; or the localizing, domestic nature of *nikki bungaku* (diary literature) as it evolved, a record kept not so much to order events chronologically but rather to arrange and ultimately to define an intimate and knowable world. Still, it is in Murasaki's tale that the question of setting and landscape first becomes a self-conscious concern of the narrator.

In the early 'Broom Tree' chapter, there is a disquisition on the art of painting through which, it seems to me, Murasaki renders an aesthetic judgment that informs her own literary style and her understanding of greater and lesser literary values:

> There are any number of masters in the academy. It is not easy to separate the good from the bad among those who work on the basic sketches. But let color be added. The painter of things no one ever sees, of paradises, of fish in angry seas, raging beasts in foreign lands, devils and demons—the painter abandons himself to his fancies and paints to terrify and astonish. What does it matter if the results seem remote from real life? It is not so with the things we know, mountains, streams, houses near and like our own. The soft unspoiled wooded hills must be painted layer on layer, the details added gently, quietly, to give a sense of affectionate familiarity. And the foreground too, the garden inside the walls, the arrangement of the stones and grasses and waters. It is here that the master has his own power. These are details a lesser painter cannot imitate.[4]

The disposition voiced here, to describe what Murasaki calls "a sense of affectionate familiarity," to meander back and forth among personal, lyrical details, determines not only the plot of the *Tale of Genji* but the future course of Japanese fiction. It is the reason why this tale is not a romance, as that term is understood in Western literary criticism. For at the heart of a romance there is a quest which takes the hero away from his home and native land, to settle a new world or to return eventually to the old one, but endowed with greater wisdom, an enlarged or simply an enraptured vision. This is as true, it seems to me, of ancient Western narratives—*The Odyssey* or *The Epic of Gilgamesh* or *The Aeneid,* for example, as it is of modern, often more sinister quests: *Moby Dick, Heart of Darkness,* and William Burroughs' *Naked Lunch.* This is not to say that in the *Genji* and in other Japanese fiction only benevolent or harmonious experience is described. We have only to think of the possession scenes and the hero's exile in Suma to realize that Murasaki's tale is not all "soft, unspoiled wooded hills" and fragrant, demure conduct. And in the modern period we can point to a cycle of writing that Japanese critics have labeled "destructive" (the work of Chikamatsu Shuko, Kamura Isota, Kasai Zenzo, Dazai Osamu, among others) where we encounter characters who, without ever straying far from the all too familiar, manage, through alcohol and an acute sense of betrayal and paranoia, to poison their own lives and the lives of those around them. There is nothing ethically or morally squeamish about Japanese fiction, only an insistence that what transpires in a story occur in a possible, knowable world, as Murasaki makes explicit in Genji's exchange with Tamakatsura:

> If the storyteller wishes to speak well, then he chooses the good things; and if he wishes to hold the reader's attention, he chooses bad things, extraordinarily bad things. Good things and bad things alike, they are part of this world and no other.[5]

There can be no quest within such a literary system; no reach for an alternative reality, a higher or simply some other world, discovered and revealed by a Utopian imagination. In Japanese literature, Exodus does not elicit dreams of a Promised Land. On the contrary, as we know from the poor, banished provincial figures in the *Genji,* and even more clearly from the depiction of exile endemic to medieval literature— exiles like the Heike, driven from the Capital and "shivering like tropical birds in a frozen clime"[6]—there is no future but only, through the agency of a powerful nostalgia, a shimmering past. Beauty is often retrieved in medieval writing, but this is contingent on the discovery of some stable, tranquil setting; the hermitage Jakkōin, for example, deep in Ohara, that near replication of a Heian garden, where the Former Empress waits for death "on a velvety green carpet of moss."[7] Otherwise, it is disorder and flux, "masterless boats drifting aimlessly with the wind and tide,"[8] and in this condition, beyond the borders of the Capital, cut off altogether from a known and beloved homeland, beauty vanishes. As we read of the Heike in their flight from Dazaifu:

> Exposed to the sea breeze, their black brows and handsome faces lost their radiance. Gazing at the blue sea, they recalled their bygone grandeurs in the Capital. The jade green hangings over their scarlet bedchambers in former days were now replaced by reed hangings in crude cottages. In place of the fragrant smoke from their incense burners rose the briny flames from fishermen's driftwood. All these changes brought the ladies of the court infinite sorrow and endless tears. Eyebrows that had glistened grew dull from weeping. Beauty that had shone faded into nothing.[9]

With the rise of a new audience and a genuinely popular fiction in the Tokugawa period, classical beauty of this kind ceased to be a primary literary value. Yet the preponderance of stories which possess sharply detailed settings, fiction as carefully circumscribed as the pleasure quarters at Yoshiwara and Shinmachi, reveals a traditional emphasis. In Saikaku and Samba and Shunsui, exploration does take place: of the body and its erotic possibilities; of commerce and the frenetic pace of the burgeoning urban centers; of language and ways to strike quick bargains between high and low diction, dazzling word play which seems, if only for an instant, to dissolve the rigidities of the class system. And yet this exploration, even that of Saikaku's *Woman Who Loved Love,* which is especially ambitious in its representation of all levels of the society, remains an exploration of the given world, and confirms the restrictiveness of it.

Paul Anderer

Since the mid-nineteenth century, as is well known, Japan has been exposed and has exposed itself to contact with the West; it is a matter of record that this contact disturbed pre-existing patterns of urban and rural life. In the large cities, especially in Tokyo, numbers of people were confronted daily with an illusionary spectacle of the strange and the unknown, with a "showcase,"[10] to use Henry Smith's word, for the display of Western gadgetry and designs. And yet in a move characteristic of and predicated on the tradition I have described, modern Japanese fiction has largely withdrawn from an imaginative exploration of this convulsive urban scene, rife with the signs of foreign influence, preferring to detail, with ever deepening psychological nuance, an inner world which, however turbulent, remains a certainty, a knowable world on which to focus. If, as I previously suggested, Thailand or the New World could not successfully be appropriated as Japanese literary landscapes, neither could the modern city of Tokyo, and for the same reason. This city, whose population doubled between 1895 and 1923, and whose topography, architecture, and transportation systems underwent change, indeed in many respects transformation, has functioned in literature as a largely alien and intrusive presence, and lies as far beyond the borders of Japanese fiction as a foreign country. If in the 1890s, Tokyo had seemed to Tokutomi Roka, as he recorded in his *Omoide no ki*, "A Promised Land inspiring fugitive dreams of glory,"[11] it had become in late Meiji and Taisho literature a city to excoriate and avoid, as Kafu repeatedly did in his elegant withdrawal to Tokyo's eastern districts, those remnants of Edo and an evocative past. Or it was a city to simply escape, as Tanizaki did, in literature and in life.

One Japanese critic, in evident exasperation, has spoken of "the provincial nihilism of Japanese prose, which glorifies material objects and ratifies inertia,"[12] and another of the "provincialization of the city"[13] by modern writers. To draw out the meaning of these charges, a literature of Tokyo scarcely exists, for it would require, in the twentieth century, a truly questing literature to confront the city's difference and otherness. As many readers have noticed, the modern literary mainstream in Japan has instead adopted a style of withdrawal and retreat—how often do we encounter a figure like Futabatei's Bunzo, who retires to an "upstairs room" and remains, emotionally, inside it? This is a pattern followed by the Japanese Naturalists, beginning with the hero of Katai's *Futon* (*The Quilt*, 1907), who by degrees withdraws from the city outside to his study, and from there in fantasy and memory to the country home to which his young pupil has herself fled. And this curtailment of movement and of vision, which socially conscious Japanese critics have repeatedly decried, has been sanctioned in the rise to dominance of the *watakushi shosetsu* or 'personal fiction,' a genre through which, it seems to me, writers have sought to find a shelter for their fiction amid the accelerating changes of their culture and society.

It may be true, as one hostile critic has noted of Shiga Naoya's *Wakai* (*Reconciliation*, 1917), that the book reveals "an unwillingness and an incapacity to understand the social and economic boundaries that determine the self and society."[14] On the other hand, it might be said, Shiga recognized certain literary boundaries very well. In *Wakai*, for example, much of the action takes place in Tokyo, and yet, except for an elaborate description of the cemetery in Aoyama, the city remains nearly invisible. It is to Abiko that the narrator withdraws to find meaning—this is where the ultimate reconciliation with his father will occur.

Shiga's example is emblematic of a whole line of modern Japanese writers, who are alert and very knowing about the borders of literary possibility. This explains, it seems to me, Tokyo's unexplored and therefore problematic status, as it does the reluctance of Japanese writers to probe other alien territories. For it is only when the city is scaled down, evoked as a cemetery or a backyard garden, a side street or a bar, a solitary room or a local shop—Tokyo, in short as a transplanted village—only in this condition does the city emerge as a landscape in most modern fiction. On any other terms it is too threatening. As Tanizaki once had a character say, "I had only three choices: to die, to go mad, or to stay away from Tokyo."[15]

I want to conclude with one further example, which we

Paul Anderer

will recognize as yet another and very characteristic flight from the city toward a more sufficient fictional space. There is an evocative passage near the close of Shiga's *An'ya Koro* (*A Dark Night's Passing*, 1937), the lyric, if not dramatic ending of this famous book. The hero, disquieted about himself and his relations in Tokyo, makes a final journey toward enlightenment. Kensaku looks toward nature, or to be more precise, toward a culturally refined landscape; and faithful to Japanese literary tradition, he projects his vision onto a space that takes shape because of the very concrete and familiar place names that surround it. The hero's epiphany, his moment of insight, occurs with the figurative brightening of this scene:

> He must have slept for some time as he sat there, his elbows resting on his knees. When he opened his eyes again, the green around him had begun to show in the light of early dawn. The stars, though fewer now, were still there. The sky was soft blue, the color of kindness, he thought. The mist below had dispersed, and there were lights here and there in the villages at the foot of the mountain. He could see lights in Yonago too, and in Sakaiminato that lay on Yomigahama Point. The big light that went on and off was surely from the lighthouse at Mihonoseki. The bay, as still as a lake, remained in the shadow of the mountain, but the sea outside had already taken on a greyish hue.[16]

It is hard to know if the light in this passage is an illumination of the hero or the setting, being at once a celebration of consciousness and a celebration of this place to which dawn comes. What is clear is that we are not out in an open field, in an unknown and untamed environment. We are on an elevation looking down from Daisen toward the sea. And Shiga is even more specific: "lights in Yonago . . . and in Sakaiminato that lay on Yomigahama Point . . . the lighthouse at Mihonoseki"—as though to have the light spread over an unmarked or unfamiliar area would mean, in substance, a loss of light. The hero sees, the scenery lightens, because of the limits at work here. The author has sanctified a character whose vision is in important ways limited, and a geography whose limits are carefully circumscribed.

Repeatedly in this most influential of modern fictions, we

encounter that "environment of feeling" which Kume Masao regarded as essential to the composition of Japanese fictional prose. It is within such an environment, of personal impressions gathered about culturally refined and domestic scenes, that Kume insisted we would find "the *furusato* of fiction, the place from which fiction originates, and the place to which it returns."[17]

If this *furusato*, this country or ancestral home, seems far from the reality of a modern and increasingly urban Japan, we should remind ourselves that no art, even the kind most desirous of verisimilitude, can ever be a precise transcription of life. The world seen from within the borders of Japanese fiction is not the whole world, or even all of Japan. It is an artificial world, as are all literary worlds, and as such possesses its own rules of artistic conduct. I have tried here to account for certain of those rules, which can help us, I think, to take pleasure in the literature we read, knowing a formidable boundary lies between any story and the life it may seem to describe.

NOTES

1. Tanizaki Junichiro, *The Makioka Sisters*, trans. Edward Seidensticker (New York, 1966), pp. 93-94.

2. Tanizaki Junichiro, p. 415.

3. Tanizaki Junichiro, p. 94.

4. Murasaki Shikibu, *The Tale of Genji*, trans. Edward Seidensticker (New York, 1976), p. 27.

5. Murasaki Shikibu, p. 437.

6. *The Tale of the Heike*, trans. Hiroshi Kitagawa and Bruce T. Tsuchida (Tokyo, 1975), p. 507.

7. *The Tale of the Heike*, p. 767.

8. *The Tale of the Heike*, p. 682.

9. *The Tale of the Heike*, p. 474.

10. Henry D. Smith, "Tokyo as an Idea," *Journal of Japanese Studies* (Winter 1978), p. 53.

11. Tokutomi Roka, *Footprints in the Snow*, trans. Kenneth Strong (New York, 1970), p. 107.

12. Eto Jun, *Sakka wa Kodo Suru*, Chosakushū 5 (Tokyo, 1967), p. 43. Unless specified, this and subsequent translations are my own.

13. Isoda Kochi, *Shiso to shite no Tokyo* (Tokyo, 1978), p. 16.

14. Honda Shugo, *Shirakaba ha no bungaku* (Tokyo, 1960), p. 106.

15. Tanizaki Junichiro, *Seven Japanese Tales*, trans. Howard Hibbett (New York, 1965), p. 65.

16. Shiga Naoya, *A Dark Night's Passing*, trans. Edwin McClellan (Tokyo, 1976), p. 401.

17. Kume Masao, "Watakushi shosetsu to Shinkyo shosetsu," in *Kindai Bungaku Hyoron Taikei 6* (Tokyo, 1973), p. 57.

Reading the Illegible:
Some Modern Representations of
Urban Experience

Steven Marcus

I have argued in the past that Friedrich Engels' representation of Manchester in the early 1840s was a paradigm for the experience of Western culture during the first period of urbanization, industrialization, and modernization.[1] This reading of the city, this perception and construction of it as a signifying structure, may be regarded, as I have intimated, as prototypical for the nineteenth century, and the first part of the twentieth as well. One finds variant representations of this vision in the Paris of Balzac, in the London of Dickens, in the St. Petersburg of Dostoevsky, in the Dublin of Joyce—not to mention the sub-versions of it in the works of lesser novelists and other writers. It is found as well, appropriately modified, in the work of such other modernist figures as T. S. Eliot, Proust, and the early Beckett. And it is this vision that has been attenuated if not lost, or that has, for the moment, ceased historically to be transmitted. What I should like to do in this essay is to look briefly at the writing of two of our most gifted and self-conscious contemporary novelists and see, for a moment, what has happened to what may be called the classical modern conception of the city.

In the work of Saul Bellow, urban experience is rendered consistently in extraordinarily self-aware terms. From the outset Bellow seems certain that urban experience is modern experience—that the two define each other. In his first novel, *Dangling Man* (1944), the chief character, an intellectual named Joseph, looks out on the urban ugliness and reflects:

> Where was there a particle of what, elsewhere, or in the past, had spoken in man's favor? There could be no doubt that these billboards, streets, tracks, houses, ugly and blind, were related

to interior life. And yet . . . there had to be a doubt . . . that they, the houses, say, were the analogue, that what men created they also were, through some transcendent means, I could not bring myself to concede. There must be a difference. . . . Otherwise the people who lived here were actually a reflection of the things they lived among.[2]

What the character is wrestling with is the fear of a simplified classical view, in which men and objects will be reduced to one another, or in which human efforts will be reified in a vision of the world of objects. Yet the power and integrity of the classical vision was such that it could recognize the analogy between city and people without diminishing either or reducing one into the other. And Bellow's character in part recognizes this difference when he adds that "we were coming to know that we had misjudged whole epochs. . . . The giants of the last century had their Liverpools and Londons, their Lilles and Hamburgs to contend against, as we have our Chicagos and Detroits."

The point to be taken is that Bellow is conscious at every moment of the tradition of discourse in which he is writing. That discourse and its self-sentience are apparent in the following:

Supply is supply, and demand is demand. They will be satisfied, be it with combs, fifes, rubber, whisky, tainted meat, canned peas, sex, or tobacco. For every need there is an entrepreneur, by a marvelous providence. You can find a man to bury your dog, rub your back, teach you Swahili, read your horoscope, murder your competitor. In the megapolis, all this is possible. There was a Parisian cripple in the days of John Law, the Scottish speculator, who stood in the streets renting out his hump for a writing desk to people who had no convenient place to take their transactions.

Within the context of the twentieth-century, modernist perspective, the city is at once sordid, corrupt, ruinous, terrible, contaminating, and still a place of wonders, magic, marvels, and "reality" in all its most startling and surprising manifestations. Within the historical conception of the corrupting market, marvels of the actual continue to occur. The city with its "treelessness," and its "unnatural, too-human deadness," with its dangerous "lack of the human in the too-human," has become humanity's new nature, and the conscious substance of Bellow's novelistic discourse.

In Bellow's second novel, *The Victim* (1947), set this time in New York, the city continues to be a text, to be read, of course, but itself commenting on the nineteenth-century city which was its pretext. The chief character, Leventhal, takes his ten-year-old nephew for a subway ride. The boy speculates to his uncle "about what there was under the street in addition to foundations: the pipes, waterpipes and sewage, gas mains, the electrical system for the subway, telephone and telegraph wires, and the cable for the Broadway trolley." To which the uncle makes this reply: "I suppose they have maps and charts at City Hall. . . . What about a drink?" What a generation or two ago was one of the wonders of the world today has become literally child's knowledge. What once constituted structural understanding has become the commonplace perception of a child's mind. The novel ceases to emphasize that kind of structural knowledge even as it is entirely aware of these developments.

In a similar sense, when Allbee, the anti-Semitic WASP antagonist of Leventhal, laments that his kind have been displaced, he says, "Try to imagine how New York affects me. . . . It's really as if the children of Caliban were running everything. You go down in the subway and Caliban gives you two nickels for your dime. You go home and he has a candy store in the street where you were born. The old breeds are out." In such a passage Bellow is deliberately playing upon the tradition of discourse he has inherited. The play, of course, consists in the transformed application of the term Caliban. In the nineteenth century it was used in this context to identify and characterize the working class. In the 1940s in New York, it is symmetrically translated into the code of Jews. A generation later it was translated yet again, back towards its original seventeenth-century usage.

One more passage of this kind will have to be enough. Here is New York on a Labor Day weekend in the 1940s.

> He started home at half-past four. The wind had dropped, the sky was cold and darkening rapidly. In the little park the

turned-up rusty shells of leaves scraped in the path and cracked underfoot. Very little green remained in those that streamed raggedly in the trees. A damp warmth, smelling of stone, rose from the subway, and through the gratings Leventhal caught a glimpse of the inert light on the roadbed and of the rails, hard and gray in their simultaneous strike. The close brownstone houses looked autumnal and so did the foot-burnished, steel manhole lids; they were glinting sharply.

Here the juxtaposition of the city and nature refers fully to the complex, classical presentation. The city refracts nature and is penetrated by it; it repels nature and yet becomes a "second" nature as well. There is no contemporary writer who is more profoundly familiar with this mode of cognition and construction than Bellow.

This mode is brought to its fullest and most explicit expression in Bellow's first major novel, *The Adventures of Augie March* (1953). In part, this work is his love song to America and to the range of urban experience in his native Chicago, "that somber city," as Augie describes it in the novel's opening sentence. That love song begins with a celebration of Augie's rough boyhood in the Chicago of the late 1920s and early 1930s and his apprenticeship to life as a youthful idler, observer, and general no-goodnik in Mr. Einhorn's—his surrogate father's—pool room. One point to be taken is that this love song is the antinomy or contrary of "The Love Song of J. Alfred Prufrock." Augie is initiated into the world by one of its denizens, a young tough called Dingbat:

> He took me under his protection in the poolroom, and we did some friendly boxing, at which I was never much good, and played snooker—a little better—and hung about there with the hoods and loudmouths. So that Grandma Lausch would have thought that the very worst she had ever said about me let me off too light, seeing me in the shoeshine seat above the green tables, in a hat with diamond airholes cut in it and decorated with brass kiss-me pins and Al Smith buttons, in sneakers and Mohawk sweatshirt, there in the frying jazz and the buzz of baseball broadcasts, the click of markers, butt thumping of cues, spat-down pollyseed shells and blue chalk crushed underfoot and dust of hand-slickening talcum hanging in the air.

Along with the blood-smelling swaggeroos, recruits for mobs, automobile thieves, stick-up men, sluggers and bouncers, punks with ambition to become torpedoes, neighborhood cowboys with Jack Holt sideburns down to the jawbone, collegiates, tinhorns and small-time racketeers and pugs, ex-servicemen, home-evading husbands, hackies, truckers and bush-league athletes. Whenever someone had a notion to work out on me— and there were plenty of touchy characters here to catch your eye in a misconstrued way—Dingbat flew around to protect me.

"This kid is a buddy of mine. . . . Monkey with him and you'll get something broke on your head. What's the matter, you tough or hungry!"

Here the hardness and crudity of Chicago are brought forward not to discredit them, but to juxtapose them in positive valence to the savagery of Chicago's European urban counterparts. As Einhorn, Augie's chief mentor and guide explains:

"But there is some kind of advantage in the roughness of a place like Chicago, of not having any illusions either. Whereas in all the great capitals of the world there's some reason to think humanity is very different. All that ancient culture and those beautiful works of art right out in public, by Michelangelo and Christopher Wren, and those ceremonies, like trooping the color at the Horse Guards' parade or burying a great man in the Pantheon over in Paris. You see those marvelous things and you think that everything savage belongs to the past. So you think. And then you have another think, and you see that after they rescued women from the coal mines, or pulled down the Bastille and got rid of Star Chambers and *lettres de cachet*, ran out the Jesuits, increased education, and built hospitals and spread courtesy and politeness, they have five or six years of war and revolutions and kill off twenty million people. And do they think there's less danger to life than here? That's a riot. Let them say rather that they blast better specimens, but not try to put it over that the only human beings who live by blood are away down on the Orinoco where they hunt heads, or out in Cicero."

But in this novel, Bellow is not satisfied with such justifications by juxtaposition. He wants to and will be satisfied with nothing less than the full spectrum of analogies and balancings between our Chicago and the entire tradition of the West, its culture and mythology:

> We went through Gary and Hammond that day, on a trailer from Flint, by docks and dumps of sulphur and coal, and flames seen by their heat, not light, in the space of noon air among the black, huge Pasiphaë cows and other columnar animals, headless, rolling a rust of smoke and connected in an enormous statuary of hearths and mills—here and there an old boiler or a hill of cinders in the bulrush spawning-holes of frogs. If you've seen a winter London open thundering mouth in its awful last minutes of river light or have come with cold clanks from the Alps into Torino in December white steam then you've known like greatness of place. Thirty crowded miles on oil-spotted road, where the furnace, gas, and machine volcanoes cooked the Empedocles fundamentals into pig iron, girders, and rails.

Here Chicago is consciously placed against the Greek world of foundational mythology and architecture and its transformation by allusion into the tragic art of Euripides. To its own credit and power, it is compared to the winter London of all of English literature, to the Alps of Hemingway's reporting and imagination and to the Empedocles of Greece, of Milton, of Matthew Arnold and hence of European culture seen in its longest perspective. Moreover, the novel is literally packed with such impressive and impassioned passages of essentially happy historical reference. Here, for example, is merely one more, chosen almost at random.

> When evening came on we were tearing out of Gary and toward South Chicago, the fire and smudge mouth of the city groping to us. As the flamy bay shivers for home-coming Neapolitans. You enter your native water like a fish. And there sits the great fish god or Dagon. You then bear your soul like a minnow before Dagon, in your familiar water.

Nor is the Chicago of the late thirties and early forties to be overlooked either. Times and internal perspectives change as well. Augie returns from Mexico, and his extended *Bildungs-romanerlebnis* there, and his brother Simon takes him to stay in his plush apartment in one of the great new towering apartment buildings.

I knew we had gone way up in the elevator but hadn't noticed to what floor. Now, after breakfast, when I strayed into one of the enormous carpeted rooms, dark as a Pullman when it sits with drawn blinds in the station, I drew a drape aside and saw we were on the twentieth story at least. I hadn't had a look at Chicago yet since my return. Well, here it was again, westward from this window, the gray snarled city with the hard black straps of rails, enormous industry cooking and its vapor shuddering to the air, the climb and fall of its stages in construction or demolition like mesas, and on these the different powers and sub-powers crouched and watched like sphinxes. Terrible dumbness covered it, like a judgment that would never find its word.

Chicago seen from this classical view is like the mesas of Texas or Mexico, or the sphinxes of non-European history and pre-history. It is a preternatural force, pre-verbal and primordial in its ancient sources of power, nature and culture compounded in a mystery that is unfathomable and inexhaustible.

Finally, and arbitrarily, there is this. To get into World War II, Augie must have an operation to repair a hernia. Here is its aftermath in County Hospital.

The hospital was mobbed and was like Lent and Carnival battling. This was Harrison Street, where Mama and I used to come for her specs . . . the thundery gloom, bare stone brown, while the red cars lumbered and clanged. Every bed, window, separate frame of accommodation, every corner was filled, like the walls of Troy or the streets of Clermont when Peter the Hermit was preaching. Shruggers, hobblers, truss and harness wearers, crutch-dancers, wall inspectors, wheelchair people in bandage helmets, wound smells and drug flowers blossoming from gauze, from colorful horrors and out of the deep sinks. Not far the booby-hatch voices would scream, sing, and chirp and sound like the tropical bird collection of Lincoln Park. On warm days I went up to the roof and had a look at the city. Around was Chicago. In its repetition it exhausted your imagination of details and units, more units than the cells of the brain and bricks of Babel. The Ezekiel caldron of wrath, stoked with bones. In time the caldron too would melt. A mysterious tremor, dust, vapor, emanation of stupendous effort traveled with the air, over me on top of the great establishment, so full as it was, and over the clinics, clinks, factories, flophouses, morgue, skid row. As before the work of Egypt and Assyria, as before a sea, you're nothing here. Nothing.

It is Europe from pre-historic Troy through all of Christendom. It is the Old Testament from Babel to the most sardonic of the prophetic poets. It is the grandiose slave-ridden empires of Egypt and Assyria. It is the Byronic ocean itself. Yet the "nothing" with which the passage ends is one of the strongest, most affirmative and positive nothings in modern literature. It is the opposite of the nothing of Beckett or Kafka. It is nothing as being part of something enormous, overwhelmingly grand, world-historically significant. It is a nothing that is full at the same time. To be nothing as part of this immensity is to be more than most somethings. One's puniness amidst all this generation of force is at the same time a very dense and packed experience. In no novel has Bellow drawn more positively and deliberately on the tradition than in *The Adventures of Augie March,* and in no novel does he affirm the values of that tradition and what it stands for more directly.

Yet somewhere in mid-career, Bellow's dealings with the city began to undergo a gradual but decided change. We can see that change occurring distinctly in *Seize the Day* (1956). Tommy Wilhelm, the feckless, weak, and quasi-incompetent protagonist of that marvelous short novel, characteristically complains, "I'm not used to New York anymore. For a native, that's very peculiar, isn't it? It was never so noisy at night as now, and every little thing is a strain, like the alternate parking." This unsettled and nervy state of mind is clearly meant to suggest both the state of being of the narrator and the world constructed by his perceptions and sensibility. Wilhelm muses that there is "no easy way to tell the sane from the mad," and that this observation holds

> in any big city and especially in New York—the end of the world, with its complexity and machinery, bricks and tubes, wires and stones, holes and heights. And was everybody crazy here? What sort of people did you see? Every other man spoke a language entirely his own, which he had figured out by private

thinking. . . . If you wanted to talk about a glass of water, you had to start back with God creating the heavens and earth; the apple; Abraham; Moses and Jesus; Rome; the Middle Ages; gunpowder; the Revolution; back to Newton; up to Einstein; then war and Lenin and Hitler. After reviewing this and getting it all straight again you could proceed to talk about a glass of water. "I'm fainting, please get me a little water." You were lucky even then to make yourself understood. And this happened over and over and over with everyone you met. You had to translate and translate, explain and explain, back and forth, and it was the punishment of hell itself not to understand or be understood, not to know the crazy from the sane, the wise from the fools, the young from the old or the sick from the well. The fathers were no fathers and the sons no sons. You had to talk with yourself in the daytime and reason with yourself at night. Who else was there to talk to in a city like New York?

I take this passage as paradigmatic of wider developments in contemporary consciousness. It is a specimen text expressive of the general and growing sense that the great modern city—or almost any great city—has gone out of control, that it has lost the signifying potencies and structural coherences that it once seemed to possess. The old structure was in considerable, though not exclusive, measure made up of relations between social groups and of functions and symbols that related to social groups, to classes and subclasses. These older structures of signification now appear to be in a state of decomposition, and newer structures are brought forward, apparently for the purpose of pronouncing that they have failed to operate. Part of the classical representation of the modern city was that it embodied, among other things, a structure of systems of communication—and that these multiple systems were part of the city's complex nature. For Bellow, these structures of messages, voices, languages, signs, lies, directions, and commands have failed in their constructive purposes as well. The city is ceasing to be readable. Or, if it is readable, the message that is being sent is getting simpler and simpler. The city is ceasing to speak in a language, and for a novelist to have language get out of hand is to be involved in a desperate undertaking.

Yet Bellow is more complex than we can so summarily account for, and in his next major work, *Henderson the Rain King* (1959), his imaginative prose poem of a novel about an imaginary Africa, he evokes New York again with a renewed and evolved sense of its ambiguous prepotencies. Here is part of his account of a tribal celebration:

> And the screams, the excitement! The roars, the deep drum noises, as if the animals were speaking again by means of the skins that had once covered their bodies. It was a great release of sound, like Coney Island or Atlantic City or Times Square on New Year's Eve; at the king's exit from the gate the great cacophony left all the previous noises in my experience far behind. . . . The frenzy was so great it was metropolitan.

In order to grasp the primordial energy and vitality of Africa, Bellow resorts to figures drawn from the concentrated energic center that is the modern city. The paradoxicality and balance recall a number of touchstonelike instances among his nineteenth-century predecessors.

Or, in a similar sense, there is this:

> Like all people who have a strong gift of life, he gave off almost an extra shadow. . . . Through his high-swelled lips a low hum occasionally came. It reminded me of the sound you sometimes hear from a power station when you pass one in New York on a summer night; the doors are open; all the brass and steel is going, lustrous under one little light, and some old character in dungarees and carpet slippers is smoking a pipe with all the greatness of the electricity behind him.

Once again, for conceptual images of the preternatural within the natural, for harnessed powers, controlled yet demonic (and hence comprehensible at least in part), he turns to his experience of the prepotent immediacies of the modern city. And he does so again to describe what it might be like to enter Hell. "After the gust of breeze came deeper darkness, like the pungent heat of the trains when they pass into Grand Central tunnel on a devastated day of August, which is like darkness eternal. At that moment I have always closed my eyes." So, Hell is a city much like New York, and so is deepest, darkest Africa, the heart of darkness, the center from which there radiates dark Lawrencian life and death.

At an even more advanced pitch of active distaste there is this comment, apropos of some of the textbooks of modern science that King Dahfu has given Henderson to read.

> The words were as thick and heavy as tombstones, and I was disheartened. It was much like taking the limousine to La Guardia Field and passing those cemeteries in Queens. So heavy. Each of the dead having been mailed away, and those stones like the postage stamps death has licked.

Even such a reference—which nudges us to think of Gray's elegy, of "Bartleby the Scrivener," of *Bleak House*, and a variety of other evocations of death harbored, apparently incongruously, at the center of life, which has turned mechanical in its driving sources of power—even such a response retains meaning, impressiveness, and coherence.

A similar arrest, or resting point, and commendable creative struggle for balance, coherence, and readability is to be found in Bellow's next novel, *Herzog* (1964). Yet, even here the battle for coherence begins detectably to be lost—particularly when Bellow compares contemporary New York or Chicago with his recreated memories of childhood urban experience. And that one of the novel's larger themes is about general loss of sanity, control, and readability, and even write-ability—as all of Herzog's written/unwritten letters to everyone and no one suggest—contributes to our more particular sense of the problematic status of the intelligible, informing, critical urban experience and its creative refraction in novelistic structure and prose.

In a number of senses, Bellow's dealings with the city are to be seen at their finest and most extended pitch in *Herzog*. In that exceptionally interesting novel, Bellow evokes three separate urban inscapes, as it were—the Montreal of his youth, the Chicago of his extended years of adolescence and maturity, and the New York of his creative crises, liberating deliverances, and destructive undergoings and apprehensions. I will take them, in abbreviation, in this order, although they do not manifest themselves creatively in this sequence in the text.

First, this is the recollection of his early Canadian years:

My ancient times. Remoter than Egypt. No dawn, the foggy
winters. In darkness, the bulb was lit. The stove was cold. Papa
shook the grates and raised an ashen dust. . . . The chimneys
in their helmets sucked in the wind. Then the milkman came in
his sleigh. The snow was spoiled and rotten with manure and
litter, dead rats, dogs. . . .
   The morning light could not free itself from gloom and frost.
Up and down the street, the brick-recessed windows were dark,
filled with darkness, and schoolgirls by twos in their black skirts
marched toward the convent. And wagons, sledges, drays, the
horses shuddering, the air drowned in leaden green, the dung-
stained ice, trails of ashes. Moses and his brothers put on their
caps and prayed together,
          "*Ma tovu ohaleha Yaakov. . . .*"
          "How goodly are thy tents, O Israel."
   Napoleon Street, rotten, toylike, crazy and filthy, riddled,
flogged with harsh weather—the bootlegger's boys reciting ancient prayers. To this Moses' heart was attached with great
power. Here was a wider range of human feelings than he had
ever again been able to find. The children of the race, by a
never-failing miracle, opened their eyes on one strange world
after another, age after age, and uttered the same prayer in
each, eagerly loving what they found.

The redemptive power is traced directly to childhood, to its
unfailing creative source of vivid emotion, to its concurrence
in the living tradition of the Jews in exile and of their vital
religious-ceremonial life, and to the traditions of Wordsworth, Blake, and Dickens as well. The smallness of scale—
the street is referred to as toylike—also helps, but the scale is
illuminated by the light that never was on land or sea, the le-
gitimate light of formative perception and undying memory
cast by childhood.
   Then there is Chicago, which comes into the novel towards
the end. There are three distinctive excursive passages about
it, from which I will choose one as exemplary:

He drove directly to Woodlawn Avenue—a dreary part of
Hyde Park, but characteristic, *his* Chicago: massive, clumsy,
amorphous, smelling of mud and decay, dog turds; sooty fa-

çades, slabs of structural *nothing,* senselessly ornamented triple porches with huge cement urns for flowers that contained only rotting cigarette butts and other stained filth; sun parlors under tiled gables, rank areaways, gray backstairs, seamed and ruptured concrete from which sprang grass; ponderous four-by-four fences that sheltered growing weeds. And among these spacious, comfortable, dowdy apartments where liberal, benevolent people lived (this was the university neighborhood) Herzog did in fact feel at home. He was perhaps as midwestern and unfocused as these same streets. (Not so much determinism, he thought, as a lack of determining elements—the absence of a formative power.)

There is no classical, concealed structure here, but there is no concealed menace or madness either. Perhaps familiarity has bred drowsiness. But, in any event, the purpose of such evocations is to put forward theatrical and drastic contrast, to thicken the context in which the "trembling energy" of New York is dramatically regarded. Fixing his gaze on "the sights of New York," Herzog finds the "square shapes . . . vivid, not inert." They are full of "fateful motion, almost of intimacy," and at the same time he senses "the danger of these multiple excitements." The danger exists both as a personal menace and as a menacing cultural portent. The portents are those of madness. Driving in a cab through the garment district, Herzog is assaulted, assailed, altogether undermined:

> Electric machines thundered in the lofts and the whole street quivered. It sounded as though cloth were being torn, not sewn. The street was plunged, drowned in these waves of thunder. Through it a Negro pushed a wagon of ladies' coats. He had a beautiful beard and blew a gilt toy trumpet. You couldn't hear him. . . .
> In the crowds of Grand Central Station, Herzog in spite of all his efforts to do what was best could not remain rational.

Then, as the train leaves Grand Central and emerges into the daylight, come "Spanish Harlem, heavy, dark, and hot, and Queens far off to the right, a thick document of brick, veiled in atmospheric dirt." The allusion to the tradition, in particular to the Dickens of Coketown in *Hard Times,* is unmistakable—but the sustaining support of such a reference is not much more than momentary.

At a later point in the novel, he refers again to Grand Central Station, or to that "ponderous stinking cavern below [it] . . . the cloaca of the city, where no mind can be sure of stability." In these infernal stygian depths, policemen "tempt and trap poor souls . . . cops now [go] in drag to lure muggers, or mashers [and homosexuals], and if they could become transvestites in the name of the law, what else could they think of! The deeper creativity of police imagination. . . ." The perversity—it is unambiguously pushed home—is characteristic and characterizing.

That is to say, the perversity goes along with the free access to a pleasurable sexuality that Herzog also finds, and takes good advantage of, in New York. And, finally, the perversity—the destructive, corrosive energies—overwhelm the freedom, the pleasure, and the creatively renewing, as in the following:

> At the corner he paused to watch the work of the wrecking crew. The great metal ball swung at the walls, passed easily through brick, and entered the rooms, the lazy weight browsing on kitchens and parlors. Everything it touched wavered and burst, spilled down. There rose a white tranquil cloud of plaster dust. The afternoon was ending, and in the widening area of demolition was a fire, fed by the wreckage. Moses heard the air, softly pulled toward the flames, felt the heat. The workmen, heaping the bonfire with wood, threw strips of molding like javelins. Paint and varnish smoked like incense. The old flooring burned gratefully—the funeral of exhausted objects. Scaffolds walled with pink, white, green doors quivered as the six-wheeled trucks carried off fallen brick. The sun, now leaving for New Jersey and the west, was surrounded by a dazzling broth of atmospheric gases. Herzog observed that people were spattered with red stains, and that he himself was flecked on the arms and chest. He crossed Seventh Avenue and entered the subway.

The scriptural, Dantesque, Bunyanesque, Blakean, and Dickensian advertings are there for the moderately alert reader to latch onto—a kind of straphanger's set of ready references to the contemporary Inferno. And when Herzog descends, we get a bit more of something very much the same:

> Waiting for his uptown express, Herzog made a tour of the platform, looking at the mutilated posters—blacked-out teeth and scribbled whiskers, comical genitals like rockets, ridiculous copulations, slogans and exhortations. *Moslems, the enemy is White. Hell with Goldwater, Jews! Spicks eat SHIT. Phone, I will go down on you if I like the sound of your voice.* And by a clever cynic, *If they smite you, turn the other face.* Filth, quarrelsome madness, the prayers and wit of the crowd. Minor works of Death. Trans-descendence—that was the new fashionable term for it.

Fashionable or not, Carlylean or not, trans-descendence is the name for it, and New York becomes, without much internal mitigation, the City of Destruction—but without a redemptive elsewhere. The resonance begins to flatten out, the response begins to be as much symptomatic as it is semi-autonomous and recreative. One senses in the writer the beginnings of a turning away from the challenges proferred by this representative condition of cultural or civilized affliction, a turning away and a weakening that is to be pursued further in his next work.

How out of hand the readable city has gotten is expressed everywhere in Bellow's novel, *Mr. Sammler's Planet* (1970). Almost all of the signifying messages have now become contradictory and cancel each other out. Mr. Sammler looks out upon brownstone houses with their black ironwork grills: "How very heavy human life was here, in forms of bourgeois solidity. Attempted permanence was sad. We were now flying to the moon. . . . But then also people exaggerated the tragic accents of their condition. They stressed too hard the disintegrated assurances; what formerly was believed, trusted, was now bitterly circled in black irony. The rejected bourgeois black of stability thus translated. That too was improper, incorrect . . . turning former respectability inside out." This admirable and continued effort at intelligence and ironic balance first seizes the positive side of the bourgeois effort or ambition of solidity. It then shows the ironic discrediting of that effort to be an illusion, only to reveal in turn the discreditation of that discrediting as an easy way out as well. The contradictory moments are brought impressively to mutual nullification. Yet what seems left out or overlooked is that the effort at change and movement was as much part of the project of bourgeois culture as were the ambitions of solidity and stability. The signifying contradiction is that the historical movements of the bourgeois urban world uprooted and overturned the very stability that it in part yearned for, a stability made, in a historical sense, momentarily possible only by the destabilizing energies that went into the great projects of social change and enterprise.

Yet, even this much balance and irony soon get dissipated in this novel, countertext as it is, in part, to the view of the world it has inherited. The city is now the scene of apocalypse:

> The dreams of nineteenth-century poets polluted the psychic atmosphere of the great boroughs and suburbs of New York. Add to this the dangerous lunging staggering crazy violence of fanatics, and the trouble was very deep. . . . The worst enemies of civilization might . . . prove to be its petted intellectuals who attacked it at its weakest moments—attacked it in the name of proletarian revolution, in the name of reason, and in the name of irrationality, in the name of visceral depth, in the name of sex, in the name of perfect instantaneous freedom.

The tendency of the whole is to collapse away from meaning (forget about systematic meaning) into incognizability and chaos. Intellect cannot give coherence to this vision. It represents, quite consciously, an incapacity of both mind and the reality that the mind imputes it is conducting its transactions with: "Sammler had learned to be careful on public paths in New York, invariably dog-fouled. Within the iron-railed plots the green lights of the grass were all but put out, burned by animal excrements. . . . Mr. Sammler was testy with White Protestant America for not keeping better order. Cowardly surrender. Not a strong ruling class. Eager in a secret humiliating way to come down and mingle with all the minority mobs, and scream against themselves." Once again, the older idea is there, but as a miscarriage, a collapse, and hence as what has become a falsehood. What was once perceived as a class structure is now re-represented as an "order" that has failed. As it has failed in this following detail: Mr. Sammler sends neither letters nor telegrams—telegrams are no longer delivered and letters may take three days to cross Manhattan. "All these local communications are in decay," he says. "Even Cracow in the days of Franz Josef was more efficient than the U.S. postal system." The unmixed tune that is being played here is that of the grand bourgeois achievement, the modern metropolis, in decline and decay—of a system which has failed. Yet that tune is really only an inversion of the other tune of the bourgeois-urban world as triumphant and oppressive. What emerges once more as a theme among these observations is the growing importance of the system of signs, of communications as a central system among those intelligibilities that are asserted as failing.

Or there is this: Mr. Sammler walks along the "fuming, heaving, fool-heaped, quivering, stinking Broadway" of the Upper West Side. Mr. Sammler, and presumably his creator, has by now abandoned his effort to be a "philosophical rambler . . . inspecting the phenomenon." The scene is, to him, self-consciously perverse and despairing, fearful and terrorized—realizing its own interest in the "pursuit of madness. . . . Madness is the attempted liberty of people who feel themselves overwhelmed by gigantic forces of organized control." On the one hand there is the late-twentieth-century evocation of anarchy, perplexity, and decay. On the other, slipping past both Mr. Sammler and his creator's animus, there are people driven mad by their ill-defined and conceived sense of giant forces of organized control. The terms of specification do not get much firmer than this. Finally, to be, perforce, brief, there is this illustration. Mr. Sammler confronts the universe on Ninety-sixth Street and Broadway.

[It] always challenged Sammler. He was never up to it. . . . For something was stated here. By a convergence of all minds and all movements the conviction transmitted by this crowd seemed to be that reality was a terrible thing, and that the final truth about mankind was overwhelming and crushing. This vulgar, cowardly conclusion, rejected by Sammler with all his heart, was the implicit local orthodoxy, the populace itself being meta-

Steven Marcus

physical and living out this interpretation of reality and this view of truth. . . . Life, when it was like this, when it was all question-and-answer from the top of intellect to the very bottom, was really a state of singular dirty misery. When it was all question-and-answer it had no charm. . . . Also, the questions were bad. Also, the answers were horrible. The poverty of soul, its abstract state, you could see in faces on the street. And he too had a touch of the same disease—the disease of the single self explaining what was what and who was who. . . . New York makes one think about the collapse of civilization, about Sodom and Gomorrah, the end of the world. The end wouldn't come as surprise here. Many people already bank on it.

So, we are called to the apocalypse again. But it is a seedy occasion indeed. There is no redemption in it, no vision of transcendence to place it in a coherent perspective. There is a devil about; but it is, as one of Bellow's masters wrote, a provincial devil. What is for me most striking in such passages is their loss of certitude, their uncertainty of tone. The distinguished novelist has been reduced to being disagreeable, querulous, and generally censorious in all directions. His tone suggests injured narcissism, befuddled superiority, frustrated expectations of understanding. What we do not understand we hasten to deplore. But that is not the whole story, of course, and it is not altogether to Bellow's discredit that the story must continue to read.

And he has continued to read it, most unhappily. In his latest novel, *The Dean's December* (1982), he is unable to decide whether the sepulchral chill and spiritual nullity of Bucharest are preferable to the lethal vitality and murderous chaos of his own Chicago, which he now regards as about as hopelessly vandalized as New York. The result is a kind of stand-off, with Chicago maybe an inch ahead, only because the Dean can return to it and leave it at will. His reading of the city has become very dim indeed.

The other writer to whom I shall direct very brief attention is, after Bellow, the most literate and widely read of our younger novelists. In the works of Thomas Pynchon, the modernist vision is metamorphosed into its latest form. This form may be characterized as a radical dichotomy. The cities that Pynchon represents most intelligibly are pure historical reconstructions. They are "Baedeker worlds," as he revealingly calls them. They include Alexandria and Florence in the late 1890s as depicted in *V* (1963), and in *Gravity's Rainbow* (1973) the London of the V-bombs of 1944–45 and the Berlin that was annihilated in 1945. Here, for example, is a moment in London, 1944, at "6:43:16 British Double Summer Time."

> It was one of those great iron afternoons in London: the yellow sun being teased apart by a thousand chimneys breathing, fawning upward without shame. This smoke is more than the day's breath, more than dark strength—it is an imperial presence that lives and moves. People were crossing the streets and squares, going everywhere. Busses were grinding off, hundreds of them, down the long concrete viaducts smeared with years' pitiless use and no pleasure, into haze-gray, grease-black, red lead and pale aluminum, between scrap heaps that towered high as blocks of flats, down side-shoving curves into roads clogged with Army convoys, other tall busses and canvas lorries, bicycles and cars, everyone here with different destinations and beginnings, all flowing, hitching now and then, over it all the enormous gas ruin of the sun among the smokestacks, the barrage balloons, power lines and chimneys brown as aging indoor wood, brown growing deeper approaching black through an instant—perhaps the true turn of the sunset—that is wine to you, wine and comfort.

There is Dickens here, and Hopkins and H. G. Wells, and T. S. Eliot, of course; but it is an imagination of an immense swarm that is still coherent in its movements and massings. The same occurs in this representation of a Victorian building in London, with its allusions to Engels, Tennyson, Ruskin, Morris, and who knows who else.

> They are approaching now a lengthy brick improvisation, a Victorian paraphrase of what once, long ago, resulted in Gothic cathedrals—but which, in its own time, arose not from any need to climb through the fashioning of suitable confusions toward any apical God, but more in a derangement of aim, a doubt as to the God's actual locus (or, in some, as to its very existence), out of a cruel network of sensuous moments that could not be transcended and so bent the intentions of the builders

not on any zenith, but back to fright, to simple escape, in whatever direction, from what the industrial smoke, street excrement, windowless warrens, shrugging leather forests of drive belts, flowing and patient shadow states of the rats and flies, were saying about the chances for mercy that year. The grimed brick sprawl is known as the Hospital of St. Veronica of the True Image for Colonic and Respiratory Diseases.

The entire historical tradition of writing about urban experience is consciously touched upon in this passage. Pynchon is letting us know exactly how aware he is of the structural qualities and intentions of that tradition. And he is doing the same in the following bravura passage about Berlin in ruins in the spring of 1945. Here, while turning the tradition inside out, he is remaining loyal to it and is doing its work.

Where's the city Slothrop used to see back in those newsreels and that *National Geographic?* Parabolas weren't all that New German Architecture went in for—there were the spaces—the necropolism of blank alabaster in the staring sun, meant to be filled with human harvests rippling out of sight, making no sense without them. If there is such a thing as the City Sacramental, the city as outward and visible sign of inward and spiritual illness or health, then there may have been, even here, some continuity of sacrament, through the terrible surface of May. The emptiness of Berlin this morning is an inverse mapping of the white and geometric capital before the destruction—the fallow and long-strewn fields of rubble, the same weight of too much featureless concrete . . . except that here everything's been turned inside out. The straight-ruled boulevards built to be marched along are now winding pathways through the waste-piles, their shapes organic now, responding, like goat trails, to laws of least discomfort. The civilians are outside now, the uniforms inside. Smooth facets of buildings have given way to cobbly insides of concrete blasted apart, all the endless-pebbled rococo just behind the shuttering. Inside is outside. Ceilingless rooms open to the sky, wall-less rooms pitched out over the sea of ruins in prows, in crow's nests. . . . Old men with their tins searching the ground for cigarette butts wear their lungs on their breasts. Advertisements for shelter, clothing, the lost, the taken, once classified, folded bürgerlich inside newspapers to be read at one's ease in the lacquered and graceful parlors are now stuck with Hitler-head stamps of blue, orange, and yellow, out in the wind, when the wind comes, stuck to trees, door-frames, planking, pieces of wall—white and fading scraps, writing spidery, trembling, smudged, thousands unseen, thousands unread or blown away. At the Winterhilfe one-course Sundays you sat outside at long tables under the swastika-draped winter trees, but outside has been brought inside and that kind of Sunday lasts all week long. Winter is coming again. All Berlin spends the daylight trying to make believe it isn't. Scarred trees are back in leaf, baby birds hatched and learning to fly, but winter's here behind the look of summer—Earth has turned over in its sleep, and the tropics are reversed.

At the same time, however, Pynchon, in another part of his mind, wants to make us aware that all of this apparent significance may be merely a kind of myth-making to which we as members of Western cultures are fatally addicted. Thus, when Tyrone Slothrop, the protagonist of *Gravity's Rainbow*, finds himself at the center of Zurich in the spring of 1945, the following reflections are set down.

He finds that he has drifted as far as the Odeon, one of the great world cafés, whose specialty is not listed anywhere—indeed has never been pinned down. Lenin, Trotsky, James Joyce, Dr. Einstein all sat out at these tables. Whatever it was *they* all had in common: whatever they'd come to this vantage to score . . . perhaps it had to do with the people somehow, with pedestrian mortality, restless crisscrossing of needs or desperations in one fateful piece of street . . . dialectics, matrices, archetypes all need to connect, once in a while, back to some of that proletarian blood, to body odors and senseless screaming across a table, to cheating and last hopes, or else all is dusty Dracularity, the dead past sucking blood from the present—fatal lustricity the West's ancient curse.

This other side of the dichotomy is brought to its fullest explicitness when Pynchon is writing about modern cities that he has actually experienced. In *V*, which is largely set in New York in the 1950s, the view of the city is largely from *underground*. This is itself no bad idea, until one recognizes in reading what Pynchon has done with it. New York in *V* is represented largely from the subways and the sewers. If people are on the subways, then they are regarded literally as yo-yos, shuttling back and forth, harmlessly, senselessly, and aimlessly—and it is better if one is drunk. "Get in there at rush hour," says one character; "There are nine million yo-yos in this town." As for sewers, a lively sport of alligator-hunting goes on in them; but here is how that activity gets represented.

Each hunter got an armband—a Zeitsuss idea. ALLIGATOR PATROL, it said, in green lettering. At the beginning of the program, Zeitsuss had moved a big plexiglass plotting board, engraved with a map of the city and overlaid with a grid coordinate sheet, into his office. Zeitsuss would sit in front of this board while a plotter—one V. A. ("Brushhook") Spugo, who claimed to be eighty-five and also to have slain 47 rats with a brushhook under the summer streets of Brownsville on 13 August 1922—would mark up with yellow grease pencil sightings, probables, hunts in progress, kills. All reports came back from roving anchor men, who would walk around a route of certain manholes and yell down and ask how it was going. Each anchor man had a walkie-talkie, tied in on a common network to Zeitsuss's office and a low-fidelity 15-inch speaker mounted on the ceiling. At the beginning it was pretty exciting business. Zeitsuss kept all the lights out except for those on the plotting board and a reading light over his desk. The place looked like a kind of combat center, and anybody walking in would immediately sense this tenseness, purpose, feeling of a great net spreading out all the way to the boondocks of the city, with this room its brains, its focus. That is, until they heard what was coming in over the radios.

"One good provolone, she says."

"I got her good provolone. Why can't she do shopping herself. She spends all day watching Mrs. Grosseria's TV."

"Did you see Ed Sullivan last night, hey Andy. He had this bunch of monkeys playing a piano with their ————."

From another part of the city; "And Speedy Gonzales says, 'Señor, please get your hand off my ass.' "

"Ha, ha."

And: "You ought to be over here on the East Side. There is stuff all over the place."

"It all has a zipper on it, over on the East Side."

"That is how come yours is so short?"

> "It is not how much you got, it's how you use it."
> Naturally there was unpleasantness from the FCC, who ride around, it's said, in little monitor cars with direction-finding antennas just looking for people like this.

In my view, such a passage is an altogether conscious parody of the classical tradition and its modes of representation and what those representations refer to. Indeed, as another character in *V* remarks about this entire *mise-en-scène,* "You don't see anything down there." That is to say, the undergirding, substructure, or ground is without content—it is radically underground. People take to "roaming the city, aimlessly, waiting for a coincidence." Indeed, everything here is a parody of the nineteenth- and twentieth-century conventions of meaning—from the underground life in *Les Misérables* and *Our Mutual Friend* to the hunting in Melville and Hemingway. When there are street gangs in *V,* they are without any "turf of their own . . . spread out all over the city; having no common or geographical ground." In order to see the contemporary urban world clearly, Pynchon asserts here, we must be able to see past "the fiction of continuity, the fiction of cause and effect, the fiction of a humanized history endowed with 'reason.' " The structural categories are, in these words, meaningless deceptions themselves. The whole has become once again destabilized, opaque, obscure, baseless, mystified—and most efforts of understanding or constructing a whole are themselves part of a mystification.

In Pynchon's second novel, *The Crying of Lot 49* (1966) this view is carried to a still further conclusion. It is set, logically, in the newer urban world of southern California, which is "less like an identifiable city than a grouping of concepts—census tracts, special purpose bond-issue districts, shopping nuclei, all overlaid with access roads to its own freeway." It is all the same, "nothing was happening." The urban landscape looks like the printed circuit of a transistor radio. It gives off "a hieroglyphic sense of concealed meaning, of an intent to communicate." Yet this latest message or revelation, this promise or hint of *meaning,* will be largely undermined and subverted. Throughout this brilliant short novel, there are hints of hierophancy, of structure, of coherence, posed within the context of the urban setting, self-consciously referring to the previous conceptual schemes against which these hints play themselves out. Finally, there is brought forth an alternate system of communication, a secret postal system, an underground network of communication, in which all the parodic elements of countersystem, counterplot, metahistory, narrative, fiction, parafiction, and so on are entailed. It is all done up once again in terms of information flow and nineteenth-century theories of thermodynamics. And the alternate system of coherent communications finds its realization in the novel in the new postal drop—a garbage can labelled *W.A.S.T.E.*—under a California freeway. The meaninglessness of one side of the coherent view is brought into factitious balance by the assertion made in the text that either the world is veritably senseless or that it is veritably paranoic, that it has the plot of a paranoid delusion. "Behind the hieroglyphic streets there would either be a transcendent meaning, . . . the orbiting ecstacy of true paranoia" or nothing. Either the world is a delusionary plot or scheme of coherence or it takes a form so insane as to make history itself into a delusionary joke. And the contours of the urban world are the text out of which this psychotic alternative is to be read.

I do not point out the distinct disablements of these two very gifted novelists for the purpose of blaming them. They are, in their different ways, symptomatic in their representation of a remystified world. They are, it seems to me, no worse off than some of their academic or journalistic counterparts who talk about overpopulation, ecology, energy, or atomic armaments—not to speak of equality, democracy, or socialism—as if these terms continued to carry clear, unmodified specific analytic meaning and coherence and had not rather become part of the higher cultural psychobabble. Throughout it all, however, the city remains the site and the text out of which such discourse emerges—and it will, in my view, continue to exert such an influence. Our ability to read it will continue to be concomitant with our ability to read our world.

NOTES

1. See Steven Marcus, "Reading the Illegible," in *The Victorian City: Images and Realities,* ed. H. J. Dyos and Michael Wolff (London, 1973), I, 257–76; and Steven Marcus, *Engels, Manchester, and the Working Class* (New York, 1974).

2. References to the Bellow and Pynchon passages quoted have not been cited, since various editions of these works are widely available.

Contributors

Paul Anderer is associate professor of Japanese literature at Columbia University. He is the author of *Other Worlds: Arishima Takeo and the Bounds of Modern Japanese Fiction.* His forthcoming book, *Literature of the Lost Home,* is a study of modern Japanese literary criticism. He has written widely on the city in literature and film for Japanese publications.

Thomas Bender is University Professor of the Humanities and professor of history at New York University. He has been a fellow of the New York Institute for the Humanities since 1977. His books include *Toward an Urban Vision, Community and Social Change in America,* and *The Making of American Society.* His most recent book is *New York Intellect: A History of Intellectual Life in New York from 1750 to the Beginnings of Our Own Era.*

Philip Collins, professor emeritus of English at the University of Leicester, is a former visiting professor at Columbia University. His publications include *Dickens and Crime, Dickens: The Critical Heritage,* the Dickens and Thackeray volumes in Macmillan's *Interviews and Recollections* series, and *Trollope's London.*

Michele Hannoosh currently holds a National Endowment for the Humanities Fellowship and is assistant professor in the departments of French and Comparative Literature at the University of California, Davis. She was a Mellon Fellow in the Society of Fellows at Columbia University from 1982 to 1985. The author of numerous articles on nineteenth-century French literature and aesthetic theory, she recently completed a book on Laforgue's *Moralités légendaires* and is writing another on Baudelaire and caricature.

Eric E. Lampard is professor of history at the State University of New York at Stony Brook. Among his many publications are *Industrial Revolution: Interpretations and Perspectives, The*

Rise of the Dairy Industry, and *Regions, Resources, and Economic Growth*, with Harvey S. Perloff *et al.* He contributed "The Urbanizing World" to *The Victorian City*, edited by H. J. Dyos and Michael Wolff. The 1986 Denman Lecturer in Land Economy at Cambridge University, he has most recently published "The New York Metropolis in Transformation: History and Prospect" in *The Future of the Metropolis*, edited by Hans-Jürgen Ewers *et al.*

Steven Marcus is George Delacorte Professor in the Humanities at Columbia University and former co-chairman of the Society of Fellows. Among his many publications are *Dickens: From Pickwick to Dombey; The Other Victorians; Engels, Manchester and the Working Class; Representations;* and *Freud and the Culture of Psychoanalysis.*

Deborah Epstein Nord is associate professor of English at Harvard University. She is the author of *The Apprenticeship of Beatrice Webb*, a study of the early life of the Fabian Socialist, and from 1980 to 1982 was the David Heyman Fellow in Urban Studies at the Society of Fellows in the Humanities at Columbia University. She is currently writing a book on literary representations of London, 1820–1850.

Theodore Reff is professor of art history at Columbia University and has lectured widely in the U.S. and abroad. His extensive publications include *Manet: Olympia, Degas: The Artist's Mind*, and *The Notebooks of Edgar Degas.* He was guest curator of "Manet and Modern Paris" at the National Gallery of Art in 1982–83 and wrote the catalogue published in conjunction with that exhibition.

William Sharpe is assistant professor of English at Barnard College, Columbia University. A former Fulbright Lecturer in France and Mellon Fellow in the Society of Fellows at Columbia, he is the recipient of a National Endowment for the Humanities Fellowship for 1987–88. He is the author of a number of articles on the city in literature and is in the process of completing a book on city poetry from Wordsworth to Williams.

William R. Taylor is acting director of the New York Institute for the Humanities, where he has been a fellow since 1978, and is professor of history at the State University of New York at Stony Brook. He has been a Distinguished Fulbright Lecturer, a Carnegie Fellow, Fellow of the Institute for Historical Research at London University, and in 1983–84 held a Rockefeller Humanities Fellowship. He has written widely on the history of urban cultures and related topics and has a book forthcoming entitled *Midway of Stone: Space and Culture in New York, 1880–1929.*

Leonard Wallock is assistant professor of history at Hunter College, City University of New York. He has been David Heyman Fellow in Urban Studies at Columbia University, Fulbright Lecturer at the University of Paris III, and Research Fellow at the Philadelphia Center for Early American Studies at the University of Pennsylvania. He is the author of articles on urban and working-class history and is currently editing *New York, 1940–1965,* a collection of essays on the relation between the city and the arts.

Index

McKim, Charles, 195, 218 n. 5
McKim, Mead, and White, 200, 201, 202, 204, 218 n. 5
Malamud, Bernard, 25
Manchester, 1, 3, 12, 19, 24, 49 n. 102, 109–10, 122, 123, 232
Manchester Strike, A (Martineau), 108
Manet, Edouard, 5, 6, 8, 19–20, 168, 169; and Paris, 135–63. Works: *The Absinthe Drinker*, 146, 151, 158; *The Balcony*, 142, 149; *Ball of the Opera*, 142, 149, 160; *Bar at the Folies-Bergère*, 150, 180–82, **180**; *A Café in the Place du Théâtre-Français*, 162; *Concert in the Tuileries*, 20, 138–39, **139**, 141, 148, 155, 156, 157, 158, 159, 169, 173–74; *Copy after Delacroix' Dante and Virgil*, **171**, 172; *Dead Toreador*, 142; *Fishing*, 139, 141; *Funeral*, 160–61; *Gare Saint-Lazare*, 142, 149, **151**; *Gypsies*, 139; *Nana*, 149; *The Old Musician*, 19–20, 139, 145, **146**, 151, 158, 160; *Olympia*, 141, 152, 158; *The Philosopher*, 147, 158; *The Races at Longchamp*, 148, **182**; *The Rag-Picker*, 148; *Rue Mosnier Decorated with Flags*, 149; *The Spanish Ballet*, 148; *The Street Singer*, 139, 146, **147**; *Women at the Races*, 139; *The World's Fair of 1867*, 149, 160
Manet, Gustave, 150
Marcus, Steven, 12, 13, 16, 23
Marin, John, 5
Martial (Marcus Valerius Martialis), 17
Martial [Adolphe Potémont], 145; *Petite Pologne*, **145**
Martineau, Harriet: *A Manchester Strike*, 108
Marville, Charles, 145
Marx, Leo, 7; *The Machine in the Garden*, 7
Massin, Léontine, 140
Mayhew, Henry, 3, 8, 12, 13, 17, 18, 19, 123; *London Labour and the London Poor*, 3, 127–33, 134 n. 52
Melville, Herman, 7, 254. Works: "Bartleby the Scrivener," 242; *Moby Dick*, 225
Meryon, Charles, 157, 174
Meuriot, Paul, 57
Milton, John, 237
Mishima Yukio, 223

Modernism, 173
Monet, Claude, 7, 169; *The Gare Saint-Lazare*, 174, **175**
Morisot, Berthe, 169
Morris, William, 250
Mumford, Lewis, 17, 216; *The Culture of Cities*, 17
Murasaki Shikibu, 224; *The Tale of Genji*, 224–25
Murillo, Bartolomé Esteban, 138
Musset, Alfred de, 141

Naked Lunch, The (Burroughs), 225
Napoleon III, 143–44, 150
New Jerusalem, 6, 7, 27
New York City, 1, 6, 8, 23, 24, 25, 38; architects, 22, 195; and architecture, 189–217; Beaux Arts style, 191–92, 194–95, 217 n. 5, 218 n. 5; in fiction, 26, 43 n. 55, 44 n. 61, 234–35, 239–42, 244–49, 252–54; Forty-second Street Development Project, 189–90; grid plan, 191, 202–3, **203**, 209, 214, 216; historical development, 196–97, 200–204, 207–8, 211–12, 216–17; Italian Renaissance style, 199, 204, 207–9, 212; City Planning Commission, 217; New York Regional Plan (*The Building of the City*), 212–13, **213**, 215–16; Regional Plan Association, 213; skyscrapers, 21, 22, 197, 199, 204, 206–9, 212–13, 214, 216; transportation, 204; urbanization of metropolitan area, 81; zoning laws, 217
—buildings: Astor House, 202; Chrysler Building, 212; Citicorp Building, 217; Columbia University, 202; Condit Building, 210, 211; Empire State Building, 207, 212, 216; Equitable Building, 200; Fifth Avenue Hotel, 202–4; Flatiron (Fuller) Building, 204–7, **206**, 211; Grand Central Terminal, 22, 201–4, 218 n. 5, 241, 244–45; Haughwout Building, 197–98, **198, 199**, 200, 202, 208; Knickerbocker Bank, 202; Lenox Library, 202; Lincoln Center, 216; Madison Square, 202–4, 206, 210, 216; Madison Square Garden, 22, 204, **205**, 208; Metropolitan Life

Printed in the United States
55507LVS00007B/4